Teaching Elementary School Mathematics

www.wadsworth.com

wadsworth.com is the World Wide Web site for Wadsworth Publishing Company and is your direct source to dozens of online resources.

At *wadsworth.com* you can find out about supplements, demonstration software, and student resources. You can also send e-mail to many of our authors and preview new publications and exciting new technologies.

wadsworth.com
Changing the way the world learns®

Teaching Elementary School Mathematics

A Problem-Solving Approach

Ruben D. Schwieger
Ohio State University

Wadsworth Publishing Company
I(T)P® An International Thomson Publishing Company

Belmont, CA • Albany, NY • Boston • Cincinnati • Johannesburg • London • Madrid
Melbourne • Mexico City • New York • Pacific Grove, CA • Scottsdale, AZ • Singapore
Tokyo • Toronto

Acquisitions Editor: Dianne Lindsay
Project Editor: Christopher Oakes

COPYRIGHT © 1999 by Wadsworth Publishing Company
A Division of International Thomson Publishing Inc.
I(T)P® The ITP logo is a registered trademark under license.

Printed in Canada

1 2 3 4 5 6 7 8 9 10

For more information, contact Wadsworth Publishing Company, 10 Davis Drive, Belmont, CA 94002, or electronically at http://www.wadsworth.com

International Thomson Publishing Europe
Berkshire House
168-173 High Holborn
London, WC1V 7AA, United Kingdom

International Thomson Editores
Seneca, 53
Colonia Polanco
11560 México D.F. México

Nelson ITP, Australia
102 Dodds Street
South Melbourne
Victoria 3205 Australia

International Thomson Publishing Asia
60 Albert Street
#15-01 Albert Complex
Singapore 189969

Nelson Canada
1120 Birchmount Road
Scarborough, Ontario
Canada M1K 5G4

International Thomson Publishing Japan
Hirakawa-cho Kyowa Building, 3F
2-2-1 Hirakawa-cho, Chiyoda-ku
Tokyo 102 Japan

International Thomson Publishing Southern Africa
Building 18, Constantia Square
138 Sixteenth Road, P.O. Box 2459
Halfway House, 1685 South Africa

Library of Congress Cataloging-in-Publication Data
Schwieger, Ruben D.
    Teaching elementary school mathematics: a problem-solving approach/Rubin D. Schwieger.
        p.   cm.
    Includes bibliographical references and index.
    ISBN 0-8273-8164-6
    1. Mathematics—Study and teaching (Elementary) I. Title.
QA135.5.S329 1999
372.7'044—dc21
                                    98-34356

*This book is dedicated to
Logan and Whitney,
two special grandchildren
just now embarking on
their mathematical journeys*

Contents

Chapter 10   Teaching Geometric Concepts   172

Chapter 11   Teaching Measurement   196

Chapter 12   Teaching Rational Number Concepts   222

Preface

Problem solving is a current major emphasis in mathematics education. One of the underlying reasons for this focus in curricula for mathematics is the need for teachers to teach and children to learn mathematics in a way that makes it meaningful and useful. Mathematics educators realize that a goal is to prepare children for life outside and after school. It is also evident that to learn to teach mathematics involves solving a number of problems. There are problems associated with finding the best methods for teaching particular topics and there are problems connected to particular children's learning styles and children's attitudes toward mathematics. How can those problems be solved?

This text places the methods of teaching mathematics in the elementary and middle school in a problem solving context. The basic understanding is that, if we can identify and understand the teaching problem, we will have a clear notion of the task, that is, finding appropriate techniques for teaching effectively. Once the problem is understood, the skills and strategies of problem solving can be applied to find a solution to the teaching problem. The chapters are divided (à la Polya) into two basic sections: "Understanding the Problem" and "Solving the Problem."

A second underlying theme is the idea that, if lessons are set in a problem solving context, three important benefits accrue. First, students can see what is to be learned as interrelated with other concepts and thus find it easier to attach meaning to new ideas. Second, students can see that the mathematical concepts and processes have real uses and applications in school subjects and daily life. Third, students are provided with an opportunity to learn problem solving skills and strategies that they may apply in problem solving generally.

A serious attempt was made in the writing of this text to make it readable, and part of that attempt involves avoiding excess verbiage and diagrams or pictures of obvious kinds of objects. Some parts of the text, therefore, may seem to be cryptic or too brief. At these points the reader is encouraged to supply his or her own images of manipulatives or objects that will extend concepts and ideas to the point necessary for clarity. It will be helpful if the reader will involve himself or herself in the issues and questions of the book by thinking carefully about how the suggestions about methodologies could be modified to meet the needs of particular students and situations.

It is clear that students in different schools and different levels will respond differently to various methods and devices for teaching mathematics.

This text, then, can serve as a starting point for exploring the great variety of possibilities in methods and materials that have been and are being shown to be effective in teaching mathematics. At the end of each chapter are references (related directly to the textual material) that can be examined for additional information about specific topics. Useful materials found in the suggested reading references and, in some chapters, a bibliography of children's reading books may be of special interest for teachers of younger children.

It is beyond the scope of this book to include reference to many items in the plethora of materials in science and social studies books and lessons that should find their way into mathematics lessons. It is assumed that prospective teachers will plan to note materials and information encountered in science and social studies education classes and in classes in various content areas.

Prospective teachers of mathematics would also be wise to adopt some of the effective methods found in other methods areas. In this text we describe the *MADS device,* which is modeled loosely after the *running record* assessment used by reading teachers. Another device used by literature teachers is called *peer editing.* It is likely that a similar device can be used to enhance the teaching of problem solving.

It is hoped that this text will encourage prospective teachers to realize that they can be among those who devise new and powerful ways of teaching mathematics. Their classroom experiences may be thought of as occurring in a learning laboratory—a laboratory for the children, but also for the teacher. And out of this laboratory should also come methodology that will affect the teaching of mathematics across the nation.

Teachers can develop this methodology as they communicate with each other within the building, across the school system, and with teachers nationwide. The Internet and teachers' conventions, especially those aimed at mathematics teachers, provide a forum for each teacher to make contributions.

CHAPTER 1

Assessing Readiness to Learn Mathematics

One of the children's problems: Jamie is not really sure that the count is still the same when the objects being counted are rearranged.

Teacher's problem: How does the teacher teach operation concepts when some of the children are not conservers?

⬚ Understanding the Problem

Regardless of grade level, it is critical that teachers understand what children bring to the task of learning in mathematics. This understanding is more important with respect to specific concepts and learning styles in mathematics than in other subjects, because new learning in much of mathematics is built on specific underlying concepts. Adding and other operations, for example, cannot be learned effectively if the underlying concept of counting is not already well established.

Jean Piaget, who was influential in the study of learning psychologies, was skeptical about the effectiveness of using counting by young children as they attempted to learn about operations such as addition. He felt that these counting skills were probably taught by the children's parents or peers without awareness that they didn't aid in learning about operations. In the book *Children and Number*, Hughes (1993) contends that experiments seem to indicate that counting strategies are frequently not taught, but rather are self-devised meaningful attempts to solve mathematical problems. Hughes was examining preschool children to determine what mathematical knowledge and abilities children brought to school.

"If we had found that children possessed very few abilities on starting school, then perhaps their subsequent difficulty with school mathematics might be easier to accept. Instead, we have something of a paradox: Young children appear to start school with more mathematical knowledge than has hitherto been thought" (Hughes, 1993). In other subject areas, children may be accustomed to learning facts and procedures that can be acquired without dependence on more basic concepts. In life science, for example, a child can learn about lions, their habitat and prey, and so forth, without first learning where lions fit into the biological classification schema. In addition, children learn mathematics differently from the way they learn other subjects. Young children find it difficult to link their understanding of *number* to the various ways it is expressed in spoken and written mathematical *language*. Statements such as "One and two makes three" or "1 + 2 = 3" are not easily connected to the young child's understanding, which is tied more directly to images of objects being manipulated. Not only are these statements abstract, as in the case of "1 + 2 = 3," but they use unfamiliar symbolism (Hughes, 1993).

Thus kindergartners and first graders are often not ready to learn in mathematics because of the difference between the way their mathematical concepts have already developed and the way beginning mathematical concepts are presented at school. They may not realize that there is any need for writing abstract expressions such as those above. Not only are they unprepared to write these expressions, but they see no reason to do so. As we will show in subsequent chapters, mathematical knowledge must be acquired (facts must be learned), mathematical concepts must be developed, and mathematical processes must be practiced.

Many children come to school already knowing bits and pieces of unrelated information, much of which is mathematical. For example, they know that some numbers are bigger than others and they may have some understanding of the concept of more and less. They have a fairly large collection of mathematical words and terms, too, but these are unorganized and lack appropriate connections and interrelationships. One might think, then, that a good foundation already exists upon which a teacher can build. There is, however, a catch. How did the children obtain that knowledge? If one examines learning at home and in the world of 3-, 4-, and 5-year-olds, it is clear that the learning has taken place through extensive repetition.

Repetition

In the sense that mathematics is a language, it may be that much of it will be learned in the same way a child's native language is learned. A child hears language spoken by parents and other adults, by older siblings, and by other children. Then the child repeats, often incorrectly at first. Parents, siblings, and others correct usage and repeat phrases. Thus, the learning is informal and natural. It is expected by both the child and by those associated with the child. Correction is provided over and over again in all sorts of settings and times during the day. Often there is positive or negative reinforcement. A child may be told repeatedly, "That's not right, say it this way"; "No, this is a nickel, that's a quarter"; "How much is 2 plus 2?" (Copeland, 1984).

A problem may develop when children enter formal education with a collection of mathematical knowledge accompanied by a well developed learning style. Subconsciously they expect to continue to learn by repetition as they always have. However, in school there isn't sufficient time for repetition to occur in the same way as before. Furthermore, the teacher cannot tailor repetition opportunities for each child with each new mathematical term or symbol. When children attempt to learn by repetition in a classroom, there is pressure to cut the repeats to a minimum. Peer pressure and teacher schedules that require moving quickly to other topics reduce the opportunities for a child to do the repetition necessary to learn a new term.

In addition, the typical homework (if indeed there is any homework in the early grades) is not likely to promote the necessary repetition. Parents and the others the child learned so well from before entering school are not able or prepared to continue their support and teaching activities with the new and much more structured material to be learned. This means that the child is left in a kind of educational limbo. Learning in mathematics and other subjects is expected, but there is no learning paradigm in place. The young child assumes that this is the way school is, may begin to believe that it is too difficult, and may decide not to learn material that is not presented with sufficient repetition. Alternatively, the child may, by observation of other students or siblings or even because of encouragement from the teacher and other adults, decide that memorization is the accepted and best mode of learning.

Memorization

Unfortunately, too many teachers and students believe that mathematics is a monolithic set of pieces of information to be memorized. When a teacher attempts to teach and students attempt to learn new material, a false kind of "learning" mode is often used. In mathematics, this false learning is typically evident as children attempt to memorize everything. Because young minds are flexible and students are eager, they can memorize a great deal. We find that many students memorize their way through science, social studies, and mathematics in the first six or seven grades quite successfully, even to the point of having straight *A*s and being regarded as very good students. Then, somewhere along the line, perhaps at the beginning of algebra (where sometimes a major shift occurs in the type of material to be learned and in the thinking necessary to learn it), the student suddenly realizes that she or he can't "learn" the new material. It is for this reason that many students experience trauma at this point and reject any further involvement with mathematics. A similar watershed point occurs when students encounter geometry, with its *proofs* and an approach to teaching and learning that is necessarily quite different from their previous experience in mathematics.

Teaching and learning are also greatly hindered when students, because of lack of background, simply cannot make sense of what is being presented. They do not know how to be involved. New ideas cannot be connected with their previous experience and concepts they already hold. Children are not sufficiently sophisticated in their thinking to know what is happening to them and why they can't learn. The only response they can make is to turn away. Some children then pretend to be learning. They exhibit the behavior of those who, they think, *are* learning. Alternatively, they may turn to cheating or find ways for someone else (a friend, parent, or someone in the cooperative group) to do their "learning" for them.

Constructing Concepts and Knowledge

Schools present three general aspects of the mathematical learning task to young children. There are concepts to be acquired, knowledge to be memorized, and processes to be learned and practiced until they become almost automatic. The constructivist philosophy and approach, which we will elaborate in a later section, holds that, especially with respect to learning mathematical concepts (but to a certain extent in learning mathematical facts as well), real learning takes place when the learner constructs the concept internally and individually. Do children come to the early grades prepared to construct the basic mathematical concepts?

Expectations

Children may also experience difficulty in learning mathematics when they do not understand the teacher's expectations. Those expectations may not coincide with the expectations the children have and the teacher may not communicate the expectations clearly. One aspect of misunderstanding arises when a teacher assumes that concepts or knowledge are being taught and learned because certain material is being presented, but in reality children are learning something different.

Specific facets of this theory are discussed in connection with concept development in the section on the construction of concepts. To illustrate, a teacher may effectively present and teach the standard algorithm for two-digit addition with multiple examples like these:

$$
\begin{array}{cccc}
12 & 34 & 32 & 25 \\
+31 & +25 & +24 & +32 \\
\end{array}
$$

The teacher may use the term *addition* consistently in connection with this process learning. The children believe that they are learning what addition is, and when the teacher tests them to find that they have successfully learned to do the process; the teacher also assumes that they understand addition. Later, when presented with other forms for addition, such as 25 + 32, children are uncertain whether this is actually addition. The children's belief that they were being taught addition did not match the teacher's belief that they were learning an algorithm for addition and that later, or in another context, they would learn other facets of the addition concept.

These concerns prompt teachers to find ways of ascertaining their students' readiness to learn mathematics. This is not an easy task for several reasons: Students may be from widely varied backgrounds; they may come from other schools with different curricula; and they typically come from earlier grades where different styles and learning requirements were part of the instructional activities. Furthermore, home environments vary widely. Some homes have state-of-the-art computers on which the students use math learning programs. These homes and others may have parental support and encouragement for learning math, while other students come from environments with no computers and no parental or other encouragement.

An additional difficulty exists in the determination of the level of mathematical knowledge and experience possessed by the student. What experience has the child had in learning mathematics? What attitudes does the child have toward mathematics in general and toward specific topics within mathematics? Not only is it difficult to answer these questions by examining records from earlier grades, but conversations with former teachers, parents, and even the students themselves are often not of much help. Some students are not good communicators either orally or with pencil and paper and cannot share what they know and are able to do.

Solving the Problem

There are three important ways to assess the status of students' mathematics learning readiness: examining past records, testing, and observing. It is likely that all three methods will be used with most students. To keep the information obtained accessible and usable, it is best to use a computer and a spreadsheet program.

Records

Two sources of records should be considered: standardized tests and grades. Math scores from standardized tests of aptitude and proficiency can form an important part of the record and provide some indication of skill and knowledge readiness. Readiness tests given prekindergarten students may include tasks with mathematical content (shapes, patterns, counting, numeral recognition, etc.). Mathematics grades from previous classes and comments of previous teachers may also be included. All of this information should be annotated with possible interpretations. For example:

> The As in math last year were attained in a mastery learning setting in which T. progressed satisfactorily in the lowest math group.

> J. was very ill and missed many days of school before the proficiency test was taken. The scores in all subjects were much lower than class work would have suggested.

Grades and statements from former teachers must be interpreted in light of several factors:

- What was the teacher's teaching style and approach? Memorizing? Teacher centered? Math favored?

- What was the nature of the mathematics presentation? Worksheets? Manipulatives? Visual?

- What was the character of the class? Showed math anxiety? Enjoyed math? Involved in math activities and projects?

This information must be recorded carefully to avoid bias toward a child or a child's ability to learn. A teacher must believe and expect that any student can and will learn the mathematics being taught in the current class. Things can be different for this child, in this year, in this class. A good mathematics teacher is essentially an optimist! The teacher wants to ensure that prejudice does not prevent a child from learning—neither in the case of a child who does not have the background to learn specific ideas, nor in the case of a child who is prepared to learn but has not been challenged to progress. A teacher should use the information about children to set the stage for the most effective learning environment. This includes helping children to understand the teacher's expectation that each one can and will learn the necessary mathematics.

The information in the math teacher's records should be concise and focused on mathematics, specifically the mathematics to be taught in the particular class. Otherwise, the volume of information could be overwhelming.

The list of topics, from the *Curriculum and Evaluation Standards* (NCTM, 1989), found in Appendix H and in the school's mathematics curriculum outline, will provide guidance in narrowing the range of information recorded. Teachers will find that a spreadsheet computer program is invaluable for keeping these records in an accessible form. If a computer is not available, the amount of information kept on each child in a notebook or files will have to be limited. Teachers should learn to use a spreadsheet for this recordkeeping and for a number of other purposes.

Records of this kind may be sensitive, and teachers must thoroughly understand school policy regarding what records may be kept by the teacher and how they are to be kept. Certain records are confidential; if confidential records are to be kept in a computer file, care must be taken that they are secure.

Testing

At the beginning of the class year and when new topics are begun, pretesting may be done with two purposes in mind: (1) to discover students' levels of readiness for the mathematics to be taught, and (2) to provide a tool for assessing progress when pretest results are compared with posttest results. One way to accomplish these goals is to use the same test both times. A potential difficulty with this approach is that it may be necessary to make changes in curriculum during the teaching period. If unplanned changes are made, it may be unfair and unproductive to use the pretest as a posttest. In these cases the tests would not be reliable, and no useful conclusions could be drawn from the differences in the results of the tests (NCTM, 1992).

In pretesting to discover the status of student readiness, it is important to focus the testing device so that it relates directly to the mathematics to be taught. It may be necessary to give several smaller focused tests, rather than trying to cover all the topics in one larger test. The tests should be general enough to include opportunities for students to demonstrate their readiness from all appropriate perspectives. For example, a test to determine a child's readiness to learn about multiplication should be designed to provide information about the following:

- Concept acquisition and understanding (multiplication operation characteristics)

- Computational skills (multiplication algorithm competence)

- Knowledge base (basic facts, when to apply multiplication, etc.)

Paper and pencil tests should include not only computational tasks requiring a certain algorithm, but examination of different algorithmic forms, multiplication terminologies, and word problems involving multiplication.

Questions such as: "How do we know that the number of students when there are 6 groups of 4 each is the same as when there are 4 groups of 6 each?" and "How can we find the total number in two different ways?" should be asked when multiplication concepts are being examined. In examining processes, arrays, algorithms, and terminology, all three areas—computation, concepts, and knowledge—need to be addressed because they are fundamental to the mathematics involving the multiplication being taught (Charles, 1987).

At the higher grade levels, it is necessary to restrict the number of test topics to specific grade-level ideas. For example, the pre- and posttests might focus on the multiplication of terminating decimals only, and not include other kinds of decimals. Typically, when the testing process deals with a narrow and restricted topic, the pre- and posttests should be administered close together rather than at the beginning and end of a term or semester. The time available for teaching the particular concept, knowledge, or process must also be a consideration.

For example, it would be cumbersome to include, in a single pretest for seventh graders, the assessment of all operations, algorithms, basic facts and other facts, and a wide range of concepts from the most basic up through the sixth grade. The focus would have to be on more general issues such as problem solving of different types or computation skills. Computers with record-keeping and testing programs installed can prove to be powerful tools that can make all this assessment manageable.

Pretests can be placed in the computer so that not only can the students take the tests by using the computer, but the test results can be stored in the computer's memory. Results will then be easily accessible, and the computer can also be used to analyze results statistically and store them in appropriate files. It is fairly simple to do the posttesting in the same way, thus avoiding much of the paperwork required to record, store, and access the information in the traditional way. Using computers allows more extensive analysis with fewer computation errors.

Observation

Ideally, the teacher can examine records, test, and observe each student for readiness in the classroom. However, in the real-world classroom all this may require more time than is available particularly because similar activities should be undertaken for subjects other than mathematics as well. If all the record examination and testing cannot be done, at least students should be observed. The intensity of the observation will vary widely, not only from class to class, but from time to time and from subject to subject. Observation can be as personal, direct, and formal as using the *Math Assessment and Diagnosis Scheme* (MADS) plan (Schwieger, 1995), or as informal as simply observing an individual child or a group of children respond during parts of a math lesson.

However structured the observation is, there should be some means of recording it. There are many interruptions and distractions in the course of a typical lesson or other classroom activity. Some teachers solve this problem at least partially by keeping an open notebook handy and having a code system so that observation information may be noted quickly with symbols. A variation of this method is to carry a previously prepared checklist on a clipboard as observations are being made. At the conclusion of the lesson or at the first opportunity, the teacher can then recall the nature of the observation and record more elaborate entries and information.

Observing and noting mathematical skills and knowledge may be difficult because many other observations are being made at the same time. During the course of a given lesson in mathematics, other activities are going on in the classroom and with individual children. Lessons and activities often integrate science and social studies concepts with mathematical content, and readiness to learn the mathematics may be obscured by a lack of readiness or background related to science or social studies. Social and psychological dynamics may also be prominent; the observer must attempt to look beyond the surface reactions. It will help to have a mental checklist of a few specific items to be looked for in the context of the lesson topic. If an aide or other adult is helping in the room, the teacher might want to ensure that a particular observation is made by instructing the adult as follows:

> While I am teaching this lesson on angles in geometry, would you please watch Kelly and Terry to see whether it's clear to them that an angle can measure to more than a right angle? Also, please make a note on how they respond to my instructions.

In unstructured observation, it is difficult to protect against bias, especially by overlooking some students or overobserving others. Bias occurs when a particular child is observed more frequently or more carefully than others because some behavior consistently draws the teacher's attention. To help with the problem of underobserving some students and overobserving others, a count of the number of observations and an estimate of the time given to a particular observation may enable the teacher to maintain an approximate balance. Teachers should not attempt to provide great detail and structure to such observation results because efforts to record details necessitate more time than is available for recording, and teachers will be distracted from teaching and from thorough observation of all students.

Observations should focus on the same issues and concerns we examined under the headings of Records and Testing. It may be helpful for the teacher to create a checklist such as the following:

The child:

—is attentive to instructions.

—attempts to follow instructions.

—has misunderstood instructions.

___is thinking about something other than the lesson.

___is math anxious with regard to this material

___is not on task;

    ___is playing with objects.

    ___is playing with others.

    ___is withdrawn.

___is having difficulty with the lesson.

(The MADS checklists in Appendix F may be used as a guide for creating more detailed or task-specific observation checklists.)

In general a teacher needs to balance time spent in readiness assessment, in recordkeeping, and in the emphasis given to instruction. A wise teacher will not shortchange instruction by spending too much time and energy on readiness assessment. With experience, a teacher will develop assessment techniques that can be accomplished concurrently with instruction.

▣ Summary

Assessing readiness to learn mathematics in a new class or in a new topic is critical to the success of teaching in mathematics. Knowing where students are in their skills and knowledge enables the teacher to plan and to teach in the manner and at the levels most likely to be effective. Three methods of making these assessments are: examining records, testing, and observing. Assessment should be focused to avoid information overload; information should be stored so that it is accessible and useful; and bias and uneven distribution of observations across the class should be avoided.

▣ Exercises

1. Perform the MADS activity with a child focusing on learning a particular mathematical concept or process. At the outset, create a test, worksheet, or list of tasks for the child to perform. See Appendix F for the MADS outline.

2. Create a pretest/posttest for assessing incoming skills and progress for a particular mathematics topic and grade level (e.g., division of two-digit numbers by one-digit numbers—4th grade; the concept of *variable* in algebra—7th grade).

3. Make an annotated list of computer software that could be used to provide pretest/posttest capability at a particular grade level. Include hardware requirements, applicability to mathematics and topics within mathematics, ease of use, and cost.

4. Create scoring schemes for the various MADS evaluations or other evaluation devices for assessing readiness.

References

Charles, Randall, Frank Lester, and Phares O'Daffer (1987). *How to Evaluate Progress in Problem Solving.* Reston, VA: National Council of Teachers of Mathematics.

Copeland, Richard W. (1984). *How Children Learn Mathematics.* Upper Saddle River, NJ: Prentice Hall/Merrill.

Hughes, Martin (1993). *Children and Number.* Cambridge, MA: Blackwell.

NCTM (1992). *Assessment Standards.* Reston, VA: National Council of Teachers of Mathematics.

NCTM (1989). *Curriculum and Evaluation Standards.* Reston, VA: National Council of Teachers of Mathematics.

Schwieger, Ruben (1995). *Mathematics Assessment and Diagnosis Scheme.* Unpublished. Lima OH: The Ohio State University.

Suggested Readings

Baratta-Lorton, Mary (1976). *Mathematics Their Way.* Menlo Park, CA: Addison-Wesley.

Barsoh, Alan (1978, October). "Task Cards," *Arithmetic Teacher*, 26, 2: 53–54.

Childs, Leigh, and Nancy Adams (1979). *Math Sponges.* San Diego, CA: National Institute for Curriculum Enrichment.

Design Group (1975). *The Way to Play.* New York: Paddington Press.

Johnson, David W., and Roger T. Johnson (1987). *Learning Together and Alone: Cooperative, Competitive, and Individualistic Learning.* Upper Saddle River, NJ: Prentice Hall.

Kohl, Herbert R. (1974). *Math, Writing, and Games.* New York: The New York Book Review.

Lane County Mathematics Project (1984). *Problem Solving in Mathematics.* Palo Alto, CA: Dale Seymour.

Peck, Donald M., Stanley M. Jencks, and Michael L. Connell (1989, November). "Improving Instruction Through Brief Interviews," *Arithmetic Teacher*, 37, 3: 15–17.

Schoen, Harold I., and Marilyn J. Zweng, Eds. (1986). *Estimation and Mental Computation*, National Council of Teachers of Mathematics, 1986 Yearbook. Reston, VA: NCTM.

Shroyer, Janet, and William Fitzgerald (1986). *Mouse and Elephant: Measuring Growth.* Menlo Park, CA: Addison-Wesley.

Webb, Norman L. (1993). "Assessment for the Mathematics Classroom," in *Assessment in the Mathematics Classroom*, National Council of Teachers of Mathematics, 1993 Yearbook, Eds., Norman L. Webb and Arthur F. Coxford. Reston, VA: NCTM.

Children's Attitudes Toward Mathematics

One of the children's problems: Kelly does not like working with numbers, especially in doing long division. What should Kelly do to feel better about doing long division?

Teacher's problem: Three children in class tune out when math class begins. How can the teacher find the reasons for their withdrawal?

🔲 Understanding the Problem

Children do not come to school and to learning mathematics with a clean slate. As will be pointed out, they have already formed some partial mathematical concepts in a wide variety of contexts. Some of them can count (up to 5 or 6) and recite numbers to 10 and beyond. They know some shape names, can draw rough forms of various shapes, and can partially describe some figures and objects such as squares, circles, and balls (spheres). Typically, however, their vocabularies are not adequate for much precision and completeness of description.

Many kindergarten children have attended preschool programs where they played with blocks, made patterns, and started adding and subtracting, though hopefully not by those names (see Developing Operations Concepts in Chapter 9). Some children have educational toys, electronic games and learning devices, and computers at home—many of these have some mathematical content. Most children come to school anxious to learn, especially to learn to read. Some are disappointed when they can't read after the first day or two of first grade. Learning mathematics does not always offer the same excitement and interest, however.

In addition to a smattering of mathematical terminology, number sense, and content knowledge, children may come to school with a fairly well-developed attitude about mathematics and mathematical ideas. This may be part of a general attitude toward school or it may be specific to mathematics. The attitudes children exhibit toward mathematics are generally specific to mathematics itself; they usually do not occur with other subjects. The attitudes may include enjoyment of numbers and counting, apathy toward numbers, or the idea that numbers are difficult and should be avoided.

Math Anxiety

While negative attitudes toward mathematics often develop into math anxiety, similar attitudes toward other subject areas do not always result in comparable anxiety. For example: One seldom hears of science anxiety, social studies anxiety, or art anxiety. Undoubtedly some children dislike these subjects and may feel anxious when required to work in these subjects, but the specific phenomenon we call *math anxiety* does not seem to be duplicated in other subjects.

In any case, the kindergarten and first grade teachers will note a wide spectrum of exposure to mathematics, awareness of mathematics, mathematical knowledge, and differences in attitudes toward mathematics when the class is examined. The teacher must try to minimize the effects of these differences so that teaching can begin. However, efforts to minimize these effects should not stifle the interest or turn away the child who already knows something. A wise teacher, by presenting activities with manipulatives and by spending individual time with children, will determine the levels of understanding of the concepts to be taught. The teacher can help children with some understanding of concepts to modify, correct, and build on those so that they can expand their knowledge as much as is possible. This effort needs to be coupled with helping children to understand the teacher's expectations concerning what is to be learned in mathematics.

First graders come expecting to learn to read. Peers, siblings, and parents have prepared them for school by talking about reading and sometimes by enabling them to gain reading skills. The same persons may not have taught them to expect to learn to count, to add, and to subtract. The teacher has to provide an awareness of the expectations for learning mathematics. Though the specific mathematical expectations are not present, some attitude factors may be. Siblings may have commented about math being hard or easy or the need for starting to do math homework. Thus, the teacher may need to correct some incorrect and damaging expectations.

For those who are clearly not prepared to learn the required mathematics, provision will have to be made for play time with manipulatives and specially designed activities to assist them in beginning to develop the necessary concepts. As will be seen, both of these conditions—significant knowledge before instruction and little knowledge before instruction—can be the precursors of math anxiety.

Children develop attitudes about mathematics before they come to school and also while in school. Felker (1974) found that there is a watershed period in a grade schooler's life which occurs typically between the end of third grade and the beginning of fifth. It seems that there are physiological and psychological changes at about those grade levels that cause a child to develop and/or change attitudes toward learning in general. Felker noted that peer and adult pressures seemed to have more of an effect at this time than at others on a child's self-esteem. He found that a child's level of interest in school and in various subjects, as well as self-esteem, usually rose steadily from kindergarten through the third grade. During fourth grade, there was a sharp drop from which many students never recovered. He recommended consistent and intentional intervention by fourth-grade teachers. The hope was that this intervention might prevent the development of significantly negative attitudes toward learning in general and various subjects specifically. This intervention, which included giving ample deserved praise to students for their work and keeping them aware of their abilities to meet high expectations, proved to be successful in several test case schools. It was possible to prevent and reverse the radical decrease in interest in school and in self-esteem.

Students' attitudes toward school, mathematics, and learning in mathematics may change at times during their school years (even through college), either in a positive or negative direction. The author has interviewed fourth-year and graduate education majors about their math attitudes and found that between 80 and 90 percent of a preservice math methods classes were significantly math anxious at some time during their studies in mathematics. While preparing to be teachers of mathematics at some level, between 35 and 50 percent are still math anxious or have developed math anxiety recently. Reasons given are as follows:

- At some grade level or class the student developed a strong dislike for a math teacher.

- The student's learning approach suddenly didn't work any more. There was too much material and it was too abstract.

- The material was presented poorly (at least as far as that student was concerned).

- The math to be learned was too difficult.

- Grades were poor and there was frustration with attempts to raise them.

- Math was taught with competitive activities in which the student was always a loser.

Anxiety developed for these students in classes ranging from first grade to the Math for Elementary Teachers class at college. Negative attitudes tended to develop, however, mostly around the fourth, seventh, eighth, and ninth grades.

A negative attitude or dislike for mathematics may not inevitably lead to math anxiety. A student may simply prefer other subjects and avoid math unless it is necessary. Some are actually quite competent in mathematical processes and concept acquisition but prefer not to work with symbols and numerical processes (Dinkmeyer, 1963). Math anxiety, however, seems to have a life of its own and can grow like a snowball.

Math Anxiety: Typically a state of fear related to learning in and working with mathematics.

Teachers need to be able to:

- Identify math anxiety in a child.

- Be equipped with activities and approaches to minimize math anxiety.

- Teach so as not to create math anxiety.

Teachers can make a difference at this point! Among the university students mentioned above, some lost their math anxiety when they were in a class with a teacher who enjoyed mathematics and enjoyed teaching it. For some this didn't happen until college, with a particularly skilled and competent mathematics teacher. In these instances, the teacher's attitude toward mathematics was a significant factor. Being a good teacher is not always the whole solution, however. Some children come to math class so conditioned by peer and family pressure that a teacher can do very little about an intense math anxiety that has existed for a long time. Some parents label their child as "dumb" or say repeatedly, "I had trouble with math when I was your age, so you won't get it either." Others refuse to help with math homework and make negative statements about math and math teachers, thus building and reinforcing negative thinking about math. It is very hard for a child to learn easily in mathematics when coming from an environment containing such negative reactions to things mathematical.

Mathematics anxiety is further exacerbated when that child does poorly on a few math assignments or tests and the child's peers label the child as "dumb" or unable to do math. This difficulty can be further strengthened by teachers who pass such labels on to subsequent teachers. A teacher must walk a fine line in deciding how to pass along helpful but not prejudicial information about a child's performance in mathematics. Since mathematics performance records may be more easily quantified than those in other subjects, teachers may feel that they are relaying objective assessment information about learning in mathematics. Even with seemingly objective data, however, it is possible to set the stage for math anxiety to develop or continue with the new teacher if information is not shared appropriately. A parallel should be drawn with receiving a math-anxious child into one's class. The current teacher should realize that the anxiety-creating conditions may not prevail in the new class. The current teacher should not assume that the math-anxious child will necessarily remain so.

Evidences of Math Anxiety

Math anxiety causes several different reactions in children, for example:

- Physiologically (sweating, crying, shaking)
- Acting out
- Pretending and cover-up
- Turning off and tuning out
- Attempting to memorize everything
- Procrastinating
- Attempting perfection

Some of the differences may be related to what caused or started the math anxiety. Anxiety expressed with obvious physical symptoms is the easiest to detect. A child may begin to perspire for no environmental or physiological reason. Crying and/or shaking at the outset of a math lesson may also indicate math anxiety. Some math-anxious children become very quiet and withdrawn. They may sit very still and stare at the wall or their papers and seem to be in a trance (Suydam, 1984). Withdrawn children may turn in blank papers or papers with only the first part written before the student *closed down*. Alternatively, papers may be scribbled on or filled with nonsense. Other math-anxious children will use avoidance techniques so that they do not actually do any mathematical tasks. They will *need* to sharpen pencils, go to the restroom, and work on other nonmathematical tasks. They become class clowns or act up sufficiently to be punished by some penalty that involves taking them away from mathematics.

Causes of Math Anxiety

There are many causes for the development of math anxiety but they may not be easily identifiable. Teachers should not attribute every difficulty with mathematics to math anxiety. Furthermore, there are varying levels of fears and reactions and these may vary from time to time with a particular child. Troubles in another part of a child's life may be evidenced in mathematics classes. Math anxiety should be dealt with primarily as an individual matter, with each child who seems to be experiencing it, and with responses appropriate to that child's situation.

Teacher-Based Anxiety

Teachers have a great deal of influence over the development of math anxiety. Students whose teacher dislikes mathematics, avoids teaching it, and demonstrates a negative attitude toward it are particularly susceptible to developing math anxiety during that class or later. Students are quick to pick up body language and subtle anti-math indicators, no matter how hard a teacher might try to disguise them (Allardice and Ginsburg, 1983).

Some teachers covertly or overtly avoid certain topics in mathematics. They may never quite get to *word problems* or certain processes or geometry. They may give only cursory attention to division by fractions (possibly because they have never really understood it well themselves). Whatever the motivation, the avoidance or inadequate coverage of important topics sets students up for math anxiety. They are aware of what the teacher is doing (and may contribute to the avoidance by keeping the teacher off track), but later will be frustrated to realize that learning necessary for new concept acquisition was not obtained. They may now be behind others and unable to learn the new material but have neither the time nor the means to acquire what they missed.

Solving the Problem of Teacher-Based Anxiety

Prospective teachers with math anxious anxiety or with negative attitudes toward math should deal with either or both prior to beginning teaching. Among ways to prevent math anxiety are:

- Spend time practicing and ensuring that you have learned the math that will be taught. This learning must be beyond the level of the children's knowledge so that you will not be uncomfortable with the math content you are teaching.

- Have a variety of teaching methods and approaches in mind so that alternatives can be used when children do not respond as desired to specific lessons and mathematical activities.

- Use manipulatives and hands-on material so that the memory does not have to be so heavily relied on. Often the teacher will learn more personally in the process of watching and helping the children.

- Express interest and excitement in the accomplishments of the students, including praising them for work well done.

- Engage the class in math projects, fairs, art-related math, problem solving, and puzzles. Problem solving with real-life situations is a particularly good vehicle for generating interest and alleviating anxiety.

- Allow and encourage children to explore, inquire and explain in their mathematics lessons, projects, and written work.

Some teaching methods and styles help create math anxiety. Lecturing and worksheet, if used day after day, make mathematics learning boring and difficult. Children realize that they are not learning at all as they do worksheet after boring worksheet. That type of activity quickly becomes a completion task rather than a learning task, especially if the worksheets are uninteresting and routine. A constant diet of "going to the board" and competition to see who's first, fastest, or "all correct" is also counterproductive. When a somewhat anxious student is forced to stand before the other students, always fails, and then is ridiculed, math anxiety only becomes worse. When math-anxious students are part of the class, teaching methods should not single them out in ways that emphasize their difficulties. If a particular method is observed to be creating math anxiety, it should be modified.

Cooperative learning is being shown effective in many learning situations and may provide a setting for relieving math anxiety. However, is also possible for math anxiety to develop in small groups. When all but one in the group seem to understand and that one is uncomfortable in group work, that individual's anxiety may be caused by the group dynamics. It sometimes happens that one student takes all the responsibility for the group work and the grade; that person may become anxious because of the pressure. Attention should be given to careful balancing of groups so that they are not the source of math anxiety. Vary the composition of the groups so that anxiety-producing situations are not perpetuated. In mathematics, certain aspects of learning occur easily and well in groups. Students can readily assist each other in reviewing factual knowledge, in practicing processes, and in working on projects. Group work, however, may not be helpful for acquiring concepts. Concepts are acquired fully when an individual internally constructs the ideas and relates them to other concepts. Thus if a student is having trouble learning math concepts, the group may be a source of frustration and anxiety. Other students are not equipped to teach, particularly since some of them are themselves struggling with the concepts. For concept learning it is preferable for students to work in settings that are not dependent on group interaction. Once concepts have been taught, group work may be used for review and for peer monitoring of progress in applying concept knowledge.

Schwieger's *Ten Commandments on Math Anxiety* (1995) may help. They are:

I. You shall keep the whole class aware of difficulties (so a child does not assume s/he alone is having difficulties).

II. You shall not communicate that math is too hard or too complex. (and shall counter others' such communications).

III. You shall assume and communicate that each child (including girls) can be successful in math.

IV. You shall exhibit an interest in, and an enjoyment of, math (and expect others to do the same).

V. You shall find ways to counter parents' and others' negative messages about math (such as: math isn't important, math is too difficult).

VI. You shall use variety in manipulatives, books, and models in teaching mathematics.

VII. You shall use a variety of methods and strategies in teaching mathematics (and avoid explain-practice-memorize).

VIII. You shall avoid excessive timed, competitive, and non-real-life-relevant activities.

IX. You shall teach, and give appropriate time to, all aspects of mathematical learning: concepts, problem solving, computation.

X. You shall use a variety of means to build self-esteem, reduce fear, and encourage creativity.

Non-Teacher-Based Anxiety

Some math anxiety is not directly connected to the teacher, but is due to the child's situation or response to other stimuli. It can be produced by pressure on the child from peers, siblings, or parents and other adults. Even imagined pressures or perceptions of what others think or might think can contribute to this phenomenon. The following sections examine several of these influences.

Learning Style Influences

Through experience in several grades, many children develop the idea that math is to be learned by memorization. It is not difficult to understand why this occurs. Because of the way math is taught in the early grades, it is quite possible for a student to progress rather successfully by memorization only. Typically, children easily memorize addition and multiplication facts, other mathematical facts about numbers, terminology, and computation processes. When such children find that they must think more than superficially about the meaning and interrelationships of facts and concepts, they may begin to experience anxiety. Suddenly the style of learning isn't adequate for the learning task. Perhaps a kind of sensory overload occurs; items are mixed up in memory and cannot be recalled in a useful way. In fact, during all the memorizing the child did previously, little actual learning occurred. The concepts and mathematical entities have not been discovered or constructed internally and thus cannot be used meaningfully by the student. A fifth or sixth grader, for example, finds it difficult to make a sudden major shift in learning style. If discovery and inquiry styles have not been a part of previous mathematics experiences, it is hard to switch to them from memorization as the main learning style.

Lack of Practice

When a child has learned through extensive repetition, math anxiety may develop when the necessary amount of repetition is no longer possible. Parents and others may no longer be able to assist in drill because of their lack of knowledge. There are too many concepts, facts, and processes to be learned in a limited amount of time. The type and style of repetition also may have changed. The teacher may require the repetition in the form of paper-and-pencil practice and exercises, or the computer may guide the drill, whereas previously the repetition was verbal and oral.

Another source of math anxiety may result from children's belief that mathematics learning is all sequential and hierarchical. This causes children to believe that they cannot grasp the idea presented or do the process required because they might have missed something in the past.

▣ Solving the Problem of Non-Teacher-Based Anxiety

From kindergarten on and at every grade level, teachers must encourage creativity and problem solving in mathematics.

Memorization

Only a small portion of what is to be learned should be memorized, and this fact should be pointed out to children. Basic addition or multiplication facts and certain formulas might be memorized, for example. However, even for these, it is best to use them extensively in a variety of contexts so that they are learned with connections and meanings rather than as abstract lists and mnemonics. Such abstractions may be forgotten or confused with other similar facts. High expectations that children will synthesize, apply, and *construct* concepts should be held by the teacher and shared with the children in appropriate and understandable ways. When problems are worked on and real-life applications made even during the earliest work in mathematics, children will learn that memorization is not effective. Obviously, the body of knowledge that would have to be memorized is immense. It is important for a teacher to realize that *concepts* cannot simply be memorized, but *must be constructed*. The teacher must provide an environment conducive to concept construction so that when students encounter new material, they will not develop math anxiety because of their use of an inadequate learning style. They will have experience with an approach which will enable them to develop concepts, to problem solve, and to understand processes.

Repetition

Teachers need to provide for all types of repetition and for a balance among the types. Assuming that sufficient repetition will occur on homework worksheets may cause students, particularly in the early grades, to miss opportunities for learning. Children need opportunities to talk about their mathematical work and to hear others discuss theirs. Such repetition, along with writing in words what they have learned and discovered, significantly reinforces and contributes to their learning (Burns, 1995).

Anxiety about Knowledge Gaps

Children can be shown how to "get back in" to math. The teacher can help a child identify a missing ingredient from previous learning when it is needed and important for current learning. The child can then quickly be taught the needed item or guided to find an alternative. The teacher and the child must be continually aware that the current lesson objective is the focus. It is neither necessary nor possible to relearn a great deal of material from the past. The belief that such learning is necessary can produce anxiety. Part of problem solving, discovering, and inquiring is to recognize gaps in knowledge and to develop a mindset that allows those gaps to be filled in so the student can continue the learning process. For example, when a particular algorithm hasn't been learned, it may be possible to teach an alternative process.

It is important for the teacher to help the child realize that he or she can do current work in most cases even without completely understanding previous material. Often, in going ahead with new material, students discover the real meaning or value of what might have been only partially learned formerly;

however, math anxiety may cause them to refuse to move on to new material. A teacher can encourage students not to let former failures or gaps in learning cause anxiety about current learning by pointing out that there are other ways of computing, different strategies for solving problems, and different approaches to various mathematical tasks. This will encourage students not to give up when they feel frustrated because a particular item cannot be recalled; they will be more likely to find information or help.

Performance Anxiety

Perfectionist tendencies and concern about classroom performance and grades may also cause anxiety. When the child encounters a new concept or topic in mathematics, he or she is unable to do perfect work from the start because the task or idea has not been practiced previously. If the child does not quickly grasp the new concept, there may be an initial period of low performance and perhaps low grades. This causes anxiety, which may develop in some children every time the teacher begins a new topic. The child may also be defining perfection in terms of knowing facts rather than in terms of concept acquisition and understanding. When a child is in the process of constructing a concept, perfection in reciting factual knowledge is not pertinent. The perfectionist model does not apply to the concept acquisition process, and this can be very frustrating to a child accustomed to always producing correct work.

Competition

Some children are naturally noncompetitive. They do not like to play highly competitive games and often lose when they do play. If mathematics lessons involve competition, those students may respond with math anxiety, which in turn may permeate other mathematics activities. Games with mathematical content and an element of competition may be a source of math anxiety. Just as some children are noncompetitive, some are intensely competitive and will turn any game into competition. When both types of children work in the same group or activity, both types are likely to be frustrated and anxious.

Concern about grades is related to competition. Because of experiences at home and in other classes where grades are a focal point, children may develop anxiety about mathematics grades. A child may be competing for grades with himself or herself or with peers or siblings. This competition may be promoted by promises of rewards (or punishment) at home, making the associated anxiety more intense.

Children can understand explanations of classroom processes, including performance assessment, when these are given at the child's level. Much of the anxiety can be alleviated when the teacher explains the grading process, even though the children may not fully understand all the details. It may be necessary to repeat the explanation in several contexts, because children may become worried if they forget that their performance is being assessed. Obviously teachers should not give the impression, either, that they expect instantaneous and complete learning of new material. Teachers should prepare good lead-in and preliminary material to avoid abrupt changes and to make clear the expectations for rate and quantity of what is to be learned. Children should be helped to understand that for some topics mastery is expected but that other parts of mathematics will be learned in a progression of steps which may require a long time to complete. For example, a teacher might tell third graders that they are expected to know the addition facts by Christmas. Fourth graders might be told that they are to work on division to a particular point, such as two-digit numbers divided by one-digit numbers. The teacher should also tell them that in the fifth and sixth grades they will return to the topic and extend their learning to two- and three-digit number division. This means that students will know what knowledge is to be assessed. Such understanding gives students learning parameters and boundaries, and helps to eliminate feelings of math anxiety stemming from a sense of lack of control over the learning process. Clearly, the teacher must maintain consistency between what students are told and the nature of the assessment. Inconsistency at this point is a source of math anxiety.

Explanations for students should include statements that:

- High performance levels are not expected at the beginning of topics.

- Define expected levels of performance.

- Grades will not be based on first trials and practice activities.

- Certain aspects of lessons will be graded and others will not (e.g., computation process, not results, will be graded).

- Describe the nature of the assessment tools and procedures (e.g., "We will have a practice quiz, then a written test which will have on it questions like these on this worksheet.")

It is also a good idea for the teacher to discuss the issue of performance anxiety with children. They should know that their teacher is aware that some are striving for perfection, that such efforts are admirable, but that they must be conditioned with reality. The teacher should describe a reasonable and common-sense approach to creating assessment tools and interpreting results. Thoughtful mathematics teachers also spend time helping children understand the nature of and reasons for the various general and standardized tests they will take. Children can also learn test-taking techniques that they can use to ease the pressure at examination time. They can be reminded that the tests will not contain material that has not been studied in class.

Cultural Issues

Students may come from significantly different cultural backgrounds. Cultural differences may greatly affect learning in reading and social studies, but typically have less effect in mathematics. Researchers have found, however, that some culture differences do seem to affect mathematics learning.

Skemp (1987) has found that Native American children tend to think of ideas globally rather than analytically and in detail. This may result in discomfort and anxiety when these children are forced to work with precision and analytical detail in mathematics class. Terminology is another focal point of difficulty for children from different cultural backgrounds, since language is an integral part of culture. For example, in the United States, we would say "5 goes into 13 how many times?" In Spanish the wording would be "13 into 5 parts is how many in each part?" Thus children with an English background would misunderstand "13 into 5," and those with a Spanish background would misunderstand "5 into 13" for the same idea: 13 ÷ 5. In East African languages, when approximate or alternative consecutive values are given, the numbers are reversed. English speakers would say, "There were 6 or 7 people present." In Kenya a native speaker would typically say, "There were 7 or 6 people present."

Solving the Problem of Culture-Based Anxiety

Teachers need to pay close attention to children from different cultures who are having difficulty in mathematics. First it should be determined from parents and former teachers if the difficulty or anxiety is in math only. If that is not the case, the problem should be tackled more broadly than in the math classroom only. If the difficulty seems to be only in math, an examination of language, learning styles, and previous experience will be necessary. In this process, the teacher should keep in mind that the source of difficulty may not be cultural at all, but a more typical math anxiety.

If a culturally based difficulty is found, the teacher should consult with parents first, helping them to understand that math anxiety is developing. The parents may be able to identify the source of the anxiety. If the parents cannot help, other members of that cultural group in the community or at a nearby university may be able to suggest ways of assisting the anxious child. Solving this problem may be very time consuming and frustrating, especially if language barriers exist, if cultural differences are extensive, and if there are no adults to assist in dealing with the difficulty.

Myth of Gender Differences

Because our society sees few girls choosing careers in science and mathematics and few girls and women in advanced science and math classes, a myth that boys are more capable of doing mathematics than girls has developed. The idea has generated considerable research, attempting to determine whether there is any truth in the conjecture either at particular age or grade levels or in particular aspects of mathematics.

There is no evidence that differences in mathematical ability can be attributed to gender differences. However, evidence suggests that the myth is believed by many parents, by both boys and girls, and even by some math teachers and other educators. Further research explores the extent of the belief and the effects of the belief on the educational system in general and the teaching of mathematics in particular. It is clear that peer, parental, and general societal influence is sufficient to convince some girls that they cannot or should not succeed in math class, so they don't. They withdraw and take no math beyond the absolute minimum required.

Solving the Gender Myth Problem

It may be helpful for the teacher to know and to share with students that there is little evidence of a gender gap in mathematics ability. Teachers should not give preferential treatment to boys in math class or in any other way indicate that gender difference is a factor in learning mathematics. Girls may be encouraged in their math learning by seeing references to women mathematicians, by listening to classroom guests who are female scientists, and by observing female teachers who are excited about, and competent with, mathematics. The myth of gender difference should be countered with fact. Fortunately, recently produced texts and other materials related to mathematical learning are carefully crafted to give balance in reference to gender in their pictures and text. Facts and information about women mathematicians and women using mathematics in daily lives and the workplace should be shared with the students as well as with their parents. Involving boys and girls equally in math problem solving, projects, and math fairs will also help. *All* students must be made aware of the teacher's expectations that *each* of them is able to learn the mathematics to be studied in the class.

Other Special Students

Visual, auditory, and other physical handicaps may also contribute to a child's negative attitude toward mathematics, because math activities may be dependent on vision, hearing, and manipulation of objects. The ability to see figures and other symbols and their relationships to one another is so critical that a child's inadequate vision can be a factor in his or her frustration and anxiety with mathematics. The influence of the handicap may not be realized by the child or parents, or they may be concealing it.

Solving Special Students' Problems

Positioning children with hearing and vision difficulties in appropriate locations in the classroom can help significantly. Classroom aides can also provide one-on-one assistance.

Various types of technology may also help. Hearing impaired children can use software with visual prompts and scripts that may be helpful. Computers with Braille and sound capabilities can assist visually impaired children. Soon voice-activated computers will be available in some classrooms to provide further capabilities for those with several different kinds of handicaps.

When a child is having difficulty manipulating objects and drawing figures and numerals because of motor skill problems, it is sometimes possible to give equivalent tasks which do not require the same level of coordination. When a child is working with computation algorithms, for example, and is unable to keep the place value, a student can be taught algorithms that are not place-value dependent if keeping columns straight and numerals appropriately lined up is a problem, for example. Teachers can work with special education personnel and use administrative guidelines to learn what adjustments they can make within the classroom to accommodate physical and other handicaps.

It is interesting to note that symptoms of dyslexia, seeing words with letters in reverse order, for example, do not necessarily occur with nonword symbols. Dyslexic children don't always reverse the order of numbers or have trouble with mathematical processes. Children who are having trouble with reading and other subjects may excel in mathematics. Teachers should resist the temptation to prejudge a child's ability to learn in mathematics on the basis of irrelevant issues such as various handicaps. On the other hand, disorders such as number reversal, similar to dyslexia, can directly affect learning in mathematics. When such disorders are noted, the teacher who suspects such disorders should seek professional help in dealing with them.

Inclusion

Inclusion in education ensures that all children are given the opportunity to learn to the extent possible for them. None should be excluded because of perceived differences of gender, culture, or handicap. This pertains to mathematics learning, too. Exclusion or fear of exclusion because a child is somehow *different* can be a factor in developing math anxiety.

Enjoying Mathematics

If the best defense is a good offense, how can math teachers preclude or counter bad attitudes toward mathematics by proactively creating enjoyable mathematics learning? In addition to avoiding boring, repetitive, noninteractive teaching methods, teachers can use devices that provide an atmosphere of excitement and interest.

Children enjoy activity. Teaching which engages students in cooperative group projects, meaningful work with manipulatives of great variety, and creative tasks captivates children's interest. The computer and other high-tech and multimedia devices also provide means of offering interesting activities using powerful teaching tools. Using these high-interest activities and tools, variety in scheduling, and elements of surprise and discovery significantly encourage and create enjoyment among children in mathematics classes. Children tend to emulate their teachers, and will begin to enjoy mathematics when they see their teachers enjoying mathematics. Teachers should set the stage for creativity and discovery; part of that is demonstrating their own pleasure and excitement in finding a solution, discovering some new fact or process, or creating an attractive design or interesting problem.

Reading books with mathematics themes can help children look at mathematics from new perspectives. Books such as *The Math Curse* (Scziescka, 1995) give a light-hearted and humorous view of mathematics and learning. The math presented is accurate and students can learn while laughing at the intriguing ideas and presentations (Silverstein, 1974). Songs such as *I know an Old Lady Who Swallowed a Fly* (Bonne, 1961) let children sing and *hear* mathematics.

In general it may be helpful for a teacher to talk to the class about math anxiety. Students need to know that the teacher knows about math anxiety and knows some ways of dealing with it. When appropriate, students may be encouraged to state their fears and concerns about mathematics (Tobias, 1978). Especially at the beginning of a class or the school year, a general sharing may prove helpful, particularly at grade levels higher than third grade. If the teacher has encountered personal math anxiety somewhere along the mathematics *super highway* and can share how it was dealt with and conquered, students can see hope for themselves and may develop less anxiety if they know that their teacher (who now knows this mathematics) has encountered and conquered math anxiety.

Most cases of math anxiety can be cured or at least made less severe if detected early. Affected students should be encouraged to talk about the problem and to find ways to work through the anxiety. Often students can identify the source of the fear and frustration, especially if it has to do with difficulty remembering, having no homework area or time at home, or having difficulty with tests. Teachers should be aware that math anxiety can develop because of the inability to do homework; a teacher may be able to help the child significantly at this point. Both parents and child should be advised to find a place and a time at home where homework can be done with reasonable consistency.

The self-esteem issues underlying some anxiety may be more difficult for students to talk about. Students sometimes do not understand the real reasons for their discomfort, and teachers need to be attentive to signals and perceptive in determining causes. Most math anxiety problems can be alleviated, so that students will not be hampered in learning or prevented from enjoying their studies in mathematics.

Summary

The difficulties some children experience in learning mathematics because of negative attitudes and anxiety are explored in this chapter. The causes and symptoms of math anxiety are examined and remedies are presented. Math anxiety causes of several kinds are detailed, including those originating with teacher, students, and culture. Schwieger's *Ten Commandments on Math Anxiety* (Schwieger, 1994) for teachers are presented as are other suggestions for preventing the development of math anxiety.

Exercises

1. Find a math-anxious student (or one who has been math anxious at some point), interview the student, and report on the symptoms, causes, and resolution techniques for the student's anxiety.

2. Choose a math anxiety with a particular cause and outline strategies and techniques for changing the learning environment sufficiently to alleviate the anxiety.

3. Outline a strategy to help a student with a negative attitude toward mathematics because of negative attitudes toward mathematics at home.

4. Outline proactive strategies for involving students in enjoyable activities (perhaps using computers) to alleviate negative attitudes toward mathematics.

References

Allardice, Barbara S., and Herbert P. Ginsburg (1983). "Children's Psychological Difficulties in Mathematics," in *The Development of Mathematical Thinking*, ed. Herbert P. Ginsburg. New York: Academic Press.

Bonne, Rose (1961). *I Know an Old Lady Who Swallowed a Fly*. New York: Scholastic.

Burns, Marilyn (1995). "Writing in the Math Class? Absolutely!" *Instructor*, 104(7), 40–44, 47

Dinkmeyer, Don, and Rudolf Dreikurs (1963). *Encouraging Children to Learn: The Encouragement Process*. Upper Saddle River, NJ: Prentice Hall.

Felker, Don (1974). *Self Concept, Divergent Thinking Abilities, and Attitudes about Creativity and Problem Solving*. Minneapolis, MN: Burgess

Schwieger, Ruben (1994). *Ten Commandments for Math Anxiety*. Lima, OH: Unpublished.

Scziescka, J. (1995) *Math Curse*. New York: Viking.

Silverstein, Shel (1974). *Where the Sidewalk Ends*. New York: Harper-Collins.

Skemp, Richard R. (1987). *The Psychology of Learning Mathematics*. Hillsdale, NJ: Lawrence Erlbaum Associates.

Suydam, Marilyn N. (November 1984). "Attitudes Towards Mathematics," *Arithmetic Teacher*, 32(3), 12. Reston, VA: National Council of Teachers of Mathematics.

Tobias, Sheila (1978). *Overcoming Math Anxiety*. New York: W. W. Norton.

🔳 Suggested Readings

Brownell, William A. (1935). "Psychological Considerations in the Learning and the Teaching of Arithmetic," *The Teaching of Arithmetic*. National Council of Teachers of Mathematics, The Tenth Yearbook. New York: Bureau of Publications, Teachers College, Columbia University.

Thiessen, Diane, and Margaret Matthia, Eds. (1992). *The Wonderful World of Mathematics*. Reston, VA: NCTM.

Whitin, David J., and Sandra Wilde (1992). *Read Any Good Math Lately?* Portsmouth, NH: Heineman.

Reading Books with Mathematics Themes

Anno, Mitsumasa (1982). *Anno's Math Games III*. New York: Philomel.

Burns, Marilyn (1975). *The I Hate Mathematics! Book*. New York: Little, Brown.

Kaplan, M. (1991) *Henry and the Boy Who Thought Numbers Were Fleas*. New York: Four Winds.

White, Laurence B., and R. Broekel (1990). *Math-a-Magic*. Martin Grove, IL: Albert Whitman.

Songs in Books which Integrate Math

Langstaff, John (1957). *Over in the Meadow*. New York: Harcourt, Brace, & World.

Raffi (1989). *Five Little Ducks*. New York: Crown Publishing.

Gerstein, Mordecai (1984). *Roll Over*. New York: Crown Publishing.

McNally, Darcie, and Robin Michal Koontz (1991). *In a Cabin in a Wood*. New York: Cobblehill Dutton.

Poetry which Integrates Math

Barnes-Murphy and G. Rowan (1978). *One Two Buckle My Shoe: A Book of Counting Rhymes*. New York: Little-Simon.

Christelow, Eileen (1989). *Five Little Monkeys Jumping On the Bed*. New York: Clarion.

Christelow, Eileen (1991). *Five Little Monkeys Sitting In a Tree*. New York: Clarion.

Learning What Children Know about Mathematics

One of the children's problems: Daric never learned his multiplication facts.

Teacher's problem: The children seem not to have the background knowledge necessary for the topics to be taught.

⊞ Understanding the Problem

Although school systems have described the mathematics curriculum in detail for each grade and have selected tests and other materials to be used, teachers still have considerable latitude in designing mathematics lessons. Teachers can decide which topics to emphasize more and which less. Manipulatives, supplies, equipment, and software will have to be selected and brought into the classroom. To provide bases for the necessary planning, teachers need to assess the knowledge base of their incoming students.

Many areas of mathematical competence should be considered and evaluated, including mathematical processing (which includes computation algorithms), concept acquisition, problem solving, and mathematical thinking (which includes fact knowledge), writing, terminology, and number and object manipulation. Of these, those that most influence the capability of a child to learn as he or she moves from one mathematics level to another are discussed here.

Mathematical Processing

For understanding the level of student competence in mathematical processing, the usual paper-and-pencil computational tasks may provide the most help. A variety of exercises should be presented, so that all aspects of the operational processes are considered. For example: In checking skills with multiplication processes, different algorithm formats and different sizes and types of numbers should be presented for the students to work with. An example of this variety is shown in Figure 3-1.

Children should have opportunities to demonstrate techniques that might be different from those most likely to be shown on the exercise sheets. There may be students who have developed some mental process which they use successfully, but which they cannot demonstrate using paper-and-pencil methods. The teacher should ask for process descriptions from those who "do math in their heads."

FIGURE 3-1. Multiplication Algorithm Formats

3×5	$\begin{array}{r} 13 \\ \times\, 6 \\ \hline \end{array}$	24×13	$3(5 + 4)$
43 times 17		5 multiplied by 12	12×5

Consideration must also be given to the use of calculators and other devices such as charts, lists, number lines, etc. The following questions should be asked and answered by the teacher:

- Are the children heavily dependent on aids for basic facts to use in computation algorithms?

- Are the children aware that there is a variety of methods and algorithms or are they dependent on a single algorithm for each operation?

- Is there concept undergirding for the algorithms the children use? (For example, do the children understand that the standard long division algorithm is essentially a device for computing using division as repeated subtraction?)

- To what extent can or do the students use manipulatives to assist them with operational computation?

- What problem solving processes are practiced by the children?

- Are manipulatives readily used to understand and work with number patterns and geometrical ideas? (Brooks, 1993)

Information gleaned from these descriptions and from written papers will guide the teacher in planning corrective and extension lessons where necessary. These lessons may be designed to correct poor procedures early or reinforce good practices. Additionally, the lessons may be designed to capitalize on already learned processes, to extend them, and to move children to learning more complex or new processes.

Concept Acquisition

Oral questions about operations and other concepts are also very important. A teacher needs to know the levels of the children's development of various critical mathematical concepts. A helpful way to make these determinations is to present children with real-life scenarios to serve as generators of discussion and as opportunities for children to express their understandings of the concepts.

Examples

John has a jar filled with pieces of candy. There is enough in the jar to give each of his seven friends and himself ten pieces of candy each. How many pieces of candy must he take out of the jar to share?

Ashley has 12 Barbie dolls to play with. If two friends come to play with her and they share the dolls so that each has the same number to play with, how many will each have?

Leading and diagnostic questions should be asked about the example situations and similar ones designed specifically at the appropriate level for the class, for example:

- Should John and Ashley use multiplication or division here?

- Why?

- Will this be a large number or small?

- How do you know? Are there different ways to count these things? etc.

The teacher should use a list of the concepts that need to be considered to guide development of the questions. The school's mathematics curriculum can provide one source for the list. Other lists of topics are found in National Council of Teachers of Mathematics publications, especially, *Curriculum and Evaluations Standards* (NCTM, 1989). This publication, a must for every school's library if not for each math teacher, lists the topics in 13 *Standards* for each grade, K–8. A partial listing for grade 3 is included here. This book also includes the NCTM's suggestions for which topics should be emphasized and which should be de-emphasized. A sample checklist based on the list of third grade level topics found in the *Curriculum and Evaluation Standards* (NCTM, 1989) is presented in Figure 3-2.

FIGURE 3-2. A Portion of the Standards Lists

Third Grade Standards
(Partial listing)

Standard 1: Mathematics as Problem Solving
          The student will be able to:
             use simple patterns to generalize.
             use multiple solving strategies.
Standard 2: Mathematics as Communication
          The student will be able to:
             use patterns to predict solutions.
             develop a convincing written argument.
Standard 3: Mathematics as Reasoning
          The student will be able to:
             use Venn diagrams.
             chain statements in a simple deductive argument.
             reason inductively.
Standard 4: Mathematical Connections
          The student will be able to:
             investigate angles by various means.
             describe different perspectives of 3-D objects.
             investigate area by covering regions.

FIGURE 3-2.   (continued)

Standard 5: Estimation

> The student will be able to:
>> understand when an estimation of measurement is sufficiently accurate.
>> estimate a calculation result.
>> use front end estimation.

Standard 6: Number Sense and Numeration

> The student will be able to:
>> record all possible arrangements of objects in a set.
>> understand the use of symbols for numbers.
>> order a few simple fractions using manipulatives.

Standard 7: Concepts of Whole Number Operations

> The student will be able to:
>> relate addition and subtraction.
>> recognize multiplication patterns.
>> understand that multiplication may be thought of as repeated addition.

Standard 8: Whole Number Computation

> The student will be able to:
>> relate skip counting and relate division by two and even numbers.
>> use front end estimation.
>> use multiples of ten in computation.

Standard 9: Geometry and Spatial Sense

> The student will be able to:
>> recognize basic geometrical shapes and recite several critical characteristics of each.
>> begin to evidence conservation of quantity and mass.

Standard 10: Measurement

> The student will be able to:
>> understand and use common units of measure.
>> use Fahrenheit and Celsius scales.
>> explore perimeter, area, and volume and basic relationships among them.

Standard 11: Statistics and Probability

> The student will be able to:
>> read, create, and interpret tables and charts and graphs.
>> use picture-symbol keys on picture maps.

Standard 12: Fractions and Decimals

> The student will be able to:
>> see the connections between a few simple fraction and decimal expressions.
>> use the relationships of just less than one and just more than one in understanding fraction size.

Standard 13: Patterns and Relationships

> The student will be able to:
>> predict the next number in simple sequences.
>> use a pattern to describe geometrical shapes.
>> understand place value in terms of patterns.

🔖 Solving the Problem

Similar checklists can be made using the appropriate grade level lists and modifying them to suit the particular examination of the incoming class. In this way a teacher can ensure that each of the critical concepts underlying the mathematical learning expected during the year, will be considered. Care must be taken to deal with concepts separately from algorithms and computation. Children may have weak concepts about operations and yet have memorized algorithms which they can perform successfully. They may know considerable terminology but be unable to use the concepts named by those words. Clearly there is much overlap between a concept and a related process (such as the concept of addition and an algorithm for computing a result of addition). Early in their mathematical experiences, children cannot and do not attempt to distinguish between a concept and processes related to that concept. They do, however, have at least partially developed concepts of the operations and other concepts such as *larger than, equal, even/odd*, etc. Teachers must remember that concept development is critical, because it is fundamental to proper understanding and use of the mathematical processes which will be taught. Among these processes are computational algorithms, constructing geometrical figures, problem solving strategies, and developing patterns. In Figure 3-2, note the strong emphasis on concepts and the lack of emphasis on processes.

Problem Solving

Since problem solving is so important, both in daily life and as a basis for real mathematical learning, its level of use among students must also be examined carefully. Hiebert, Carpenter, and others (1996, p. 12) write that problem solving can also serve as a basis for reform in mathematics curriculum and instruction. Consequently, it is essential for the teacher to learn early what experience and background in problem solving the children have. The current situation in mathematics education is still a very mixed bag. Although the National Council of Teachers of Mathematics, in its *Standards* (NCTM, 1989, 1991, 1995) publications, has emphasized the teaching and learning of problem solving, some teachers do little with problem solving. Thus children coming to the new class may have had little experience in, and no direct teaching about, problem solving. This is particularly true for the early grades, because some teachers assume that problem solving should not begin until the fourth or fifth grade. The idea grows out of a misunderstanding of what constitutes problem solving. An emphasis on problem solving should begin in kindergarten (and even before) and continue through high school. Children naturally solve problems at their level in kindergarten and do so using the skills they have available to them.

Note

Problem solving involves working with any situation where there is not an immediate solution or algorithmic rule for reaching solution and where mathematical tools can be applied to achieve resolution. Very young children can solve problems at their level with their tools.

In good mathematics learning environments, children will continue to solve problems and develop more and more skill and sophistication in finding solutions. Furthermore, as they become skilled with additional tools and acquire more mathematical concepts, their ability to solve a greater variety of problems will increase. An important facet of the teacher's responsibility here is to encourage problem solving and keep the expectation level high. The teacher should be very open and clear in helping children to know that they can solve problems at their level and with the tools they have.

To assess awareness of problem solving, children and their previous teachers should be asked at least the following:

- What problem solving was done previously?

- What approaches were used?

- What success did the students have?

- What are their attitudes toward problem solving?

- Were problem solving techniques taught directly?

The children's problem solving interest, approaches, and abilities can be examined directly by giving them interesting puzzles and problems to solve. An alternative approach is to use the *MADS* (Schwieger, 1995) outlined in Appendix F. This device enables the teacher to check an individual child's skills and responses in problem solving.

The teacher may then observe the children's behaviors involving the use (or nonuse) of manipulatives and other tools in addition to the children's paper-and-pencil work. It should be remembered that Hughes' research with young children showed that "although they see written numerals around them all the time, children in most Western societies are not usually introduced to written arithmetic until they start school" (p. 143). Then they must learn to translate between their own concrete understanding of number and the abstract written symbolism. This is shown to be very difficult for children early in their school careers (Hughes, 1993). This means that teachers must take care in designing and interpreting the paper-and-pencil responses children make in assessment environments. Children should be instructed to use whatever methods they wish, to write or draw anything that might help organize their work in some way, and not to erase their rough work. The teacher will look at all of these for evidence of the use of the various problem solving skills and strategies. (Checklists found in Chapter 8 and in the appendixes may be helpful at this point.)

The teacher should not focus on some particular *answer* or *method*; the focus should rather be on the overall process and on whether a child is making some progress using problem solving. As the reader will note in the study of problem solving, *translation* is a critical part of successful problem solving. This translation can be from the words of the problem statement to the student's own words or to diagrams or charts. Translations are usually obvious in the child's paper-and-pencil work and should be carefully observed by the teacher. Even when children come from classrooms where there has been no overt teaching about problem solving, it will be of interest to know what children have acquired *on their own*. To make thorough assessments, three aspects of problem solving should be addressed:

- As children are questioned or given sample problems to work on, they should have access to various tools as they indicate their knowledge and skills. (In addition to paper, drawing instruments, and appropriate manipulatives, calculators should be provided.)

- Problems which are appropriate and drawn from real life, that is, in the environment of the children, should be presented. For comments on real-life expressions and appropriate problems and sample problems, see Chapter 8 and the appendixes.

- The problems presented should cover a variety in topics and in the skills and strategies which are likely to be used in solving them.

    Good sources of problems at appropriate levels are:

- Various problem solving Internet sites

- Mathematics teachers' bulletin boards and information exchanges on the Internet

- Calendar problems (*Mathematics Teacher*, NCTM). (These are for advanced middle school and high school students.)

- Menu of problems (*Teaching Mathematics in the Middle School*, NCTM)

- NCTM conferences and conventions

- State mathematics teachers' organizations and meetings

Mathematical Thinking

It is important that the teacher know what mathematical thinking and knowledge the children bring to their new class. Again, a checklist of mathematical knowledge assumed to have been acquired in the former grade will be helpful. The teacher may formulate questions, tasks, games, and activities to gather this information as the new school year begins. Games and activities are additional places where a teacher can look for evidence of the level of mathematical thinking and knowledge (Carpenter, 1985). Teachers in the early grades should ask the following questions:

- Do the children recognize and use numerical order appropriately?

- Are they able to count accurately using a variety of methods including skip counting, addition, and multiplication?

- Do they recognize fractional concepts in a variety of connections: rate, ratio, division, etc.?

- Have they developed conservation of number and part/whole at some level or in some aspect of mathematics?

- Do they show evidence of recognizing interrelationships and connections between various mathematical ideas?

Reasoning

A teacher will want to know, too, the level of reasoning ability present in the class. Are the children comfortable with chaining together *if-then* statements so that the reasoning leads effectively to certain conclusions? (NCTM, Feb. 1995) An activity for the whole class that will help the teacher check this kind of reasoning is to present problems in which the teacher has in mind a certain number or mathematical entity and the children are asked to discover what it is by asking questions which may be answered only by "yes" or "no." For example, the teacher may say:

"I am thinking of a geometrical figure."

"I am thinking of a large number."

"I am thinking of a small number."

"I am thinking of an operation."

Depending on their grade level, the children may ask such questions as: Is it round? Is it circular? Is it a solid? Is it larger than 1000? Is it smaller than 1? The terminology, complexity of the concept, and nature of the questions will depend on the grade level. When the puzzle has been solved, the teacher or a student should summarize with a statement such as: "If it has this characteristic and that too, then it must be . . ." and obtain class agreement. Multiple game scenarios and concluding statements of this kind by the class will help the teacher to know whether the children are capable of performing deductive reasoning and at what level. The activity can easily be made into a game, and students can take turns selecting a concept and answering questions.

Inductive reasoning ability should be examined by presenting incomplete number and other patterns and asking students to solve the puzzles (i.e., complete or extend the patterns). The reasoning ability here concerns facility with considering multiple specific examples and drawing a general conclusion from them. This reasoning ability is very important as the basis for a powerful problem solving strategy and has many directly practical applications. Most children have some ability to reason in this way. They may not, however, have exercised it very much in connection with mathematics learning and use (Brooks, 1993).

 Examples

Extend the following sequences:

2,4,6,8,_,_,   1,3,5,7,_,_,   O,T,T,F,_,_,
J,A,S,O,N,_,_,   2,4,8,_,_, not the same as 2,4,8,_,_,

$$\triangle, \square, \hexagon, \_\_\_ , \_\_\_ \qquad \uparrow, \text{2S}, \text{3E}, \text{4}, \_\_\_ , \_\_\_$$

A triangle has no diagnonals, a rectangle has two, and a pentagon has five. How many does a hexagon have? How many does a 20-sided polygon have?

Two lines may have 0 or 1 intersections. Two lines may have 0, 1, 2, or 3 intersections. How many intersections are possible with 3 lines? How many with 7 lines?

Summary

As students enter school or a specific class, teachers must ascertain the status of children's knowledge and ability. Four general areas of concern were discussed: mathematical processing, problem solving, mathematical thinking, and concept acquisition. Suggestions were given for assessing the level of competence and the level of knowledge in the four aspects of mathematical learning.

Exercises

1. Find a child to interview about mathematical concepts. Use a series of questions carefully worded to enable discovery of whether the child has good understanding of the four operations concepts, the concept of numerical order, large and small numbers, fractional numbers, or other concepts. Record the results of the interview(s) and the conclusions you draw about the level of concept development.

2. Prepare checklists for assessing, at a particular grade level, three of the following:
   - Understanding of counting
   - Fractional value concepts
   - Competence in the use of algorithms
   - Ability to solve problems

- ■ Deductive reasoning with number concepts
- ■ Knowledge of basic facts interrelationships

3. Prepare a description of a workstation, including the tools and manipulatives that should be present for adequate assessment of a student's level of problem solving skills.

4. Prepare a whole-class activity such as: *I have . . . Who has? . .* which would enable a teacher to see at a glance the level of knowledge or awareness of a particular topic or concept in a class. An individual chalk-slate activity may also serve this purpose.

5. In consultation with a group of four or five classmates, write a definition of *understanding mathematics.*

🔃 References

Brooks, Jacqueline Grennon, and Martin G. Brooks (1993). *The Case for Constructivist Classrooms.* Alexandria, VA: Association for Supervision and Curriculum Development.

Carpenter, Thomas P. (1985, February). "Research on the Role of Structure in Thinking," *Arithmetic Teacher,* 32(6), 58–60.

Hiebert, James, and Thomas P. Carpenter, et. al. (1996, May). "Problem Solving as a Basis for Reform in Curriculum and Instruction: The Case of Mathematics," *Educational Researcher.* Washington, DC: Association for Educational Research.

Hughes, Martin (1993). *Children and Number.* Cambridge, MA. Blackwell.

National Council of Teachers of Mathematics (1989). *Curriculum and Evaluation Standards for School Mathematics Education.* Washington, DC: National Academy Press.

National Council of Teachers of Mathematics (1991). *Professional Standards for Teaching Mathematics.* Reston, VA: NCTM.

National Council of Teachers of Mathematics (1995). *Assessment Standards for School Mathematics.* Reston, VA: NCTM.

🔃 Suggested Readings

Baratta-Lorton, Mary (1976). *Mathematics Their Way.* Menlo Park, CA: Addison-Wesley.

Burger, William F., and J. Michael Shaughnessy (1986, January). "Characterizing the Van Hiele Levels of Development in Geometry," *Journal for Research in Mathematics Education,* 17(1), 31–48.

Clark, Faye B., and Constance Kamii (1996). "Identification of Multiplicative Thinking," *Journal for Research in Mathematics Education,* Reston, VA: NCTM.

Dienes, Zoltan P., and E. W. Golding. *Learning Mathematics.* Boston: Allyn & Bacon

Dossey, John A., Ina V.S. Mullis, and C.O. Jones (1993). "Can Students Do Mathematical Problem Solving? Results from Constructed-response Questions in NAEP's 1992 Mathematics Assessment" (Report No. 23-FR01). Washington, DC: Government Printing Office.

Gibb, Glenadine, and Alberta Castaneda (1975). "Experiences for Young Children," in *Mathematics Learning in Early Childhood*. National Council of Teachers of Mathematics, 37th Yearbook. Reston, VA: NCTM.

Kamii, Constance (1990). "Constructivism and Beginning Arithmetic (K-2)," in *Teaching and Learning Math in the 1990s*. Eds. Thomas J. Cooney and Christian Hirsch. Reston, VA: NCTM.

"Mathematical Thinking" (Focus Issue). (1985, February). *Arithmetic Teacher*, 32(6). Reston, VA: NCTM

National Research Council (1989). *Everybody Counts: A Report to the Nation on the Future of Mathematics Education*. Washington, DC: National Academy Press.

Payne, Joseph N., Ed. (1975). *Mathematics Learning in Early Childhood*. National Council of Teachers of Mathematics, 37th Yearbook. Reston, VA: NCTM.

Webb, Laurye M. (1996). "How to turn Oranges into Moolah," *Mathematics Teaching in the Middle School*. Reston, VA: NCTM

Teaching Sequenced, Nonsequenced, and Mandated Topics

One of the children's problems: Teri believes that all mathematics is nicely ordered and has difficulty when topics do not build neatly on previously learned material.

Teacher's problem: The mandated topics contained in the proficiency examinations are not well coordinated with the mathematics texts.

Understanding the Problem

Many people believe that mathematics is a very tightly ordered system in which topics are neatly sequenced and that to learn or to teach math requires students and teachers always to organize their work from the simple to the complex. The idea is that children will master simple concepts and processes and, using those as a foundation, build ever more complex ideas and concepts on them. A natural consequence of this view is the belief that if a child does not learn sufficiently at some rudimentary level, he or she will then be unable to learn in the next and higher stages. This belief is evident when students are placed in remediation classes and kept there until able to master a particular skill.

Some topics and even some concepts are necessarily learned after others. For example, formal learning about fractions depends on good understanding of whole numbers. Multiplication usually follows addition, especially where multiplication is defined as repeated addition. Algebra follows arithmetic. Generally, mathematical concepts and processes are more involved and complex for children in the upper grades than they are for children in the lower grades. But this sequencing does not hold uniformly within mathematical topics or even within the mathematics of a particular grade level. Children learn about some fractions and about the process of sharing evenly (dividing) before they learn about adding and subtracting.

Sequenced topics are those which fit into an order; one part of the topic follows another in a clearly specified pattern. For example, the study of the standard division algorithm must follow learning the standard algorithm for subtraction. Hierarchical topics are those which increase in complexity and dependence on former topics: learning to write and read decimal numbers depends on a good understanding of place value in the numeration system, for example.

Many topics studied in elementary and middle school mathematics are not necessarily taught in a particular order and are not dependent on other knowledge or skills being learned first.

Example

Geometrical concepts such as shapes, symmetry, and topological ideas can be taught before, simultaneously, or with operations.

One aspect of the problem of teaching sequenced topics is that sequences are not uniform throughout individual topics, and the interrelationships between topics are not always clearly in linear sequence (Brooks, 1990). One part of a topic may be dependent on part of another while others are not. A familiar example occurs in fraction operation algorithms.

Example

The *invert-and-multiply* algorithm for dividing by a fraction is dependent on knowledge of how to multiply by a fraction. The *standard* algorithm for adding two fractions is not dependent on any other learning about operating with fractions. Furthermore, both of these processes can be done (and too often are) without any real understanding of the actual operations.

Much emphasis in teaching mathematics to young children has been given to computation and, later, to algebra. Because many of the *processes* in these mathematical topics are sequential and hierarchical, students and teachers have the impression that mathematics topics and teaching and learning in mathematics are predominantly sequential. This assumption leads teachers, and children too, to believe that any learning in mathematics is heavily dependent on prerequisite learning of simpler facts and processes. Homework in mathematics and foreign language is almost always described as strongly sequential (Brooks, 1990), implying that missing even one homework assignment will permanently damage future learning. As noted earlier, this belief is often an important cause of math anxiety. A child who realizes that a previously presented concept or process was not mastered assumes, therefore, that new ideas cannot be learned. Math anxiety develops, then, not because of the nature of the mathematics to be learned, but because of perceptions and beliefs about mathematics teaching and learning.

Even in areas where there is obvious sequencing, options which are not dependent on previous learning can and should be presented to students (and perhaps explained to parents as well). For example, within the sequence of learning the standard algorithms for subtraction and multiplication in order to cope with the long division algorithm, a student may be given an alternative algorithm for division. This will be important when the student is struggling with the long division process. The student may be making errors in division because of difficulty with the subtraction algorithm. The alternate division process might be one using the distributive property.

Illustration

$$\frac{4683}{23} = \frac{4600}{23} + \frac{83}{23} = 200 + \frac{69}{23} + \frac{14}{23} =$$

$$
\begin{array}{r}
203 \\
23\overline{)4683} \\
46 \\
\hline
83 \\
69 \\
\hline
\end{array}
$$

$$200 + 3 + \frac{14}{23} = 203 \ \text{R} \ 14$$

In formal learning about fractions, a typical procedure involving relative size of fractions is to convert the fractions to their decimal equivalents and compare the decimal values. This procedure is obviously highly dependent on the learning sequence:

1. Place value and relative size of decimals

2. Understanding a fraction as division

3. Accurate division procedure

4. Comparison of decimal values

When there is a weak link in this chain (a student may be uncertain about place value and number size determination by examining decimal place values), the sequence cannot be used effectively. The alternative method of examining the equivalence classes for two fractions and finding equivalents with the same denominator (or the same numerator) and comparing numerators (denominators) may be a much better option.

Illustration: Is 7/9 greater than 3/4?

$7/9 = .7777$ $3/4 = .7500$ $.7777 > .75$ because $7 > 5$ in the hundredths place, therefore $7/9 > 3/4$.

Option: $\dfrac{7}{9} = \left\{ \dfrac{7}{9}, \dfrac{14}{18}, \dfrac{21}{27}, \dfrac{28}{36}, \dfrac{35}{45} \cdots \right\}$

$\dfrac{3}{4} = \left\{ \dfrac{3}{4}, \dfrac{6}{8}, \dfrac{9}{12}, \dfrac{12}{16}, \dfrac{15}{20}, \dfrac{18}{24}, \dfrac{21}{28}, \dfrac{24}{32}, \dfrac{27}{36}, \dfrac{30}{40} \cdots \right\}$

The equivalents to compare are $\dfrac{28}{36}$ and $\dfrac{27}{36}$. Thus $7/9 > 3/4$. Alternatively, the numbers $\dfrac{21}{27}$ and $\dfrac{21}{28}$ can be compared with the same result.

Clearly, saying the number names and writing the numerals in counting are partially dependent on the ability to build on more basic knowledge and to identify patterns. The numeral 185 cannot be understood and written before the numeral 85 is understood, for example. The name *forty-three* has little meaning before the concept of naming group of 10s and adding the units to create number names and numerals is understood. Similarly, the standard algorithm for two-digit multiplication cannot be taught before algorithms for adding two- and three-digit numbers have been learned. These are sequential and hierarchical. In the next section, we examine teaching of the many concepts and processes of mathematics that are not necessarily sequential or hierarchical.

Solving the Problem

In teaching sequenced and hierarchical topics, four major considerations must be attended to. These are:

- Ensuring that the learners know the prerequisite information.

- Presenting adequate information about how the new material connects with and builds on other ideas.

- Giving an understanding of the integrated whole that is being created by the addition of the new material.

- Indicating the direction for further building the system.

We will examine each of these concerns as we find solutions to the difficulties encountered in teaching the most obviously sequenced topics: counting, the number system, operation algorithms, and linear-area-volume measure. The principles which apply in teaching these will be important in teaching in other wholly or partially sequenced topics.

Note

Teaching fractions may also be considered sequenced. We begin teaching fraction ideas in the first grade with $\frac{1}{2}$, $\frac{1}{3}$, and $\frac{1}{4}$ and then wait until later to work with $\frac{1}{8}$, $\frac{1}{10}$, and $\frac{1}{16}$, etc. We wait until still later to operate with fractions. However, as no definitive order is necessary, we will discuss teaching fractions in later sections.

Counting

What is counting? When a 4-year-old correctly recites the sequence of names of numbers 1 to 10 or beyond, is this counting? Not really. That 4-year-old probably can actually count to 3 or 4. That is, the child can accurately recite the names in order while identifying each of four objects and establishing a one-to-one correspondence between the number names and the objects. Beyond three or four objects, often depending on the arrangement of the objects, the child may skip some objects and count others twice. Thus the child is not actually counting beyond 4. The sequence of skills in learning to count is:

1. Establishing direct one-to-one correspondence

2. Using operations of adding and multiplying

3. Recognizing numbers up to 5 or 6

4. Comparison counting

After first making a clear classification, a student can use the ability to establish one-to-one correspondence to devise and carry out a scheme that will avoid skipping or double counting. This enables the student to be definitive and consistent in counting. The next stages in the sequence of learning to count involve the use of the operations (especially addition and multiplication), indirect methods, and estimation. Addition is used when counts are made for portions of the set, and the results are added to complete the count. Similarly, the objects in the set may be placed in arrays (subsets of equal sizes) and multiplication used to obtain a total. Indirect methods include comparison of the set to be counted with sets with known counts and the use of measuring devices. Students need to learn that, for large numbers, estimates are often appropriate. Estimates are adequate for many other practical counts.

A second stage in counting occurs when a child is able to recognize immediately the numbers of objects in sets of 0, 1, 2, and 3 items without some sort of counting *process*. When a child does this with three objects, the child is said to have the concept of *threeness* as an attribute of a given set. He or she simply knows that there are three objects or entities present. The child can state that categorically without attaching number names starting from one or moving attention from one object to another. Studies show that most adults have this kind of concept of number up to 5 or 6 for most objects in any arrangement. Beyond 6, the objects must be in arrays or familiar arrangements and must be neither too small nor too large. Children should be assisted in developing *fourness*, *fiveness*, and *sixness* gradually, by giving appropriate experiences. There is no need to encourage children to develop this kind of recognition beyond *sixness*. Some children, however, may be able to recognize other set numbers because of some common sight in that child's experience. An example of instant recognition is *twelveness* when a child sees a dozen cans of cola in a package. These skills are taught by providing multiple opportunities for children to identify number with sets in a wide variety of contexts. Teachers should take advantage of the many opportunities to provide these experiences that occur in all aspects of classroom life, in studies in science, social studies, and music, as well as in the routines of scheduled activities.

Comparison counting is last in the sequence of developing counting skills for young children. Comparison counting occurs when a person notes a relationship between the set being counted and comparable sets of known number. In elementary classrooms, attendance charts or other devices may allow children to *count* the number of the class present by noting that all the indicators corresponding to individuals in the class are marked in some way. This process might be combined with an operation by noting that on another occasion, two indicators are missing, so that the count is two less than the number of the full class.

 ## Activities

Students can fill coin tubes and determine whether the correct number of coins is in a tube by comparing it with a correctly filled tube.

Students can count the number of desks in a room by noting that there are the same numbers of desks in the same number of rows as in a room known to have 24 desks.

Children can count money required for a class project or event by comparing amounts required for purchases of small amounts of known quantity.

The predominant teaching technique in teaching counting is to provide ample opportunity for practice. It is a process, and processes are *constructed* by practice and repetition. Counting techniques can be demonstrated; students can then emulate as they are given opportunities to count many different kinds of manipulatives. At first the manipulatives used should include objects the children are familiar with, such as toy cars, pieces of candy, books, pencils, markers, and crayons. Items of different sizes should be counted: marbles, coins, and other small objects as well as large things like chairs, tables, and people. Mixtures of small and large things should be included. The objects to be counted should be a mixture of discrete objects and representations (that is, abstractions) such as sketches and pictures of objects. Colors, shapes, textures and object arrangement should also vary. Sets of objects to be counted should appear in arrays, random arrangements, closely packed settings, and loosely scattered collections.

If variety on all these fronts is not provided, young children who are just developing conservation of number can get the idea that a count may vary according to the attributes or the arrangement of the objects. All this variation ensures that students realize that a count is not to be thought of as dependent on noncritical attributes of the set such as color, size, or shapes of the objects. Otherwise they might believe, for example, that large numbers are for large objects and small numbers for small objects. Teachers should remember, too, that the early stages of learning to count come while children are developing *conservation* abilities. When children are not *conservers*, their counting is inconsistent and often depends on the type of the objects or the arrangement of objects within the set rather than on number alone.

Thus, teaching counting involves sequencing activities and tasks which will bring children from the simplest forms (reciting names in one-to-one correspondence with fingers pointed to objects) to counting with large numbers of items. Skip counting, instant recognition of certain numbers, comparison counting, and counting using computation are more advanced forms. At each level, variety in experience is vital. These experiences with manipulatives and the environment of the classroom must be connected directly to the children's lives inside and outside the classroom. It is also important to arrange for student-generated counting situations in addition to the teacher-created counting tasks so that the children learn to exert control over the counting processes. All of these will enable children to progress from simple to more complex counting abilities.

The Number System

Students begin with the *natural numbers* (the counting numbers) and, through their counting experiences, build increasing complexity into their concept of numbers. First, the concept of *zero* is added, and the slightly larger system is called the *whole numbers*. Negative numbers are added to the wholes and the resulting set is called the *integers.* Next, the noninteger *rationals* are added to the integers to form the *rational numbers,* and finally (in grades 7 and 8) some *irrationals* such as $\sqrt{2}$ and π are added. Thus each larger set contains each of the previous smaller sets. Figure 4-1 depicts a Venn diagram, showing relationships between types of numbers.

Note

The concentric rings indicate successively inclusive sets. This means, for example, that the naturals are also whole, integers, rationals, and reals.

It is clear that many children have heard of, and know something about, certain fractions before there is formal teaching about fractions, but the basic approach to developing the number system concept is to move in the sequence cited above from the *naturals* to the *reals.* (The *real numbers* consist of the *irrationals* added to the *rationals.*) This learning is hierarchical in obvious ways; a student would have difficulty learning fraction and decimal forms without first learning whole numbers.

Teaching numbers in this sequence means attempting to ensure that students have a good grasp of the whole numbers before they are confronted with negatives and fractions. This involves providing wide-ranging experiences with the numbers being studied. Care should be taken to make these experiences as practical as possible. Children often bring examples to class from their homes

---

FIGURE 4-1 Venn Diagram Showing Relationships Between Types of Numbers

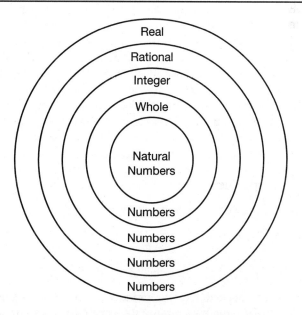

and play. Whenever numbers can be connected with situations in which the children themselves would naturally use those numbers, real learning is more likely. The teacher should explain the idea that the numbers presently being studied are not *all* the numbers. Students will understand that the collection of numbers to be learned about and used will be expanded as necessary, particularly as different numbers are needed to solve new problems. The teacher might remind the class about past experiences with certain numbers. For example, the teacher might say,

> Remember when we needed numbers to express parts of wholes, so we wrote $^1/_2$ and $^4/_5$? Now we need a number to represent the relationship between the diameter and circumference of a circle. None of the numbers we have will work. The new number isn't exactly one we know, so we have a new number we call *pi*. The symbol for it is π. We can estimate it with $^{22}/_7$ or 3.14 but we must estimate because it does not have the exact value of any fraction or terminating decimal.

Similar introductions should be made as zero, negative numbers, and other new numbers are presented to students. It is important that children understand that these numbers are not just abstract constructs, but are developed because of need and because they work well to meet those needs.

There is a kind of expression used by many teachers at certain stages of working with numbers that is not only misleading but actually untrue. Examples are: "You *can't* subtract 5 from 3, because five is bigger than three," and "Six *can't* be divided into 2 because 6 is bigger than 2." Teachers may use these statements when students have not yet learned about the next set of numbers—the negative numbers in the case of the first statement and the rational numbers in the case of the statement about division. It may be difficult for students to grasp concepts such as: "Now we can subtract 5 from 3 and get negative 2," and "Two divided by 6 is one-third," because the teacher has said "You can't," then later, "You can." Teachers should discontinue the use of the phrase "You can't," replacing it with an expression such as "We don't have the numbers to do this with," or "We will learn how to do this when we need it later or in a more advanced class."

Examples

- The need to express parts of wholes

- The need to express the result of division when "it does not come out even"

- The need to solve certain kinds of problems

- The need to express practical situations such as those involving money, very large measurements, very small measurements, and certain physical entities

If lessons are designed so that children construct the number ideas for themselves and understand that they are building on foundational numbers, they will more easily grasp the idea of increasingly complex numbers (Russell, 1990). In the process, the teacher should not make confusing or misleading statements about what can and can't be done. Children are quite accustomed to understanding that they will be able to do some tasks later when they know more.

The concept of a *number system* is a partially sequenced study. Children begin to pay attention to the base 10 number system and its place value format as they start to count and write numerals for 10 and beyond. As they learn the place value system, the pattern of place value for larger and larger numbers becomes evident. This sequence of powers of 10 is further expanded when decimals are studied. This latter part of the sequence of learning about the base 10 system is interrupted so that fractions and powers of numbers can be studied. This constitutes one example, among many in mathematics, of learning in a sequenced subject being interrupted so that another topic may be studied and the knowledge applied to the sequenced topic when it is again taken up.

Teaching numbers and number systems, then, requires a teacher to know how to build one more complex concept on another which is less complex. Not only should lessons emphasize sequencing and structure, but students should be reminded that they are building understanding of the number system. The teacher must also be aware when a "break in the action" is necessary to prepare students for the next concept development stage with additional information. Students should be told straightforwardly that a particular idea fits into a sequence and will need to be built step by step. They should also be told what the steps are and how they are going to be put together. Students function better when they understand something of the structure that predominates in an environment (Dinkmeyer, 1975).

Teachers will find, though, that children are different in this respect. One group is better organized and enjoys working within structure and patterned activity, including sequenced learning. They will benefit significantly from being told about the sequence structures and how they will work within them. Some other children are generally more disorganized in their approach to life, cannot see structure easily, and do not directly benefit as much from knowing about the sequence and organization of mathematical topics (Allardice, 1983). These children still can and do learn the concepts and ideas, but from a different perspective. Even so, this latter group can benefit from the teacher's structured approach and from knowing that there is a structure.

Operation Algorithms

Teaching and learning operation algorithms are covered extensively in Chapter 9, so the discussion here will focus on sequencing in algorithms. There is very little general sequencing in algorithms from operation to operation. That is, one does not have to learn an addition algorithm before one can learn a division algorithm. Some algorithms, however, such as the standard algorithm for multiplication of base 10 numbers, involves the use of some addition algorithms. A particular addition algorithm is not necessary; however, it must be column- and place-value-based for this particular multiplication process.

Within algorithms for one operation, some sequencing is necessary. Students move from the algorithm for two-digit addition

$$
\begin{array}{r}
45 \\
39 \\
+78 \\
\hline
\end{array}
$$

to three- and on to four-digit algorithms, which are simply extensions of the two-digit form. Additional sequencing is involved as the process is extended by repeating the *carrying* device to the columns to the left. Similar sequencing is found in other addition algorithms and in those such as the standard algorithms for subtraction and multiplication. In the standard long division algorithm, the process is to use a sequence of operations and placement of results in a particular form repeatedly. The sequence is:

1. Try a division.

2. Multiply (placing the result in particular columns).

3. Subtract.

4. Repeat the sequence.

Within this sequence is a subsequence at the first step:

1. Try a partial quotient.

2. If the result is too large (because the multiplication result is too large to subtract), try a smaller quotient.

3. If the result is too small (because the multiplication result when subtracted yields a value too large), try a larger quotient.

The sequence is further elaborated when numbers in decimal form are divided using this process. A step involving moving decimal points is inserted. Furthermore, different teachers teach different variations in the form.

 Illustration

$$
\begin{array}{r}
9 \\
42\overline{)386} \\
378 \\
\hline
8
\end{array}
\qquad
\begin{array}{r}
9\ R\ 8 \\
42\overline{)386} \\
378 \\
\hline
8
\end{array}
\qquad
42\overline{)386}\ (9\ R\ 8 \\
\underline{378}
\qquad
\begin{array}{r}
9.01 \\
4.2\overline{)38.6}
\end{array}
$$

It is evident that some of the sequenced material taught can involve rather complicated sequences. It is also clear that the difficulty children have with learning long division (one of these complicated sequenced processes), for example, may stem from the complexity of the process rather than from the difficulty of the concept. Over the years, teachers have discovered and taught variations to such sequences in order to make them easier to learn and remember. For example, in division with decimal numbers, the step of moving decimal points can be omitted in favor of recognizing (in the instance shown above) that 10 times 4.2 is 42. This means that the result of division will be close to 9, and the decimal point can simply be placed immediately after the 9 when the process, ignoring the decimal points, is complete.

Recent research and teaching practice suggest that teachers avoid complex sequences like the one described above and choose alternative algorithms or limit the use of complex algorithms. The *Curriculum and Evaluation Standards* (NCTM, 1989), for example, recommends that the long division algorithm be taught and used for single digit divisors only. For divisors with two or more digits other algorithms or calculators should be used. One of the significant dangers involved in teaching a concept or process with a complex sequence of steps is that teachers and students can be sidetracked from the central learning task into spending excess time and energy on teaching and learning the sequence itself. Learning the sequence may be too much for the students and make it difficult to learn the main material. The essential task in the instance cited above is to learn to divide accurately and consistently; and focus on that can be lost if too much attention is given to the complex sequence of the standard long division algorithm.

Measurement

Measurement concepts and techniques can be taught as sequenced topics. This is true especially where measurements are made using linear measure and multiplication as the basis. Students must learn to measure length with inches before they can measure area in square inches and volume in cubic inches.

In the metric system, sequenced names are based mostly on names for powers of 10. Students need to learn the sequence: millimeter, centimeter, decimeter, meter, decameter, centameter, kilometer. In common usage, however, some of these (decimeter, decameter, and centameter) seldom appear. The sequence is left with gaps unless those left out are learned too, and there is no apparent value in learning them. Furthermore, learning those must be done by rote memorization because there is no application or common use to help give them meaning. Although the progressions described occur in names and dimension measurement, there is measurement that is not taught in a particular sequence. Children learn to measure for recipes with cups and spoons at the same time that they are learning about one- two- and three-liter bottles of cola.

They may also be simultaneously measuring their heights in inches and discussing Olympic races that are measured in meters.

Sequentially teaching dimensional measuring requires the teacher to help students realize that the measuring unit for length can be used as a basis for developing area and volume measuring units. This avoids the necessity of inventing units of measurement that would not have obvious direct relationships to other units. Children need work with manipulatives and real-life situations to help them grasp the concepts of area and volume and with the approximations that must take place in any measurement activity. In considering the sequenced aspect of measurement, emphasis must be given to building dimensionally on length measurement, squaring, then cubing.

Activity for fourth- through eighth-graders

Students will begin with a toothpick on a line segment drawn on a paper and then "move" that segment perpendicularly (leaving an imaginary trace) and use more toothpicks glued at the ends (or attached with miniature marshmallows) to create a square. They will then create a second square, lay it on the first, then move it perpendicularly to the plane of the first to form a cube. They will attach edge pieces to form the cube. Finally, students will measure in the three dimensions—length, area, and volume—on this cube and list their measurements. (One toothpick could be the unit of measure, or standard units could be used.) Straws, multijointed cubes, or Cuisenaire rods could also be used to do the same or a similar activity.

> **Subproblem 2:** *Some topics to be taught are not inherently sequenced.*

Understanding Subproblem 2

Just as some topics seem to have an inherent hierarchical or natural sequencing, other topics in elementary school mathematics have no implied or necessary natural teaching sequences. The teacher must be aware of which topics lack natural sequencing. To try to force order, where there is none, confuses students and gives them false impressions about what is important to learn. A topic such as geometrical shapes does not come before or after the topic of addition of whole numbers, for example.

It would be a good idea to teach counting before teaching geometrical shapes if part of the teaching about geometrical shapes involved describing them by counting the number of sides. Although knowledge of adding might be a useful tool at some points in the study of geometry, it is not necessary for learning basic ideas about geometrical shapes. When considering mathematics topics from the perspective of sequencing, teachers will realize that not much of mathematics is inherently sequenced. *This means that natural sequencing of topics or within topics cannot always be relied upon to provide direction for instruction.*

🔲 Solving Subproblem 2

When teachers have no natural sequencing to provide guidance for instruction, they may rely on documents such as the *Curriculum and Evaluation Standards* (NCTM, 1989), textual materials, and their own experience. This lack of prescribed scheduling frees teachers to work more directly from the perspective of the children's needs. Documents such as the *Curriculum and Evaluation Standards* (NCTM, 1989) provide lists of topics which must be covered at some point during classes at specific grade levels. Within that general framework, and where sequencing is not critical, teachers can adapt the schedule of particular lessons to events in the school and community. When the 100th day of school is approaching, the class may plan *hundreds* activities, though they may not be called for in the text. If there is a basketball tournament in the offing, a teacher may want to leave the study of three-dimensional geometrical figures to provide some lessons on probability, data collection, and statistics in connection with teams and scores.

Again, teachers should let students know that for particular topics, sequence is not a major concern. They should also know when sequence clues are not helpful for learning certain concepts. In learning concepts where there are no clues and guidance from sequence ideas, students will be free to use other tools and concepts they have acquired; their learning approaches do not have to be based on what was studied yesterday or on what is in the current section of the textbook. Some students get into the habit of frequent reference to *this* chapter or *this* section of the text as they look for clues to help them with their work. When these are not found, students sometimes give up even though they have the skills and information they need from a previous chapter or mathematical lesson. Realizing that information from a variety of sources can be searched for and used is important when students are solving problems. Problem solving is not a sequenced activity; solving certain problems doesn't necessarily allow direct progress to more complex or difficult problems. A simply worded problem may be based on simple ideas and yet be difficult to solve while one that requires much description and explanation may have a simple solution. In problem solving, a student is expected to bring ideas, concepts, and skills from various sources and levels.

The level of difficulty or of complexity of these resources is not an issue when working in nonsequenced topics. The focus is rather on what is needed for understanding, progress toward concept acquisition, or progress toward solving a problem.

> **Subproblem 3:** *Certain topics are mandated by outside agencies.*

🔲 Understanding Subproblem 3

Typically a state's department of education issues standards for content of the mathematics curriculum for kindergarten through eighth grade. In recent years, state standards have relied heavily on the National Council of Teachers of Mathematics' *Standards for Curriculum and Evaluation* (1989). Mathematics educators also provide recommendations for topics to be taught in mathematics classrooms. In some states, these guidelines are quite prescriptive, in others more general. Math teachers and school staff should examine their state and local prescriptions carefully. The classroom texts, if old, may not coordinate very closely with state requirements. Even the newest texts do not always match closely what the state or the local school requires. In either case, the teacher will need to use the text more as a reference book than as a daily guide. To meet the state requirements, it may be necessary to alter emphasis or order of teaching certain topics. Teachers, particularly at the same grade or subject level, should discuss the mandates and decide together how and when to teach various topics. If the school or system has a mathematics coordinator, he or she can provide invaluable help.

An indirect mandate to teach certain topics in mathematics may come as a result of state proficiency examinations that students take at various grade levels. Some states give math, social studies, science, and language skills examinations to students at grades 4, 6, 8, and 12. Practice tests available to teachers indicate that certain topics will be emphasized on the examinations. Wanting their students to do well and to enhance teachers' and schools' reputations, teachers are tempted to *teach to the exam.* This can result in children learning only what teachers think will be on the examination. A danger is that material not needed specifically for the examination may be omitted or de-emphasized. If teachers must give extra emphasis to preparation for the examination, they should ensure that they do not omit other critical topics from their instruction.

🔲 Solving Subproblem 3

Teachers need to learn the precise nature of the mandated requirements. This will involve discussions with school administrators and colleagues as well as efforts to obtain pertinent documents from the state department of education. After examining the requirements, the teacher can plan to meet both the general and specific mandates. Specific topics such as *ordering fractions* and themes and general issues such as *problem solving* are usually covered. Typically school systems try to choose texts that deal with the topics and themes as prescribed, but the textbook selection process may make this difficult. Teachers may need to fill the gaps between the textual materials and the curriculum by consulting with colleagues and administrators and planning to obtain additional materials or to design and create missing pieces. Lesson plans and units which meet the needs directly can be devised. The NCTM materials are especially helpful because they cover thoroughly all the topics which might be at issue. Other important sources for materials and for teaching ideas and strategies are teacher's journals and computer networks. The *Eisenhower National Clearinghouse for Science and Mathematics Education,* for example, is readily accessible through various networks and contains extensive resources of many kinds for mathematics teachers. The ENC may be accessed by entering Eisenhower National Clearinghouse in an Internet search engine such as Yahoo or by entering the website www.enc.org/

Students coming into a new class may have gaps in their mathematical preparation. They may come from schools that emphasize or cover the same materials. This may cause gaps that create a real difficulty for the learners and the teacher in the new school year. In preparation for the new class, the teacher should examine, if possible, the math curricula in the schools from which the students come. This will help the teacher adjust the curriculum for the new year to compensate for differences in requirements and emphasis.

Summary

This chapter discussed the issue of determining what mathematics to teach and when. It was noted that some topics in mathematics have inherent sequencing while others do not. Four topics with natural sequencing were discussed, along with the response of teachers and students to sequencing. Teaching nonsequenced material was described and issues in teaching mandated subjects were discussed.

Exercises

1. Obtain a copy of the state mathematics curriculum and its requirements for a particular grade level. Compare this with the *Standards'* suggestions (NCTM, 1989). Write a compare-and-contrast paragraph.

2. List three topics in mathematics where children assume an order when one is not present. Could those topics be taught helpfully with an artificial order or sequence imposed?

3. Describe the difficulty encountered in attempts to teach various fraction concepts and/or operations with fractions using a sequenced scheme.

4. Describe a teaching strategy that would help students prepare for a proficiency examination but that would not involve teaching strictly *to the exam.*

🔲 References

Allardice, Barbara S., and Herbert P. Ginsburg (1983). Children's Psychological Difficulties in Mathematics, in *Development of Mathematical Thinking*, Ed., Herbert P. Ginsburg. New York: Academic Press.

Brooks, Jacqueline Grennon (1990, February). Teachers and Students: Constructivists Forging New Connections, *Educational Leadership*, 47(5), 68–71.

Dinkmeyer, Don, and Rudolf Dreikurs (1963). *Encouraging Children to Learn: The Encouragement Process*. Upper Saddle River, NJ: Prentice Hall.

NCTM (1989). *Curriculum and Evaluation Standards for School Mathematics*. Reston, VA: National Council of Teachers of Mathematics.

Russell, Susan Jo, and Antonia Stone (1990). *Used Numbers: Counting: Ourselves and Our Families*. Palo Alto, CA: Dale Seymour.

🔲 Suggested Readings

Abrohms, Alison (1992). *Literature-Based Math Activities: An Integrated Approach*. New York: Scholastic Professional Books.

Brownell, William A. (1935). Psychological Considerations in the Learning and the Teaching of Arithmetic, *The Teaching of Arithmetic*. National Council of Teachers of Mathematics, The 10th Yearbook. New York: Bureau of Publications, Teachers College, Columbia University.

Dienes, Zoltan, P. (1971). An Example of the Passage from the Concrete to the Manipulation of Formal Systems, in *Educational Studies in Mathematics*, vol. 3, Ed. H. Freudenthal. Upper Saddle River, NJ: Prentice Hall.

Gibb, Glenadine, and Alberta Castaneda (1975). Experiences for Young Children, in *Mathematics Learning in Early Childhood*. National Council of Teachers of Mathematics, 37th Yearbook. Reston, VA: NCTM.

National Council of Teachers of Mathematics (1995). *Assessment Standards for School Mathematics*. Reston, VA: NCTM.

——— (1993). *Assessment Standards for School Mathematics* (working draft). Reston, VA: NCTM.

——— (1991). *Professional Standards for Teaching Mathematics*. Reston, VA: NCTM.

Skemp, Richard R. (1987). *The Psychology of Learning Mathematics*. Hillsdale, NJ: Lawrence Erlbaum.

Schwartz, David M. (1989). *If You Made a Million*. New York: Lothrop, Lee, and Shepard.

Wahl, John, and Stacey Wahl (1977). *I Can Count the Petals of a Flower*. Reston, VA: NCTM.

Equity in the Mathematics Classroom

One of the children's problems: Joy feels that because she is a girl, she is unable to learn mathematics.

Teacher's problem: Minority children in the classroom are experiencing difficulty in learning mathematics.

⊞ Understanding the Problem

To provide equitable treatment for all students regardless of their background or status differences, many schools practice various forms of *inclusion.* Formerly called *mainstreaming,* inclusion brings back into the regular classroom students who need remedial instruction or who have special physical or mental needs. Along with this trend, there are efforts to deal with ethnic and cultural diversity. Many of our classrooms are made up partially of children from minority groups within the United States population as well as with children from other nations and a wide variety of cultures. The following questions are important:

- Can and do children from diverse backgrounds learn mathematics in the same ways?

- Are there topics which are more easily learned by children from one ethnic background than by children from another?

- Do physically handicapped children have any special needs relative to learning mathematics?

These questions are among those of concern to mathematics educators. When these questions are connected to studies purporting to show that children from certain countries are ahead of or behind American children in math skills or knowledge, the issues become even more intriguing.

An issue of equal concern is whether gender influences students' abilities to learn mathematics. Study after study show that girls (after certain age and grade levels) do more poorly in mathematics than boys (Hood, 1994; McCoy, 1994). After certain points in schooling, fewer and fewer girls choose courses in upper level mathematics. This means that few women are found in the mathematical professions, such as engineering, science, and astronomy. Studies are underway to find reasons for this phenomenon. Are females less apt in mathematics at any point in their physical and mental development or are the differences caused by cultural and societal factors only? If the causes are purely cultural, then math educators should encourage and aid girls in learning mathematics, in showing themselves to be equally capable with boys, and in pursuing mathematically related careers. What strategies can be used to achieve this?

If, on the other hand, there are differences inherent to gender, what are they and how should these differences affect the way mathematics is taught? Should boys and girls be separated for mathematics classes at certain grade levels? This has been tried in an effort to remove the social stigma and peer pressure related to boys' and girls' performances in the same mathematics class (McCoy, 1994). Such practices obviously run directly counter to the inclusion philosophy. Alternatively, can an individual teacher give more attention to girls than to boys when both are struggling with particular topics in mathematics? Should girls be exempted from studying certain topics in mathematics? While some solutions might be found in teaching girls and boys differently, school and societal philosophies of education will not permit the discrimination that is likely to occur as a result. Furthermore, it is difficult to design and conduct research studies to directly answer some of these tough questions.

The issues described above are affected by the attitudes of students and parents as well as teachers and school systems. The prevailing philosophy and policy may be inclusion, but if parents, teachers, and children believe that culture, ethnicity, and gender are really the factors that determine the ability to learn mathematics, inclusion may have little effect in the math classroom. The mere fact that diverse groups share the same classroom, curriculum and teaching may have little effect on whether the students learn mathematics. The myths that all Asian children do well in mathematics and that girls cannot learn mathematics persist and affect all parties in the learning experience.

In studying mental computation, Reys and others found that although scores for Japanese boys were higher than those for girls in each of grades 2, 4, 6, and 8, they were *significantly* higher in grade 2 only (Reys et al., 1995). They further found that mental computation scores ranged widely among Japanese students, dispelling the notion that Japanese students are uniform in their ability to compute mentally. This study also confirmed that in Japan, as in the United States, students express the tendency to rely on paper-and-pencil algorithms even when doing mental computation. A study by Cai and Silver (1995) found that Chinese children, while more successful in executing a long division algorithm than American children, were far less successful in their attempts to solve the division-with-remainder problem of which the division computation was the main ingredient. Adetula (1989) found that Nigerian children experience most of their difficulty in problem solving because of the language used in problem statement presentation. The choice of language—English or Yoruba—affected both their skills and strategies. From these examples teachers realize that the issues are more complex than simply attributing a skill or lack of ability to a particular cultural or ethnic group. Language, cultural traditions, regional differences, previous schooling, parental involvement, type of mathematical task, and sociological pressures are all factors that may influence a child's effectiveness in learning mathematics.

For children in American classrooms, the consensus is that neither boys nor girls have any inherent advantage as they learn mathematics. The reasons that children of equal abilities do not enjoy mathematics and choose not to continue in mathematics beyond required levels seem to be primarily cultural and sociological (Lo, 1994). At certain ages many girls come to believe that their peers will disapprove of them if they show interest and success in mathematics. They may pretend not to understand even when they do and intentionally score low on tests and homework papers in efforts to seek approval from certain peers or family members.

In classrooms where manipulatives are used extensively, a physically handicapped person may be unable to use the objects as effectively as necessary to work on learning a particular concept. Similar difficulties are encountered with paper-and-pencil work. Keeping columns straight for certain algorithms may prove difficult for some physically handicapped students, for example. This can be true for students who have visual impairments and for those with muscle coordination difficulties. Classes oriented to cooperative learning may be a struggle for students who are hearing impaired because of difficulty in participating in discussion (O'Melia, 1994).

It is important to help these students appropriately so that they can learn as effectively as they are able while others in the class proceed at their best rates. How does a teacher, especially in a self-contained classroom, deal effectively with this diversity as well as with the other children who also differ in their learning rates and learning styles?

Solving the Equity Problem

A teacher must be open and clear in the expectation that both boys and girls can learn mathematics. The teacher should also be alert to peer comments and expressions about girls' learning. These expressions can come from both boys and girls and are most likely to originate outside the classroom. It may be necessary to work directly with parents to counter misconceptions that may influence girls' learning. Some girls respond well to unexpected success. Others require significant amounts of persuasion to believe they can learn because they tend to believe what is commonly said. (The same applies to boys, though their perceived reasons for being unable to learn in mathematics are not gender based.)

For the special learner, the teacher's first task is to discover just what the child needs. Both readiness to learn and attitudes must be assessed. If the child's background is not adequate to the tasks ahead, the teacher may want to arrange remedial assistance through an aide, parents, the school's remediation programs, or the use of specially designed computer programs. A child who cannot manipulate pencil and paper or other objects may be able to use a computer in some cases to keep pace with the rest of the class (Hart-Davis, 1995).

Physically rearranging the classroom can assist children in wheelchairs by giving them access to books and manipulatives. Students with impaired hearing may be positioned so that noises and distance do not make hearing too difficult. To accommodate students who cannot easily move about, the teacher may decide to discontinue or modify contests and activities that involve moving around the room. A slate for each student to write on and display might work just as well as going to the board to write, for example.

Children will respond helpfully if the teacher can share openly with the class what the special needs of other children are. In fact, a very effective approach is to solicit the children's help in deciding how to provide the best possible learning environment for their classmate who has special needs. Children will volunteer to assist in ways directly helpful to the classmate with special needs. Accommodations the special child has used in previous classes may be helpful in the current class.

In discussions with the class, the teacher can counter myths and falsehoods by giving examples to show what is really true. The class should be encouraged to discuss issues in learning mathematics for all members of the class. If the teacher needs to make grading accommodations, that should also be explained to the class and discussed in appropriate terms and at a depth the students can handle. It is usually possible to give compensatory assignments to students with special needs when they are excused from some particular assignment or activity in mathematics. Teachers can explore the possibility of acquiring additional equipment such as specially designed tables and chairs, touch screens, and computer overhead projector units to help meet the special needs of certain students (Inkpen et al., 1994).

Consideration of Textual Materials

Though there is not as much difficulty with mathematics textual materials as there might be with those in other subject areas, teachers should be alert to gender, ethnic, and culturally sensitive materials. The Racism and Sexism Resource Center has published *Ten Quick Ways* (1992) to check documents for possible culturally insensitive material:

- Look for stereotypes.
- Check the story line.
- Look at the lifestyles.
- Weigh the relationships between people.
- Note the heroes.
- Consider the effects on a child's self-image.
- Consider the author's background.
- Check out the author's perspective.
- Watch for loaded words.
- Consider the copyright date.

Current textbooks are very careful about the considerations listed above, but other materials such as worksheets and reading books should also be checked for offensive content that might hinder particular children in their learning of mathematics. When possible, Internet sites that the children access and videos that will be used in the classroom should be examined in advance. Some of these are produced by organizations and individuals who are not aware of the care that must be taken to ensure that materials are unbiased.

Equal time should be given to girls and boys. Examples and problem statements should be in generic terms or set in a variety of cultural backgrounds. Many good reading books have mathematics themes and different cultural settings. If the classroom contains children from differing ethnic backgrounds, the teacher should find ways to emphasize each and to accommodate differences. Such accommodation should be based on thoughtful understanding by the teacher of the special characteristics of the various cultures. It may require considerable research to learn how characteristics of a child's culture affect learning in mathematics (and other subjects). Parents provide an important source of information. If ethnically or culturally different parents can be invited to the classroom to talk about how they or their relatives learned mathematics differently, that event could significantly increase interest in a particular mathematics topic. It could also alleviate math anxiety on the part of children struggling to learn mathematics in an unfamiliar cultural setting.

Language and Classroom Practices

The language and terminology that the teacher uses may be the most important factor in promoting equity in the mathematics classroom. Some children from non-English-speaking families may experience translation difficulties. For example, in Spanish the phrase, "nine into three" would be used, where English speakers would say, "three into nine." Others say "three by nine" meaning "three times nine." African children use hand symbols for numbers that are different from those used by American children. The symbol for three, for example, is made by holding down the index finger with the thumb and extending the other fingers; a closed fist is the symbol for five. Translation devices for computers and software in Spanish and other languages are available to help children who have not yet learned English well enough to function in the mathematics classroom (MSEB, 1990). Wise teachers will avoid using terms and practices that might be misunderstood or prejudicial.

Some teachers, in teaching classifying for descriptive or graphing purposes, use exercises which involve classifying children according to hair or eye color. These activities can be offensive to African-American or Asian children, all of whom have dark hair and dark eyes (Gerdes, 1994). This is a subtle issue, but easily dealt with by avoiding even indirect references to differences in appearance, clothing, or socioeconomic status that might be due to culture or ethnicity differences. Intriguing differences in culture and customs can be used instead of personal differences, as the latter can be sources of peer prejudice among children. When teachers are working on classifying techniques and statistical concepts, children's clothing colors and characteristics such as height and reach might be used, thus making the tasks interesting and meaningful for the children without distracting or creating offense.

Home conditions related to culture also can present difficulties for individual children and their parents. Teachers cannot assume that all homes have telephones, televisions, VCRs, and computers. Homework assignments should not be made in the expectation that each child will be able to use certain tools and materials such as computers and newspapers at home.

Technological Solutions

Sheppo (1995), writing in *Educational Leadership,* reports that Lincoln School in Springfield, Illinois, promotes inclusion by using an integrated curriculum anchored in science and technology. The multimedia technologies are incorporated into the curriculum because they support the integrated curriculum. The school feels that this integration enables students to construct their own knowledge and understanding. Mathematics students use projects such as weather analysis and geographical studies as a basis for working with numbers in real problem solving settings; they use computers with databases and spreadsheets extensively for data analysis and reporting. Computer Assisted Instruction (CAI) has been shown to improve language facility and word recognition skills (Askov et al., 1989) and students who are deaf or hearing impaired learn more quickly and show better retention of material when using CAI (Hart-Davis, 1985). Advantages of using the computer include privacy, individualization and immediate feedback, flexibility of scheduling, and ready access to the curriculum. These may be of special value to students with handicaps. For those with vision impairment, the Macintosh offers *CloseView,* a screen magnifying device. Braille embossers and printers are available. Though these are very expensive, Braille translators are not. Speech synthesizers, which read text aloud; screen readers, which speak what is on the screen; reading or scanning machines; and keyboard kits with large print or Braille keys are also available to assist students in mathematics as well as in other classes (Woods, 1994).

Talented Students

It is sometimes easy for math teachers to focus their attention on students who are having difficulty, while gifted and talented students are left on their own. These children often tend to finish their work early, and may become bored or may create problems in the class. A number of schemes including magnet schools, magnet classes, special tracks, and other innovative treatments are being used to help talented and gifted students. Many, though, must be included with the other students in the classroom. Computers provide some solutions to the problem of dealing with students who are advanced mathematically. There are extremely interesting software programs with which students can explore mathematical ideas, solve problems, and work on projects that do not take them to subject matter that the class as a whole will study in the future. The teacher should provide opportunities for gifted students (and others) to explore laterally in mathematical content. The material should complement what is currently being studied. For example, when operation algorithms are being studied, advanced students might consider a variety of alternative algorithms and use the algorithms with different number bases. In addition to software, books with mathematical themes, puzzles, and a variety of manipulatives with a mathematical basis can be valuable (Carle, 1988). These can be used by students who have the time and inclination to do more in mathematics than is possible for the whole class. The gifted and talented should be treated equitably too. Every student in the mathematics classroom should have the opportunity to learn all the mathematics possible and be prepared for the highly mathematical society in which we live.

▣ Summary

In this chapter the problems of providing appropriate mathematics education for all students is explored. The special needs presented by diversity in ethnicity, culture, gender, and mental and physical handicaps are discussed along with the reasons for some of the difficulties special students face. Suggested remedies and techniques, including the use of technological devices, are presented for teaching mathematics in very diverse classrooms. Finally, the needs of the gifted and talented are mentioned and teaching approaches presented.

▣ Exercises

1. Prepare a report on the ways computers can be used to facilitate learning in mathematics by:
   - physically handicapped students
   - students from non-English-speaking backgrounds
   - dyslexic students
   - children with Attention Deficit Syndrome (ADS) and other disorders
2. Find and evaluate software that enables manipulation of objects by students who cannot physically manipulate concrete objects.
3. Describe a classroom environment and scheduling that would foster appropriate involvement by students who are gifted in mathematics.
4. Create two lists.
   a. Manipulatives, games, and activities for students who are very weak in mathematics.
   b. Manipulatives, games, and activities for students who are gifted and talented in mathematics.

🔲 References

Adetula, Lewal O. (1989) Solutions of Simple Word Problems by Nigerian Children: Language and Schooling Factors, *Journal for Research in Mathematics Education*. Reston, VA: National Council of Teachers of Mathematics.

Askov, E., et al. (1989). Adult literacy, computer technology and the hearing impaired, *Literacy and Hearing Impaired Conference Proceedings*. ERIC: ED 353 733.

Carle, Eric, Raymond Briggs, Ye Popov Nicolai, Akiko Hayashi, Gian Calvi, Leon Dillon, Diane Dillon, Zhu Chengliang, Ron Brooks, and Mitsumasa Anno. (1988). *All in a Day*, New Greenwillow, NJ:

Cai, Jinfa, and Edward Silver (1995, November). Solution Processes and Interpretations of Solutions in Solving a Division-With-Remainder Problem: Do Chinese and U.S. Students have Similar Difficulties? *Journal for Research in Mathematics Education*. Reston, VA: National Council of Teachers of Mathematics.

Gerdes, Paulus (1994, June). Reflections on ethnomathematics. *For the Learning of Mathematics*, 14(2), 119–122.

Hart-Davis, S. (1985). The classroom computer as a partner in teaching basic skills to hearing impaired children. *American Annals of the Deaf*, 130(5), 410–414.

Hood, Jacqueline N., and Dennis F. Togo. (1994, Winter). Gender effects of graphics presentation, *Journal of Research on Computing in Education*, 26(2), 176–184.

Inkpen, Kori, and others (1994). We have never-forgetful flowers in our garden: Girls' responses to electronic games. *Journal of Computers in Mathematics and Science Teaching*, 13(4), 383–403.

Lo, Jane-Kane, and Grayson H. Wheatley (1994, September). Learning opportunities and negotiating social norms in mathematics class discussion. *Educational Studies in Mathematics*, 27(2), 145–164.

Mathematical Sciences Education Board (1990). *Making Mathematics Work for Minorities*. Washington, DC: Mathematical Sciences Education Board.

McCoy, Leah P. (1994, May). Mathematical problem-solving processes of elementary male and female students. *School Science and Mathematics*, 94(5), 266–270.

O'Melia, Mary C., and Michael S. Rosenberg (1994, May). Effects of cooperative homework teams on the acquisition of mathematics skills by secondary students with mild disabilities. *Exceptional Children*, 60(6), 538–548.

Racism and Sexism Resource Center (1992). *Ten Quick Ways*. New York: RSRC.

Reys, R.E., B.J. Reys, N. Nohoda, and H. Emori (1995, July). Mental Computation Performance in Japan, *Journal for Research in Mathematics Education*. Reston, VA: National Council of Teachers of Mathematics.

Sheppo, Karen Groves, et al. (1995, December–January). How an Urban School Promotes Inclusion, *Educational Leadership*. Washington, D.C.: Association for Supervision and Curriculum Development.

Woods, Rodney W., and Jimmy D. Lindsey (1994, February). Perceived and actual mathematical competencies of children with visual impairments and learning disabilities, *Psychological Reports*, 74, 238.

🔳 Suggested Readings

Baroody, Arthur J. (1986, November). Basic Counting Principles Used by Mentally Retarded Children, *Journal for Research in Mathematics Education*, 17(5), 382–389.

Hiebert, James (1984, March). Why Do Some Children Have Trouble Learning Measurement Concepts? *Arithmetic Teacher*, 31(7), 19–24.

Moore, Charles G. (1994, June). Research in Native American mathematics education, *For the Learning of Mathematics*, 14(2), 9–14.

Pajares, Frank, and M. David Miller. (1994, June). Role of self-efficacy and self-concept beliefs in mathematical problem solving: A path analysis, *Journal of Educational Psychology*, 86(2), 193–203.

Parmar, Rene S., John F. Cawley, and James H. Meller (1994, May). Differences in mathematics performance between students with learning disabilities and students with mild retardation, *Exceptional Children*, 60(6), 549–563.

Randhawa, Bikkar S. (1994, October). Self-efficacy in mathematics, attitudes, and achievement of boys and girls from restricted samples in two countries, *Perceptual and Motor Skills*, 79, 1011–1018.

Samimy, Keiko, et al. (1994, September). *Gambare, amae*, and *giri*: A cultural explanation for Japanese children's success in mathematics, *The Journal of Mathematical Behavior*, 13(3), 261–271.

Shroyer, M. Gail, et al. (1994, February). Science and mathematics equity issues at a local school district level, *School Science and Mathematics*, 94(2), 65–77.

Skaalvik, Einar M., and Richard J. Rankin (1994, November). Gender differences in mathematics and verbal achievement, self-perception and motivation, *British Journal of Educational Psychology*, 64, 419–428.

Woodward, John, and Lisa Howard (1994, October–November). The misconceptions of youth: Errors and their mathematical meaning, *Exceptional Children*, 61(2), 126–136.

Yankel, Erna, et al. (1990). The Importance of Social Interaction in Children's Construction of Mathematical Knowledge, in *Teaching and Learning in the 1990s*, Ed. Thomas J. Cooney and Christian Hirsch. Reston, VA: National Council of Teachers of Mathematics.

Zambo, Ron, and John Follman (1994, Spring). Gender-related differences in problem solving at the 6th and the 8th grade levels, *Focus on Learning Problems in Mathematics*, 16(2).

Children's Reading Books

Feelings, Muriel (1994). *Moja Means One*. New York: Puffin Books

Gillen, P. (1988). *My Signing Book of Numbers*. Washington, DC: Little, Brown.

Munsch, Robert (1987). *Moira's Birthday*. Toronto: Annick

Grifalconi, Ann (1986). *The Village of Round and Square Houses*. Boston: Little, Brown.

Tompert, Ann (1990). *Grandfather Tang's Story*. Toronto: Crown.

General Methods for Teaching Mathematics

One of the children's problems: Jimmy feels that if math were taught the way science is taught, he could "get" math too.

Teacher's problem: Are there some general methods for teaching mathematics that are different from the methods for teaching other subjects?

🔲 Understanding the Problem

Research by major psychologists has yielded theories of educational development and learning that can be useful to teachers of mathematics. Piaget's perspective, which views children as passing through certain physiological-psychological stages, can have direct application to methods of teaching mathematics, as teachers realize that a child's developmental stage may determine what can be learned. Piaget says that, if a child is developmentally not ready to learn at a certain level, intensity of teaching, time spent, and even significant experience with concrete objects will not promote learning. He writes that children progress through the stages at different rates when they are internally ready, and that passage from one stage to another happens only when the experience base is sufficient (Piaget, 1954, 1964).

Researcher Jerome Bruner holds that real learning cannot take place without the existence of a mental infrastructure, a framework, into which a learner can place new ideas. This infrastructure provides interconnecting links with concepts already learned, and these links and interrelationships enable the learner to attach meaning to the new learning. Thus, new material is not "learned" in isolation, where it might become merely memorization of a nonsense symbol (Bruner, 1960).

The Developmental researcher Dienes (1960) has examined learning as it involves extracting conceptual ideas from interaction with concrete objects, the environment, and their interrelationships. Most mathematics educators base their understanding of effective mathematics teaching methods on these themes or on variations of them. In doing this they are subscribing to the *constructivist* philosophy. Essentially this is the belief that true learning takes place only as learners construct in their own minds the concepts which form the building blocks for the learned material (Steffe, 1994). Other ways of stating this are:

- The ability to cite memorized facts and trivia does not indicate that learning has taken place.

- If the learner is not actively involved in the learning process, learning will not occur.

- Learning is not synonymous with memorization.

Dissonance

Another facet of the stage set for learning is the level of disparity between what the learner knows and what is to be learned. This disparity may be called *dissonance*. Psychologist Vigotsky calls this the *zone of proximal development*. As children construct knowledge and concepts, the mind functions not as a camera, taking isolated snapshots of reality, but rather as an organizer of information toward coherence, stability, economy, and generalizability (Pirie, 1994). In attempting to organize ideas, the learner encounters dissonance. This is a moderate mismatch between interrelated ideas within the fabric of the learner's knowledge or between the knowledge/concept fabric and the outside reality. For effective learning, the disparity must be neither too small or too great. If there is little or no dissonance, the learner is bored; there is no challenge, and learning cannot take place. Trivial computation tasks, for example, are of no value for a fifth grader. The student doing such tasks does not learn, because there is not sufficient dissonance between what the leaner can do easily and the difficulty of the computation task.

On the other hand, if the gap is too great, the student may feel that bridging the gap is impossible. Problems which can be solved only by using algebraic equations, for example, do not provide a learning environment for the average fifth grader because the dissonance between the background, knowledge, and skills of the learner and the ability to use algebra is too great.

Unfortunately, the only dissonance some teachers provide for their students in found in competition against other students and against the system (for grades, etc.). Much better settings for dissonance include self-competition in learning, challenge, surprise, novelty, mystery, ambiguity, and moderate complexity. In these settings students can use their abilities appropriately and can accept the challenge of a task that is just beyond them. The teacher is responsible for creating a classroom with the appropriate amounts of dissonance so that children learn naturally and at an appropriate level. Recently a number of inservice training opportunities focusing on discovery and inquiry have been developed to assist teachers and departments in providing the moderate dissonance needed to engender learning. Prominent among these is the *Discovery* program funded in part by Eisenhower funds through the National Science Foundation.

With this background, we examine several general issues relative to teaching methods based on constructivist philosophy. We will consider those that seem to have the greatest direct application to mathematics teaching generally. The specific applications will be considered in the various chapters.

Terminology

In many respects, mathematics is a language. The fourth goal for mathematics educators in the five-goal set described by the National Council of Teachers of Mathematics in the *Standards for Curriculum and Evaluation* (NCTM, 1989) describes the language and communication aspects of mathematics. Certainly there is a vocabulary to learn and a general syntax to go with it. For this part of mathematics learning, the methods used successfully in teaching language can be applied.

- Repetition both in writing and speaking are important.

- Meanings of words must be carefully attached using appropriate contextual information and a variety of applications.

Because many mathematical words are taken from English and given special meanings and significance, it is necessary to help children understand those terms as they are needed in mathematics (Lo, 1994).

Examples

- times   (4 times 3)

- of   (one-half of 5)

- equals   (three-fourths equals six-eighths)

The difficulty of learning special meanings is compounded by what children encounter when they find mathematics terms used inappropriately in daily language. *Circle, square, average,* and *probability* are words often used inaccurately. *Percentage* and various fraction terms such as one-half also have ambiguous usages.

Methodologically, a teacher must keep his or her own language clear and appropriate. Of first importance is to avoid using ambiguous terms and to use the correct, precise words, such as *mean* instead of *average* and *numeral* instead of *number.* A teacher should not refer to exercises as *problems* and solutions to problems as *answers.* Thus the teacher instructs by example as well as by directing specific attention to correct wording. In Chapters 11 and 12 aspects of terminology usage in specific instruction are discussed in more detail.

Memorizing

Developmental and educational psychologists recognize the critical importance of experience in children's learning. Outside school children learn through repetition and from a wide variety of naturally occurring experiences and structured events scheduled for them by others such as parents and friends. In school we attempt to shorten that process because there is so much to be learned. We try to abstract the essentials from actual experience and express them symbolically in concise and easily remembered forms. This sets the stage for memorization as a means of learning. Children are good at memorizing and quickly adopt this approach to learning for several reasons:

- Our society values extensive knowledge of trivia.

- Peers respect knowledge of many facts.

- Math is often taught as a collection of facts.

- Math is often reduced to remembering steps of a process.

- Evaluation often requires no more than recitation of facts.

Mathematics teachers need to deal with two important questions about methodology in relation to memorization:

- To what extent should memorizing be a part of teaching and learning in mathematics at a particular level or for a particular topic in mathematics?

- Should memorizing and memory techniques be specifically taught?

When we think of education as preparation for life outside of school we realize that students should be prepared

- To solve problems

- To synthesize known information

- To communicate ideas based on knowledge

- To integrate concepts from a variety of subject areas in various applications of knowledge

A student who has only *memorized* facts and processes, however successfully, is not well educated. Memorized information often cannot be remembered even long enough to be reproduced on a test.

Some mathematics educators feel that memorization never facilitates learning. In their view mathematical facts and processes such as algorithms (where memorizing is most regularly applied) are not really learned until students are presented with those ideas in various contexts and repeatedly *experience* contextually oriented processes. They point out the obvious difficulties with memorized material.

- Memorized material is not easily recalled after time.

- Memorized material is not easily applied practically.

- Memory overload occurs at some point.

- Complex processes and problem solving activities cannot be effectively memorized.

Another view is that some aspects of mathematics learning can be acquired effectively and efficiently through memorization and that memorization should be used for those. Educators who hold this view would argue that learning the basic multiplication facts and certain standard algorithms can be best achieved by memorization. They feel that trying to teach these by providing contextual experience is not only too idealistic but impractical. The hope is that students would commit these tools and facts to memory and then learn them through repeated recall and use.

Children do, in fact, learn these building blocks when they are presented in context and application; it is true that there is not sufficient time in typical mathematics curricula to provide all the experience needed for contextual learning. However, children can often memorize prodigiously. When mathematics is presented as material to be memorized, they move along rapidly and appear to be learning a great deal. Furthermore since mathematics is taught, evaluated, and widely regarded as a set of items that can be memorized, the whole system encourages and rewards memorization.

Difficulties arise, though, in limiting memorizing to appropriate levels. Once a child is rewarded for successful work in mathematics through memorizing at beginning levels, that child will find it difficult to transition to more involved methods and approaches using synthesis and application. Especially in mathematics, children may adopt memorization as their sole mode of learning. Using this technique, children may be successful until they encounter algebra or some other major topic change. Suddenly they are confronted with a significantly different aspect of mathematics. As the new subject begins, students find that the memorization approach doesn't work. Since students then have no effective learning technique available for work in the new topic, they are tempted to stop trying to learn in mathematics. Some students formally drop out of mathematics at this point, or they may tune out when in mathematics class. This traumatic event, something like an athlete's "hitting the wall," can occur at various points. Some students can continue their memorizing through algebra and experience the trauma when they come to geometry. Others experience this difficulty when a new teacher emphasizes problem solving and does not approach it using memorization schemes.

Solving the Problem

The best approach for teachers is probably to permit memorization of some basics but to incorporate any memorizing within as many contextual experiences as possible. Memorizing should be de-emphasized in contrast to the application, meanings, and connections with other facts and concepts. Teaching from a problem solving perspective will assist this approach. Not only will this help greatly in providing context, motivation, and meaning, it will also directly indicate the necessity of learning more than isolated facts. Teachers must not create or perpetuate a *memorization* environment. Teachers should avoid:

- Teaching memorizing as a primary method of learning
- Making the activities memory oriented
- Preparing evaluative instruments which are based on memory only

The mathematics being taught should not be reduced to sets of facts and steps of processes to be memorized.

Teaching Memorization

If some memorizing is to be included in the learning process, either intentionally by the teacher or naturally by the students, the following principles are important:

- It should be made clear to the students which material will be memorized.

- Techniques of memorization that are assisted by context and connections with other material should be used.

- Giving the false impression that *memorizing* is *learning* should be avoided.

- Students should understand that memory is only one tool to be used in learning and applying mathematics.

If these principles are followed, any good memorization techniques can be used. Classifying, attending to patterns, using mnemonics, reciting, using flash cards, and playing games are all good strategies that can be used effectively.

Using Manipulatives

Some mathematics educators believe that mathematics learning cannot take place without reference to concrete objects, either the actual objects or some material representation of them. Even if we don't agree fully with that broad statement, we believe that, for initial instruction and learning of particular mathematical concepts, manipulatives are essential (Hatfield, 1994). This is especially true for students in kindergarten through sixth grade, who are generally classified as in the *concrete* and *pre-operational* stages of mental development. It is also true for adults (who in many ways have become operational thinkers) who encounter a new concept. Most adults use concrete objects whenever possible to make learning efficient. Since children, especially, benefit from the use of manipulatives, teachers in elementary and middle school mathematics must find ways to provide hands-on activities of all sorts to promote concept learning in mathematics (Hatfield, 1994). Some aspects to be considered in attempting to make the use of manipulatives as effective as possible are:

- Manipulatives should be pertinent specifically to the concept being learned.

- The manipulative-concept connection should be natural and not forced.

- The manipulatives should not be dangerous in any way to the students (not readily swallowed, have loose paint, etc.)

- If possible the manipulative should be applicable to multiple concepts. (For example, geoboards and C-rods are usable for counting, shapes, measurement, and fraction concepts.)

- Manipulatives should not be over-used. They don't always teach everything to every student.

- Manipulatives should not be used so that they present wrong concepts or misleading ideas.

- Typically manipulatives alone cannot teach a concept from the beginning. Students will work and play with the manipulatives but may never think of the particular concept to be learned without being coached.

- Generally, manipulatives should be used after or in the process of teaching a concept and as examples and for practice. (Thompson, 1994)

When used properly, manipulatives are powerful tools for both teachers and students. Like any tools, manipulatives must be applied to the appropriate tasks in appropriate ways; the user must learn how to use them most effectively. The learning, however, must be guided. Teachers should explain how students are to use the objects, give them hints about what to look for, and provide instruction on how to experiment with the manipulatives (Hatfield, 1994). Manipulatives do not necessarily have to be sets of objects usable on a desktop. In fact, translation of pertinent characteristics of a problem or concept learning task to pencil sketches often allows a more efficient and wider range of manipulation than working with the objects themselves. Furthermore, computer software is now available that amplifies the possibilities significantly beyond either of these two approaches. Using the mouse or joystick, a student can move, enlarge, flip, and rotate representations of objects and even create objects to be manipulated. The same principles for use apply, however, whether the medium is the real world, paper and pencil, or the computer.

Constructivism

We believe that the *constructivist* approach to teaching and learning mathematics is the most powerful and effective force for real learning. This view holds that learning takes place when a student *constructs* a concept in his or her own mind. To construct a concept means to mentally receive various facts, see patterns, and reason about those so that they are attached and interrelated to other facts and concepts. When those interconnections have been created, a concept construct has been developed. That basic framework may essentially complete the construction of the concept. If not, it may be necessary to add other information and make additional connections with more concepts in order to flesh out the mathematical construct. Some mathematical concepts can be fully constructed in the early grades, and others are added to gradually over a number of years. Many children can complete the concept of a counting number in the first and second grade. However the construction of the concept of a fraction begins in the first grade, is added to through the grades, and may not be complete even during high school mathematics classes (Brooks, 1993). There are significant differences in how construction takes place in three different aspects of mathematical learning: Mathematical Concepts, Mathematical Facts, and Mathematical Processes.

FIGURE 6-1 Triangles with the Same Orientation

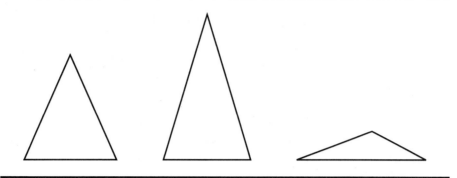

Constructing Concepts

In order for a person to acquire a concept, both concept examples and concept counter-examples must be examined.

Concept Examples.   Concept examples must vary over a wide range of non-critical attributes. To illustrate: a noncritical attribute of the concept of *triangle* is the figure's orientation. If triangle examples are all as shown in Figure 6-1, a child might gain the impression that Figure 6-2 is not really a triangle.

In fact, there is a similar and very real difficulty for some students in geometry who are distressed when the *base* of the triangle is not *down* (in the lower portion of the triangle) and horizontal. All the examples they have been given show the base horizontal and at the bottom of the triangles. However, problems in geometry often refer to bases which are not down, not horizontal

FIGURE 6-2 Triangle with Different Orientation

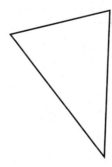

FIGURE 6-3 Squares of Same Orientation and Different Sizes

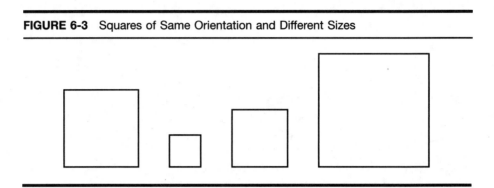

and which, in the case of trapezoids, occur in pairs, one *down* and one *up*. Other noncritical attributes of triangles are size, shape, color, angle size (<180 degrees), and, in the case of three dimensional objects, the texture and substance of which triangles are made. Concept examples that vary by one noncritical attribute should be given before more complex examples are examined. For example, if the concept of *square* is being constructed, two noncritical attributes are size and orientation. The teacher might present examples of squares of different sizes, but without differences in orientation, as in Figure 6-3.

After students understand that size is not critical, then variations in orientation can be shown, as in Figure 6-4.

Other noncritical attribute variations may be added later as the concept of square is further constructed. A teacher should carefully examine concepts for their critical and noncritical attributes so that these can be included appropriately in examples and counter-examples. Planning for lessons should include designing the use of manipulatives and activities to illustrate the various attributes. In the case of geometrical shape concepts, manipulatives such as geoboards and paper folding are invaluable tools to use in demonstrating the various examples and counter examples.

FIGURE 6-4 Squares of Different Sizes and Orientations

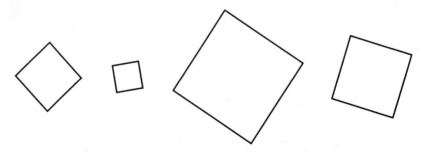

FIGURE 6-5 Triangle Concept Counter-Examples

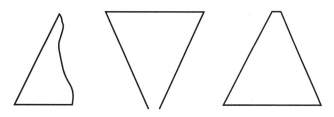

Concept Counter-Examples.   Counter-examples, on the other hand, must vary across critical attributes. In Figure 6-5 shapes are presented that have some of the features of triangles, but with some critical attribute missing.

The critical attributes of triangles not present in Figure 6-5 are:

- Straight line segments for sides

- Closure of figure

- Exactly three sides

Part of concept development is clearly understanding the nature of the concept and knowing precise, accurate names and descriptors to attach to the concept. In the case of the concept of triangle, a fully developed concept will enable the child to clearly recognize triangular shapes and to describe them. The child also can recognize variations and state what's "wrong" with a shape (Wright, 1994).

When giving counter examples, the teacher must identify the critical attributes clearly and help students to focus on what is necessarily present in the concept. Special care should be taken *not* to identify as critical those attributes that are not critical. A common error of this type is committed by teachers while teaching subtraction. Some teachers, for example when teaching a subtraction algorithm for 74 − 38, will say, "You can't take 8 from 4, so you regroup to make 14 from which 8 can be subtracted." Students quickly get the idea that a critical attribute in the subtraction concept is that the number subtracted *from* must be larger than the number subtracted. This is not a critical attribute unless subtraction is limited to results in whole numbers. Teachers know that 4 − 8 will yield −4 for students in the 6th grade and beyond as they continue constructing the subtraction concept.

The approach of first identifying the pertinent attributes should be used early in the effort to teach concepts. First graders may not be able to develop the full concept of triangle, but if the approach is consistent with sound concept development, the concept will be correctly fleshed out naturally later on.

Poor approaches to teaching concepts may preclude the student's being able to acquire the concept at all. Poor approaches include:

- Giving abstract definitions before experimentation and exploration with the concepts

- Giving no variety in examples

- Giving no variety in counter-examples

- Encouraging only memorization of facts and definitions

Operations Concept Development

Since the operations form the basis of much that is to be learned in mathematics, especially in the early grades, it is appropriate to mention specifically this set of concepts and their construction. Teaching the operations is discussed in detail in Chapter 12, so this section will deal with the construction aspect of teaching and learning of operations concepts. Six important considerations are:

- Begin operations with manipulatives carefully, giving attention to salient characteristics such as conservation of number and the binary attribute.

- Build the application of the operation to include different types of numbers: small, large, fractional, and in different forms.

- Modify the operations as needed to achieve results appropriate to the situation (e.g., use regroupings, commutativity, distributivity, related operations).

- Gradually abstract the operation from its concrete representations, but return on occasion to the manipulatives to confirm and reinforce.

- Point out to the learner multiple ways of regarding an operation. (Multiplication is repeated addition but is also the inverse of division.)

- Take care with terminology. (One example: Operations yield *results*, not *answers*, since questions are not always involved.)

It is essential that as students move from manipulation of objects to symbolic forms (algorithms) in order to operate, they do not equate the algorithm to the operation. It seems natural to make them synonymous, but when operation and algorithm are not clearly distinguished, the concept of the operation is lost. Often a student may have difficulty in applying the operation in a practical way, even though the student has memorized an algorithm for the operation.

Problem solving depends on the ability of the problem solver to identify the need for particular operations. Typically, there are no direct instructions such as "add these numbers and multiply those" in problem statements

(Fernandez, 1994). Furthermore, it is often the case that no specific algorithms are called for or necessary for successful progress toward solution. (For more on this issue, see Chapter 7 on problem solving and Chapter 9 on operations.) Mastery of operation concepts should not be expected or emphasized in the early stages even though a particular operation algorithm might be fully constructed in the first two or three grades. Operation concepts mature gradually over the course of several months or years and require an exposure to a wide variety of mathematical ideas, different numbers, and types of applications.

Constructing Facts

Earlier in this chapter we discussed making connections among facts as a critical part of mathematics learning. It is important when teaching facts to provide information about those connections and interrelationships. These connections provide meaning and a framework to which the other sets of facts can be attached. The framework provides a structure to enable recall and mental manipulation of various facts in the process of constructing new facts.

The best way for children to construct facts is to discover the facts for themselves. In order to discover a fact, students must be placed in an environment where this will occur naturally. The environment may be a number game, guided manipulation of concrete objects, step-by-step instruction by the teacher, a computer program, or the Internet. Environments may need to be combined so that one particular fact will be discovered. Younger children who have not developed some of the investigative skills necessary to conduct discovery processes need significant teacher guidance and environments directly conducive to discovery, exploration, and inquiry. Part of the environment may need to be carefully structured to lead students directly to the specific concept to be constructed.

Children come to school with significant repertoires of factual information, much of it mathematical. It is, however, largely unorganized and not very useful to them. The construction of the *house* of facts is begun by:

- Enabling them to develop classification skills

- Helping them with the associated terminology

- Guiding them in the organization of known facts

- Modifying and reconnecting what is known

Following that, new facts are presented with special attention to terminology and to relationships to known facts. Children struggle with terminology relative to mathematical fact construction because words they use and hear in daily life usually have fuzzy and ambiguous meanings. In mathematics, names and fact statements must be much more precise and unambiguous. It will help if the teacher points this out to students and reminds them often to be as careful and precise with language as possible.

To help children construct facts, teachers will:

- Provide experiences and an environment where children will discover as many facts as possible.

- Present the children with facts that are not easily discoverable or which would require excessive environmental manipulation in order to be discoverable.

- Help children make connections and relationships between new and already known facts.

- Provide opportunities for children to state, write, and use the facts in applications, especially in problem solving.

Children should be expected to master certain facts at each level. Other facts, though, may take time to construct fully since some of the connections and relationships may not be made until later grades.

Constructing Processes

Processes are not constructed in the same way as facts and concepts. The word *process* itself connotes the idea of several steps linked together in some sequence. A fact may be noted and committed to memory as a single entity, but a process requires consideration of a number of entities, linkages, and sequencing. Children begin to build processes as they manipulate concrete objects and learn the steps necessary to accomplish a task. Focusing on the order of steps and whether or not order is critical, will assist the student later in learning more complex and abstract processes.

Children can be helped to recognize well-known processes from their daily lives. Such procedures as operating a VCR, using a microwave, constructing a model, and cooking from a recipe are known to children and can be used to help them understand how processes are learned. They should then be shown that mathematical processes can be learned similarly. Examples should include situations in which different sets of processes can be used to accomplish the same task. For example, multiplication can be done using many different algorithms: a place-value-based vertical form, use of the distributive property, or adjust-and-compensate techniques. The teacher should demonstrate that within a given process, variations may be used to shorten the procedure or to make verifications as needed. For example, in comparing fractions using equivalence classes, two fractions may be compared by examining the difference between denominators rather than numerators if that is more convenient. This is part of preparing students for problem solving.

Students need to learn that while some processes do have wide application (e.g., standard algorithms can be applied with all place-value-expressed numbers including decimal forms and nondecimal-based numbers), one cannot memorize all the processes one will need and use. There is no set of *basic* processes which one can learn and then choose from for any task. An important basic understanding is that processes are actually tools for students to use in mathematical tasks, and they should be constructed for that reason. They are not to be learned as one would learn trivia. Furthermore, in doing these tasks, it may be necessary for students to construct a process for a specific task. There is also the need to refine and modify processes to meet the needs of particular tasks. Just as students learn to use calculators and computers, they need to learn to regard mathematical processes as tools to be used in problem solving and other mathematical tasks.

Constructing processes involves being told and shown the steps of the process and then practicing the steps. Thus, to assist students in constructing a process such as an algorithm, a teacher will:

- Demonstrate the process step by step, commenting on important steps and order, including the points at which students typically have difficulty.

- Guide students through the process, again noting the more difficult steps.

- Give students opportunities to practice completing the process.

- Remind students, in the case of an algorithm, that this is but one of the available processes, simply the one chosen for all to learn at this time.

- Discuss the appropriate use of the process: the numbers for which it works, when it can be used, and when it should not be used.

- Examine the students' practice work to determine what difficulties they are experiencing and help them make corrections.

- Give additional practice helping students to understand that mastery/ perfection is the expected goal.

Terminology is a significant concern here, too. There is a dangerous tendency among some teachers to make mathematics into a study of tools (processes, in this case) rather than a study of mathematical concepts. Exotic terminology may become the focus and draw students' attention and learning away from the important material. For example, the following scenario represents a poor environment for teaching subtraction:

Objective:	Learning and using the operation—subtraction
Setting:	Subtracting whole numbers
Procedure:	Use the standard algorithm and place value concepts
Teaching:	Emphasis on the terms *minuend* and *subtrahend:* placing them properly in a format, memorizing the words, spelling them correctly, using them in mathematical sentences, and explaining procedure to others using this terminology.

The terms *minuend* and *subtrahend* are particular to only one subtraction algorithm. To emphasize or even to use them, will not help students to learn subtraction. The words are completely abstract, unrelated to the process of subtracting, and not connectable to other words which would help to provide meaning. If the teacher emphasizes these words (and other similar ones) for mathematical processes, children will think that they are important and try to memorize what are essentially nonsense symbols. In trying to learn these abstract terms, children neither construct the process nor learn the mathematics to be processed. Their attention is directed away from the mathematics and focused on abstract learning about the tool.

Integration

Mathematics has often been taught in isolation from other subjects and even from the real world. This is natural because much of mathematics can be handled abstractly and, by its appearance and structure, it seems quite different from other subjects. When mathematics is compartmentalized as it is taught, students gain wrong impressions, for example:

- Mathematics has no real-life application.
- Mathematics has no connection to any other subjects.
- Mathematics can be learned as an isolated subject.
- Learning mathematics is like learning trivia.

Integrating mathematics into other subjects and integrating other subject material into mathematics lessons are powerful ways to provide a number of benefits:

- Motivation and interest
- Connections that give meaning
- Support for memory and recall
- Awareness of application
- Understanding of problem solving

The extent of integration will vary from lesson to lesson and is dependent on a variety of factors. The lesson topic, the length of the lesson, and the focus of the lesson all affect the amount of integration possible. Some topics lend themselves naturally to integration. A social studies lesson on the decision to purchase the Louisiana Territory, for example, could include the mathematics of finding area and cost per square mile. A mathematics lesson on percentages could include economics issues or social demographics.

Very brief lessons, on the other hand, and lessons on specific mathematical issues such as the long division algorithm, would be difficult to integrate. Thus, even though integration is desirable, teachers should not attempt to achieve significant integration of some other subject in every math lesson or mathematics in every other subject's lessons. Integration should be natural, not forced or contrived. Chapter 8 includes a section on problem solving where contrived problems are discussed. It is difficult to find a good real-life problem to illustrate neatly each mathematical entity being taught. It may be tempting to create problems like: "Tom was 3 times as old as Kelly 4 years ago. In how many years will Tom be twice as old as Kelly?" Even though Tom and Kelly might be real people and children are interested in ages, problems like these are actually puzzles contrived to fit an algebraic procedure. Problems that describe actual situations do provide real support for mathematical constructions because they are set in a meaningful context.

Lesson Plans

Lesson plans take two basic forms: the *block* plan (a concise sketch of the lesson's main point, written in the teacher's daily plan book) and the full-length lesson plan with details of objectives, procedures, and evaluation written out. A model of a full-length form is found in Appendix G.

Mathematics lesson plans may be substantively different from other subject area lesson plans because they need to include several important parts.

- A clear objective (usually fairly narrow in scope)

- A clear picture of the readiness of the students

- Obvious direct relationships between procedures and objective

- Obvious direct relationships between the objective and the evaluation

In other subjects, students' readiness to learn may not be as important. The success of mathematics lessons often depends on whether students know certain prerequisite facts, skills, and concepts. When the lesson is not well coordinated with student readiness, students will resort to memorizing nonsense symbols and processes. That is, what they are asked to *learn* will have no real meaning or connection to anything real or any other mathematical idea.

Some teachers allow math lessons to "just happen" by using the mathbook, assuming that the author of the book had a good objective in mind, which students will meet by "going through the book." That is unlikely. Any lesson, no matter how simply carried out, needs to be based on a very specific objective. The objective may be as simple as exposing students to a mathematical idea or as complex as demonstrating competence in finding square roots using a particular algorithm.

If the lesson's objective is not clear, it may be difficult to design appropriate procedures and even more difficult to evaluate the results of the lesson. This lack of clear objectives is especially obvious when operations are taught. Often sheets containing 15 or 20 algorithmic forms for a particular operation are given to students for completion. This work follows lessons in which those kinds of exercises were illustrated by the teacher and practiced by the students. The *test* is graded and students are rated on their abilities to *do* the operation. In reality, the students were tested on their memory of what *steps* they were to show, because that was what the teacher wanted to see on the paper. Because of the way they took the test, students were not actually tested on their concept of the operation, their understanding of the algorithm, or their ability to perform the algorithmic process.

When the author's son was in fifth grade he was given the test shown (partially) in Figure 6-6.

FIGURE 6-6 A Portion of Kevin's Paper

$$27 \quad 34 \quad 48 \quad 59 \quad 63$$
$$+45 \quad +67 \quad +72 \quad +46 \quad +28$$
$$72$$

First Kevin went through the whole paper and put little numeral 1's between and above the two digits at the top. Then he went back and wrote all the results using mental computation. Apparently the teacher never knew what Kevin was really doing and thought that Kevin's skills in using the standard addition algorithm were being tested. Based on his paper, Kevin was judged to have mastered addition with two-digit numbers where trading (carrying) from the righthand column is required. Kevin, however, had not "carried" at all; certainly he had not performed all the steps of the algorithm he was being taught. He had put all the 1's in the proper places because he knew that was what the teacher wanted to see. Obviously, the objective of the lesson was not being evaluated by this test.

Classroom Environment

Setting the stage for teaching mathematics effectively involves preparing a classroom to promote and encourage mathematics learning. Attractive posters highlighting various facets of mathematics will help children notice uses of mathematics in daily life, architecture, and business. Some posters also contain pictures and information about men and women mathematicians. Many classrooms have not only reading and language arts texts but many interesting books on a variety of subjects to encourage reading. However, they have only one book on mathematics—the math text. This is unfortunate, because many well-written, interesting books with mathematics themes for children are available. A number of these are listed in the suggested readings at the ends of the chapters.

Art and Mathematics

The connection between mathematics and art should not be neglected. The art and math teachers can cooperate in helping the students work with geometric shapes to create designs and, with paper folding and other techniques, to create intriguing three-dimensional objects. These may be put on display in the classroom and in other parts of the school building. The mathematics teacher can accomplish much in teaching geometrical concepts in the context of these highly motivating and creative activities. Students should be encouraged to bring to the classroom containers and objects that illustrate geometrical and other mathematical concepts. These objects can be added to the manipulatives the teacher has collected and can be used for counting, classifying, measuring, and studying many different mathematical ideas. They also form a part of the environment of the classroom and subtly remind the students that mathematics is interesting and applicable to real life situations.

Cooperative Learning

Teachers have been encouraged recently to implement cooperative learning environments in their classrooms. The advantages of teaching and learning cooperatively are obvious. Students can help each other, work on class projects together, and prepare themselves for the job market where much work is done in team formats.

On the other hand, members of cooperative groups cannot introduce and teach new concepts in mathematics to each other. The teacher may teach the ideas to the students while they are in groups, and the students can profit from group discussion and manipulation of objects. Without the teacher's guidance, the group would simply share ignorance. A related problem is that group members might develop wrong and/or incomplete concepts and, if left to themselves, have no way of knowing their inadequacies. Following teaching and learning, however, cooperative activity can be very powerful in mathematics process and fact construction. Discussion and exchange is helpful as students practice processes, review facts, and check and cross-check with each other. Students who have already constructed concepts, processes, and facts may assist others, using easily understood terminology and student-level communication. Cooperative grouping will not automatically function effectively. Teachers have to provide for group structure, including well defined tasks and instructions, or timid students will tend not to participate and aggressive students to dominate and do all the activities themselves (Norwood, 1994).

Teachers should use cooperative groupings in the classroom to explore, discover, inquire, problem solve, and practice skills, but they should not assume that groups will help students learn new mathematical concepts and ideas. The teacher should structure the groups carefully and give clear instructions to guide the groups' work.

Competition

Intense competition and the resulting social and learning difficulties (including, in the case of mathematics, math anxiety) should not be a part of the classroom environment. Some children are not naturally competitive and they suffer in a subject area where highly competitive games are a regular part of teaching and learning. There are also serious questions about the value of such games to learning in general. Highly competitive games may contribute only excitement for some children. Having fun in the competition may be substituted for the actual learning that was intended. Students may feel good about the mathematics lesson but not realize that they have not learned any mathematics.

Difficulties with competition should not, however, completely prevent mathematics teachers from using games for teaching and learning. Gentle games can also provide strong motivation for learning. Interesting and challenging mathematics games are available for all grade levels, and they should be used where appropriate in the mathematics classroom. These games usually involve manipulation of objects and numbers and may be valuable in helping children construct concepts and develop factual knowledge.

Software games provide the additional benefit of practice using the computer and knowledge about computers and software. If a game is to be used for instructional or practice purposes, the teacher should examine the game carefully to be sure that it will actually help children meet the objectives for its use. Children often figure out how to play games and avoid learning in the process. Not every game, though, must be used only to meet some highly structured mathematical objective. Filling time with enjoyable activity in which some math is used is a legitimate objective. Almost any mathematics oriented game can meet that criterion.

To defuse the competitive aspects of some games, the teacher can

- Modify or remove the scoring scheme

- Choose games in which winning is based on chance rather than skill

- Make arrangements so that every child can win

- Reduce the value of rewards (both physical and psychological) for winning

- Encourage competition with oneself

- Keep the amount of competitive activity at appropriate levels.

Advanced Students

Pace of learning often differs from one student to another. It is tempting to let the quicker students move ahead to the next topic or to more advanced material. Generally, this is not a good idea, because as the gap between the slower and quicker students widens it becomes difficult to teach the whole class. An effective method of dealing with the more advanced students is to send them on lateral excursions. Fortunately, in most mathematics topics, there are many lateral routes containing challenging and fascinating material. Many of these are in the realm of problem solving (Mills et al., 1994). Challenging problems can be given that do not require any advanced concepts. For example, when the class is studying algorithms, advanced students can be given cryptarithms (algorithmic forms that contain letters instead of numerals, forming a problem that involves finding the numerals that make a complete correct statement).

 Example

$$
\begin{array}{r}
\text{S E N D} \\
+ \ \underline{\text{M O R E}} \\
\text{M O N E Y}
\end{array}
\qquad
\begin{array}{r}
\text{Solution:} \ \ 9567 \\
+ \ \underline{1085} \\
10652
\end{array}
\qquad
\begin{array}{l}
\text{(Are there} \\
\text{other} \\
\text{solutions?)}
\end{array}
$$

It is counterproductive to give faster learners and advanced students more of what they have already mastered. A wise teacher will have a collection of tasks, projects, problems, puzzles, reading books, software, and Internet addresses that advanced students can use in taking lateral mathematical excursions.

Summary

This chapter considered the general methods that apply to teaching mathematics in all topics and areas. First the underlying learning and psychological theories were examined. Memorizing, the importance of terminology, the use of manipulatives, and constructivism were all detailed. Attention was given, too, to what teaching is involved in helping students to construct concepts, processes, and facts. Math lesson plan construction and developing appropriate classroom environments were studied, along with comments about the place of cooperative grouping and competition in teaching mathematics.

Exercises

1. Choose a topic to be taught in mathematics and identify three different lateral tasks to give advanced students so that they don't become bored or need to move beyond their peers.

2. Identify and explain three significant differences in the ways concepts in mathematics and concepts in other subjects are learned.

3. Using a particular mathematics concept to be taught at a certain grade level, give brief descriptions of lessons containing insufficient dissonance, appropriate dissonance, and excessive dissonance.

4. Consider a particular concept in mathematics and describe the part memorization should play in learning that concept. Explain how the teacher will enable students to move beyond memorizing at the right stage in learning that concept.

▣ References

Brooks, Jacqueline Grennon, and Martin G. (1993). *The Case for Constructivist Classrooms.* Alexandria, VA: ASCE

Bruner, Jerome S. (1960). *The Process of Education.* Cambridge, MA: Harvard University Press.

Dienes, Z. P. (1960). *Building Up Mathematics.* London: Hulchison Education.

Fernandez, Maria L., et al. (1994, March). Connecting research to teaching: Problem solving: Managing it all. *Mathematics Teacher,* 87(3), 195–199.

Hatfield, Mary M. (1994, October). Use of manipulative devices: Elementary school cooperating teachers self-report. *School Science and Mathematics,* 94(6), 303–309.

Lo, Jane-Kale, et al. (1994, January). The participation, beliefs and development of arithmetic meaning of a third-grade student in mathematics class discussions. *Journal for Research in Mathematics Education,* 25(1), 3–49.

Lowery, L. (1974). *Learning about Learning: Classification Abilities.* Berkley, CA: University of California.

Mills, Carol J., et al. (1994, November). Academically talented students' achievement in a flexibly paced mathematics program. *Journal for Research in Mathematics Education,* 25(5), 495–511.

Norwood, Karen S. (1994, May). The effect of instructional approach on mathematics anxiety and achievement. *School Science and Mathematics,* 94(5), 248–254.

Piaget, Jean. (1954). *The Construction of Reality in the Child.* New York: Harcourt Brace.

Piaget, Jean. (1964). Development and Learning. *The Journal of Research in Science Education,* 2(3), 126–135.

Pirie, Susan, and Thomas Kieren. (1994, March). Growth in mathematical understanding: How can we characterize it and how can we represent it? *Educational Studies in Mathematics,* 26(2–3), 165–190.

Steffe, Leslie, P., and Thomas Kieren. (1994, December). Radical constructivism and mathematics education. *Journal for Research in Mathematics Education,* 25(6), 711–733.

Thompson, Patrick W., and Diana Lambdin. (1994, May). Research into practice: Concrete materials and teaching for mathematical understanding. *Arithmetic Teacher,* 41(9), 556–558.

Wright, Bob. (1994, July). Mathematics in the lower primary years: A research-based perspective on curricula and teaching practice. *Journal for Research in Mathematics Education*, 25(3), 324–336.

🔲 Suggested Readings

Chandler, Donald G., and Patricia A. Brosnan. (1994, Fall). Mathematics textbook changes from before to after 1989. *Focus on Learning Problems in Mathematics*, 16(4), 1–9.

Carroll, Jean. (1994, December). What makes a person mathphobic? A case study investigating affective, cognitive and social aspects of a trainee teacher's mathematical understanding and thinking. *Mathematics Education Research Journal*, 6(2), 131–143.

Kohler, Frank W., Helen Ezell, Kathryn Hoel, and Phillip S. Strain. (1994, March). Supplemental peer practice in a first-grade math class: Effects on teacher behavior and five low achievers' responding and acquisition of content. *The Elementary School Journal*, 94(4), 389–403.

Smock, C. D. (1981). Constructivism and Educational Practices, in *New Directions in Piagetian Theory and Practice* Eds. I.E. Siegel, D.M. Brodzinsky, and R.M. Golinkoff. Hillsdale, NJ: Lawrence Erlbaum Associates.

Developing Number Sense

One of the children's problems: Sholan believes that large numbers are somehow connected to large objects and small numbers are for small objects.

Teacher's problem: Many of the children are not conservers and are having difficulty with adding since they are trying to memorize "what to do."

🔳 Understanding the Problem

Children who approach learning mathematics from a rote memory perspective and teachers who teach purely algorithmic rules produce students who cannot function effectively in mathematics classes or in our technical society. To do so, children must develop what mathematics educators call *number sense.* Mathematics education researcher Robert Reys defines number sense as an intuitive idea about numbers and their uses, including an appreciation for accuracy, an ability to detect errors, and common sense when working in mathematics (Reys, 1980). Extensions of this basic notion include the properties of different kinds of numbers such as primes and odds and evens, numerical order, and understanding of big and small numbers. Additional considerations are understandings of number systems and counting schemes.

The *Curriculum and Evaluation Standards* lists categories under which ideas of number sense fall. They are *Standard 5: Estimation* and *Standard 6: Number Sense and Numeration.* Standard 5 for K–4 lists the following curriculum goals: Students will:

- Explore estimation strategies.

- Recognize when an estimate is appropriate.

- Determine reasonableness of results.

- Apply estimation when working with quantities, measurement, computation, and problem solving. (NCTM, 1989, 36)

For grades 5 through 8 the list includes:

- Develop number sense for whole numbers . . . integers. (NCTM, 1989, 87)

The Standard 6 list for K–4 is:

- Construct number meanings through real world experiences with the use of physical materials.

- Understand our numeration system by relating counting, grouping, and place value concepts.

- Develop number sense.

- Interpret multiple uses of numbers encountered in the real world. (NCTM, 1989, 38)

For grades 5 through 8 the list includes:

- Develop and use order relations for whole numbers . . . . integers.

■ Develop and apply number theory concepts (e.g. primes, . . .) in real world and mathematical problem situations. (NCTM, 1989, 91)

As these lists show, there are significant tasks concerning the idea of number sense outlined for both student and teacher. This vital aspect of mathematics learning cannot be glossed over under the assumption that, if basic facts and operation algorithms are well taught, children will automatically assimilate a sense of number. Using a gloss-over approach, schools have produced many students who blithely accept the reading on the calculator window, with no sense of whether a computation result is even close to what it ought to be. Some high school students cannot measure accurately and do not understand when different levels of accuracy are appropriate. Children without number sense in the early grades mention number names at random. When asked, for example, how many people are in the school, they will say, "fifty," or "one hundred," or "one thousand," obviously with no idea of the appropriate number. For them, *one-half* describes one of two parts of something regardless of whether the two parts are the same size. Students who have not thought deeply about the interrelationships of numbers and the different types of numbers have difficulty with problem solving, because the ability to solve often depends on understanding the characteristics of the numbers involved. Those who do not understand that mathematics is systematic and structured are relegated to thinking of numbers as erratic and whimsical.

Piaget's theory informs us about children's psychological development and points out that it is necessary for a child to learn mathematical concepts from activities in a contextual environment. From this theory we also understand that the ability to use, understand, and manipulate symbols does not automatically develop in a child's mind. It comes about, rather, through interrelated experiences with physical objects and variety in attempts to develop and use representations of those objects (Piaget and Inhelder, 1969, 1971). These experiences in arranging, counting, classifying objects, and taking their various attributes into consideration are what help children to develop number sense.

Counting and Classifying

Some objects children should *play* with and use for counting and classifying are:

Marbles	Coins
C-rods of all sizes and colors	Science objects
C-rods of particular color	(leaves, seeds, etc.)
Base-10 blocks of all sizes	Pieces of chalk
Counters	Crayons/markers
Pennies	Attribute blocks
Magazine cutouts	Books
People	Small toys

FIGURE 7-1   Sets of Objects of the Same Size and Kind, but Arranged Differently

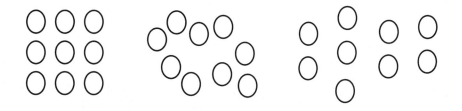

Children should count with objects under different arrangements and orders. See Figure 7-1.

Children should be guided to take control of the manipulatives and to construct and arrange objects in ways of interest to themselves. One of the immediate goals is to have children classify objects and place them in sets or groups. These sets should be named, described, and counted. For example, a collection of buttons may be grouped into sets called the *reds*, the *blues*, and the *greens* or the *no-holes*, the *two-holes*, and the *four-holes*. Then the sets can be described with statements like, "There are 12 buttons in the set of the reds and the same number in each of the sets of the blues and the greens." Classification with reference to many different attributes is important. Children usually focus first on color, but should be encouraged to use size, shape, thickness, and texture classifications as well. At first these ideas need to be teacher generated, but children will quickly enjoy generating their own classifications. Many children's reading books provide interesting stories using numeracy concepts including classifying as their focus. These are helpful for setting the stage for classifying and encouraging children to develop their own ways of sorting and classifying. *Shoes* (Winthrop, 1986) and *Sorting* (Philomel, 1988) are appropriate for kindergarten and first grade students. Teachers will find that children, on their own, will create some unusual and intriguing categories. These will provide opportunities for discussion and correction of misconceptions students may have.

Among the difficulties students have with classification tasks are:

- Not recognizing overlapping categories

- Losing track of classification criteria and mixing classes

- Focusing on subsets rather than essential classification criteria

- Using multiple criteria simultaneously (Piaget, 1969)

They should practice justifying the placement of certain objects in certain sets, explaining their reasons both orally and in writing. Writing of this kind should start in the first grade with children encouraged to write what they can and to use drawings and sketches to represent sets of various kinds. These sets should include those with no elements so that when numbers (the measures of the sets) are assigned to the sets, zero is included.

Cardinal Number

The number that describes this important characteristic of the set (the number of the set) is called the *cardinal number* of the set. It should be explained to students that number is one of the ways of describing a set. A set might be described as containing 10 large, blue, square-shaped objects. Reading books that can be used effectively when children are learning about cardinal numbers include: *Anno's Counting Book* (Anno, 1977), *Anno's Counting House* (Anno, 1982), *Ten Black Dots* (Crew, 1986), and *Moja Means One* (Feelings, 1994). The idea of order should be introduced along with cardinal number ideas but not overemphasized; the idea of the number of a set should be well developed before the concept of order is given significant emphasis. Sets should be described as larger, smaller, or the same size (the same measure, having the same cardinal number). Multiple variations in set construction must be given along the lines of conservation experiments.

Solving the Problem

Students should be asked not only to describe and discuss sets such as those in Figure 7-2 but also to create sets with various kinds of objects, according to a variety of criteria.

They should then be asked questions such as, "Which set is larger?" and Which has more in it?" Books with mathematical order concepts as their basis that will be enjoyed by children are, among others: *Always Room for One More* (Leodhas, 1965) and *The Very Busy Spider* (Carle, 1989).

Activities in constructing sets, counting, and ordering help children to begin to think about sets and their numbers and to develop conservation con-

FIGURE 7-2 Sets with Variety in Number and Types of Objects

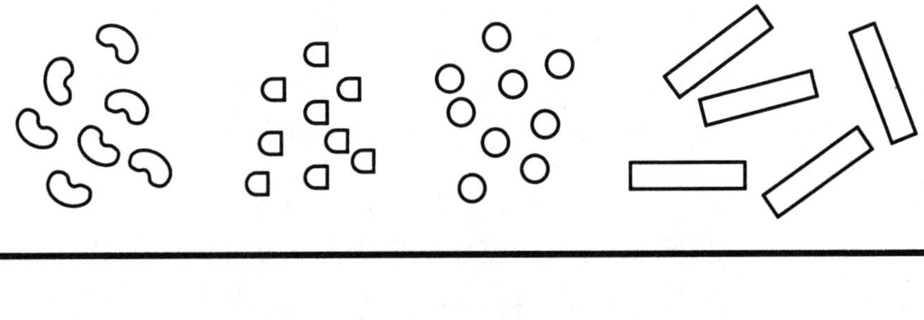

FIGURE 7-3 Sets with the Same Number but Different Arrangements

cepts. It is important to help them realize that the numerical count of a set is a fixed attribute; it does not change with rearrangement of the members of the set. See Figure 7-3. Also, the apparent size of the figure drawn to represent a boundary of the set should not be considered as a factor influencing the number of the set. See Figure 7-4.

Once the idea of a cardinal number of the set is fairly well developed, teachers and students can move on to more formal consideration of order among the counting numbers. They begin with examination of which sets have larger counts than others and with the idea that the number of a set is independent of the characteristics of the objects in the set. It must be clear that this independence exists, even though non-number attributes usually attract attention when the set is first examined. The items in the set must actually be counted. Examples of sets of a few big things and sets of many small things should be used and the usual questions asked. "Which is larger or smaller?"

FIGURE 7-4 The Sets Are the Same Size but the Loops Designating the Sets Are Different Sizes and Shapes

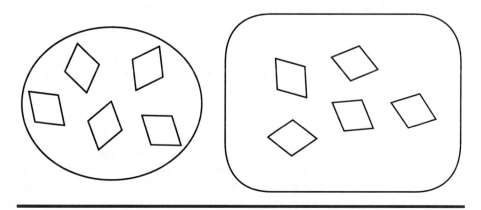

FIGURE 7-5 Sets Showing One-to-One Correspondence and Remainders

and "Do they have the same number of items in them?" Students should practice establishing one-to-one correspondence to answer these questions.

The teacher should also have the students manipulate and create various sets themselves and then ask other students questions relative to the numbers of the sets. A game of "I can trick you!" can be played with the students in pairs. This game would include rearranging items and asking, "Now how many are there?" There need be no winners or losers.

In kindergarten and first grade, when one-to-one correspondence understandings are being developed, teachers should make reference to the *remainder* or lack thereof. At this early stage the idea of *remainder* should not be overemphasized, but if children encounter the idea at this time, it will serve as a building block for work in subtraction and division in later grades. An algorithm formalizing the remainder should not be mentioned too early, typically not before the third grade.

Number Systems

Having examined sets and counted to determine the numbers of various sets, students will move on to think seriously about the organizational structure of number systems. Children are first introduced to the base-10 place value system. The first sense of a pattern in number names is presented to kindergarten children and first graders when they are shown that there is a way to remember what comes after 20, 30, 40, and so on. Children realize that they can repeat the number names *one* through *nine* after the decade designation: 21, 22, etc. and so make their way all the way to 100 and beyond.

Children usually struggle with the names in the teens even though something of a pattern can be detected here too. English took part of the pattern from the German so that *tsvelf* became *twelve,* and our students simply have to learn these aberrations and remember them. Perhaps *eleven* and *twelve* have to be memorized while *thirteen, fourteen,* etc. can be related to the *three, four, five, . . .* number pattern. *Fifteen* may be something of a problem because young children are learning by hearing and *fifteen* may not sound very much like *five,* certainly not with the obvious connection of *fourteen* and *four.* Another related difficulty is the word pattern in the teen numbers, the decade designation *teen* after the word portion for the particular number as in the *four* in *fourteen* and the *six* in *sixteen.* The pattern changes at twenty so that the decade designation comes before the specific number portion (as in *forty*-five). Since children learn at the beginning by hearing and speaking rather than by reading and writing, the visual clues obtained by examining the written numerals are not meaningful to them.

Teachers should note that, in the case of decade designations, the pattern shown by the numerals for counting the decades begins with 0. The first decade has no number (or 0 in some applications) before the specific number designation. The second decade numerals begin with 1, the third with 2, etc. The teacher should point out the pattern 0,1,2,3, etc. in the written forms of the numbers. Awareness of this pattern is an important starting point for developing measurement concepts. As students begin measuring tasks, they use rulers which require aligning the initial point of a line segment with 0 on the ruler. Many of them struggle with this and make measuring errors because they do not begin at 0. Up to this time much of their learning in mathematics has involved counting, which always began with 1. This is an instance of the shifts teachers make at many points in mathematics. Such shifts (in this case, giving examples only of starting a pattern with 1, then shifting to a very similar pattern but now beginning with 0) are difficult for young children to accommodate.

Along with these basic patterns, teachers encourage students to write two-digit numerals and show the side-by-side form of base 10 numeration. Students quickly learn that the relative positioning of the digit is important and that meaning is attached to a position (Jones, 1994). It is important not to confuse the learning of place-value numeration concepts with learning place-value-based algorithmic procedures for operations. At this point the focus must be on the place-value concept itself. It should be pointed out to children that the base-10 system is really a shortcut device—a system by which we can write any number, no matter how large, using just 10 digits. To do this we have created a system in which a digit takes on meaning dependent on its position in the numeral. Examples (really counter-examples of the base 10 system) of other systems should be given along with discussion of the reasons why those systems are more cumbersome and difficult to work with. Students should be given opportunities to experiment with those nonbase 10 systems. They can try to compute, experiment with possible algorithms, or invent algorithms. See Figure 7-6

FIGURE 7-6 Differing Numeration Systems

The tally system: | one,)| two,

 twenty-three, etc.

Hieroglyphics:

 Examples

- The tally system: | one, ‖ two,

  ‖‖ ‖‖ ‖‖ ‖‖ ||| twenty-three, etc.

- Roman numerals: I, II, III, IV, V, VI, . . .

  CMDXLIX = ?

- Hieroglyphics:

- Bushman: one, two, three, many

- Mayan: (Base 60)

    Unfortunately there are not many naturally occurring base 10 objects and measures in our society and culture. Money designations are good examples, but even there one must be careful to omit nickels and quarters. One other somewhat familiar example is the mileage odometer in a car, which reads in tenths. The disadvantage is the necessity of watching it for extended periods of time to see the cylinders turn over and the numbers move up through the numeration system, regularly trading 9's for 0's. For older children the metric measuring system can provide some examples. (Ironically there are many examples of nonbase 10 systems: days of the week—base 7, months and eggs— base 12, weeks and months—base 4, etc.) Nonbase 10 examples can be used (but sparingly) to illustrate the place value concept as a basis for a system. They should be used sparingly because they are not used much in real life, at least in terms of written numerals, and studying them extensively could be confusing (Sowder, 1994).

    Preservice teachers should experiment with nonbase 10 systems because this experimentation can help prospective teachers understand the nature of the place-value numeration system. It is particularly instructive for prospective teachers to use the standard algorithms with different bases when studying the teaching of algorithms. The only two daily life applications of the base-10 system which involve trading from one place value position to another are money and counters such as car odometers. Thus teachers should obtain and / or make a number of manipulatives to illustrate the base 10 system. Children should work with these repeatedly, trading from one position to the next until the idea of the powers-of-ten positions are well understood. Some helpful devices are:

- C-rods (units and tens)
- Base 10 blocks
- Beansticks
- Bundles of 10 tongue depressors.
- Pennies, dimes, and dollars
- 'Trains' of Unifix cubes (Thompson, 1994)

Unifix Train Trading Activity

1. Students in pairs count out 15 "cars" (cubes).

2. Students in pairs use cubes to create "trains" of ten "cars" each.

3. Ask students how many cars are left over (i.e., don't go into making a train).

4. Have students count out 23 cubes and make trains.

5. Ask students how many trains they now have and how many cars are left.

6. Have students record the number of cars, number of trains, and number of cars left.

7. Ask students to give each other certain numbers of cubes, then create and record the trains information.

Beanstick Trading Activity

1. Students in groups create bean sticks by gluing 10 beans to a stick.

2. When dry, the sticks are used with loose beans to count a large set of beans.

3. Students place the bean sticks in a column on a paper or in a box for the 10s place, and place bundles of 10 sticks (100) in the 100's place, trading until the set is counted.

4. Students record results and explain to the class how they proceeded.

Zero

Special attention should be given to *zero*. Containers (sets), which contain no items, should be provided, but care should be taken with semantics. Students who pass through this section of learning number sense and come away with the notion that *zero* means *nothing* have not properly developed this part of the sense of number. Zero must be identified as a specific number. Many examples should be given to show, that zero is an important and necessary place holder.

 ### Examples of Set Numbers

(Their numbers are listed below the set designations.)

{ 0, 1 },   { 0 },   {   },   { 0, 1, 3, 5 },   { 0, 1, 2, 3, }
  2   1   0   4   4

(Note that the second set in the list, { 0 }, contains one item, a "0," so the set number is 1.)

 ### Examples of 0 Place Holders

In the numbers 230, 203, and 1013, "0" is a place holder indicating no units, no tens, and no hundreds in the respective cases. Those sets are empty, so 0 is needed to indicate that condition. The number of units, tens, etc. is 0 in each case.

The teacher should provide such examples because students will, at first, feel it necessary to put a numeral between 1 and 9 (for place holders) in every column. They need to understand that zero is a legitimate place holder, expressing a precise value for that place.

Ordering

Children come to school with an incomplete ordering concept. They know that there are large and small numbers. They do not, however, know how to write the numerals to represent those numbers and so have no means of comparing them by examining their numerals. This is further confused by the fact that children do not distinguish between the numeral and the number it represents. So, for example, the expression $3 > 5$ would not present a difficulty for them. The symbol for three is obviously larger than the symbol for five. The *more than* and *less than* concepts must be formalized and made definitive. In addition, what seems like a large number to a child is not necessarily a large number to an adult. The idea of *large* or *small* is relative and may be relative to circumstances outside of mathematics. For example, one dollar may be a large amount of money when buying candy, but a very small amount when considering the purchase of a bicycle. The measurement of 0.1 inch is insignificant when considering the distance from the house to the school but a very large value to a machinist (Hiebert, 1980).

Large and Small Number Activity:

The students will write the largest number they can.

The students will next write the largest number they can name. They will write out its name.

The students will write the smallest number they can.

The students will write the smallest number they can name. They will write out its name.

The students will write a description of how they know when one number is larger than another using place value ideas.

In pairs, students will challenge each other by writing a number and challenging the partner to write a larger number.

In pairs, students will challenge each other by writing a number and challenging the partner to write a smaller number.

Discovering Other Numbers

Ideally, teachers should present students with real problems whose solutions require finding or inventing new numbers. When children discover numbers such as negative and fraction numbers naturally while solving a problem, the concepts are not as easily forgotten or misunderstood. The power of discovery techniques is that they provide motivation and contexts in which the invented or discovered entity has meaning and value.

 Examples

Problem: The temperature is 8 degrees Fahrenheit. Because of a coming snowstorm, the temperature is to drop by 15 degrees. After the temperature drop, what will the temperature reading be?

Problem: Keel owes Mom $1.50 from an allowance but needs $2.00 for a ticket. He borrows the $2.00 from Mom. How much does Keel owe now!

(Students with no experience working with negative numbers may not know what these number are called, but if encouraged to explore the ideas with subtraction can develop the concept of negative numbers even though the formal name is not used.)

Problem: Shell and three friends are eating two pizzas of the same size, each of which has been cut into 6 equal sized pieces. If they eat 9 pieces altogether, how many whole and part pizzas did they eat? If they eat 10 pieces, what portion of a pizza is left?

Problem: Find the missing number in the sequence:

    3   7   15   _____   63   127

Problem: Use exactly six 5s and other mathematical symbols to represent the numbers between 1 and 10.

 Examples

$$\frac{5}{5} + \frac{5}{5} + \frac{5}{5} = 3 \qquad \frac{5 + 5 + 5 + 5}{5 + 5} = 2$$

(The formal teaching of fractions is discussed in Chapter 11. Here the issue is for students to think about what do with the situation in which division does not "come out even." What numbers express that? How can those numbers be manipulated? How does the system of numeration for fractions differ from the base-10 numeration system?)

After discovering some of these "other" numbers, the students should be shown an overview of the numbers and systems we use. Some of this will be beyond their current understanding, but it will help students to visualize the general relationships among these different numbers. The Venn diagram, illustrating this connection, is presented in Figure 7-7. Discussion about the relationships among the different types of numbers available to students for solving problems and about understanding numbers generally should be a regular part of planned classroom mathematics lessons.

Definitions

Counting numbers: Beginning with one, the numbers used for counting

Whole numbers: Counting numbers with zero added

Integers: Whole numbers with negative whole numbers

Rational numbers: Integers with fractional numbers (including decimal and percentage forms)

Real numbers: Rationals with numbers which cannot be expressed as rationals (includes such numbers as π and $\sqrt{2}$)

(The Venn diagram (Fig. 7-7), with sets diagrammed within sets, shows that integers are contained in the rationals. That is, all the integers are also rationals, and so forth.)

Special Numbers

Further number sense understandings include awareness of numbers with special characteristics. These include odd and even numbers, prime numbers, composite numbers, perfect numbers, and those with certain divisibility properties. These are concepts from number theory. The study of some number theory concepts is valuable in the elementary school because:

FIGURE 7-7 Venn Diagram Showing Number Relationships

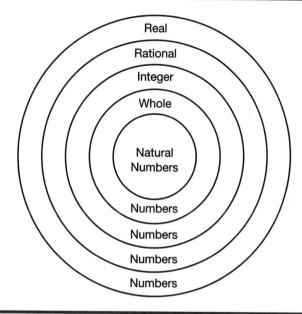

- It provides arenas for exploration and discovery of which elementary students are capable.
- It provides motivational and challenging problems at the students' level.
- It provides information and skills children can use in operations.
- It provides knowledge helpful to students in problem solving.

 Hundreds Chart Activity

1. Provide students with a hundreds chart.
2. Instruct students to ring the "1" on the chart.
3. Instruct students to cross out every even number (divisible by 2) after 2 on the chart.
4. Instruct students to cross out every number after 3 which is divisible by 3.
5. Ask the students to continue the process using 4, 5, 6, etc.
6. Ask the students to comment on any patterns they notice.
7. Ask the students to give a reason for a pattern they notice.
8. Ask the students how far one has to go before one knows that all the numbers (which will be crossed out) have been crossed out.

9. Ask the students to characterize all those numbers which have been crossed out.

10. Ask the students to characterize all those number which haven't been crossed out.

11. Discuss with students the concept of *prime* and *composite*.

12. Discuss other ways of finding prime numbers.

Goldbach's Conjecture Activity

1. State Goldbach's conjecture: *Every composite number can be written as a sum of two prime numbers.*

2. Ask students to confirm or deny this by experimentation.

3. Discuss and inform students that the conjecture is unproven.

(Note: Here is an idea which is very easily stated, verifiable for many numbers, and easily understood by young children, but very difficult to prove true for all composite numbers.)

Numbers-at-Home Activity

Students record different kinds of numbers and their uses in the home, including numbers on the phone, clock, VCR, microwave, mailbox, etc.

Students write a statement of reasons why those numbers are appropriate in each case and what system the numbers are a part of.

Special Numbers Activity

Perfect numbers are those whose prime factors add to a sum equal to the number itself. Have students find perfect numbers (all the perfect numbers between 0 and 100).

Abundant numbers are those for which the sum of the prime factors is larger than the number. Deficient numbers are those for which the sum of the prime factors is smaller than the number. For a further investigation, students may explore these.

Pascal's Triangle Activity

Explore and extend Pascal's triangle, searching for patterns.

```
            1
         1     1
      1     2     1
   1     3     3     1
1     4     6     4     1
```

Nines Experiment Activity:

Check addition, subtraction, and multiplication by "casting out nines."

$$\begin{array}{rr} 723 & 3 \\ +\ 628 & \underline{7} \\ \hline 1351 & 10 \end{array}$$ (Add the digits and write the remainder on division by 9)

($7 + 3 = 10$ leaves a remainder of 1 on division by 9, just as does $1 + 3 + 5 + 1$)

Each number in the operation is "checked" by adding its digits. The number to be used in checking is the remainder when the sum of the digits is divided by 9.

$$\begin{array}{rr} 723 & 13 \\ -\ 628 & \underline{-8} \\ \hline 96 & 5 \end{array}$$ (But $9 + 6$ leaves a remainder of 6, not 5, when divided by 9—thus there is an error in subtraction.)

Students should experiment with this method of working with mod 9 numbers.

Estimation

The ability to examine numbers and to think about the approximate results of an operation is strengthened by multiple experiences in operating with numbers like those being studied at a particular time. The use of a calculator to do rapid repetitive computation is recommended to provide quick reference to many computation results as estimation is practiced (Reys, 1980). A student with good number sense relative to estimations will probably establish some *benchmarks* to serve as indicators of number location. These *benchmarks* are related to the nature of operations. Students should be encouraged to generate this kind of thinking and use the information to assist them in computing. Perhaps the most frequently used benchmarks are 0, 1, 10, 50, and 100.

Examples

Adding: $46 + 59$. These are both near 50.
$50 + 50 = 100$. Estimate: A little more than 100.

Subtracting: $76 - 29$. $70 - 20 = 50$. The result should be a little less than 50.

Multiplying: 0.78×13.78. 0.78 is a little less than 1, so the result should be something less than 13—about 11.

Dividing: $4.6 \div 0.3$. There are about three 0.3s in 1, $3 \times 5 = 15$, so the result should be somewhere around 15.

The fractions $\frac{1}{2}$, $1\frac{1}{2}$, $2\frac{1}{2}$, etc., as well as $\frac{1}{4}$ and $\frac{3}{4}$, are typical *benchmarks* for computing and measuring with fractional values. Depending on the setting for practical applications of computations, other numbers may be even more useful. Machinists use 1/1000 and national economists use billions, while astronomers use lightyears. A good understanding of the various operations will indicate to the estimator whether the result of the operation will be large or small relative to the numbers involved in the operation. This is part of the number sense to be gained by the student, combining to give a sense of what is reasonable for the result of an operation (Leutzinger, 1986). Students should understand that it is not possible to determine what would be a reasonable estimate in every operation situation. They also should not spend excess amounts of time and effort in developing better and better approximations for estimates of operation results or measurement. An estimate is intended to be quick and to yield its assistance to the task without becoming the focus of the task. Students should have sufficient experience with operations with numbers in the range 0 to 100, so that the results of operations with these numbers can be seen as reasonable.

A further aspect of number sense requiring more sophisticated thinking and experience is the understanding of when a certain level of accuracy is sufficient to solve a problem involving a particular computing or measurement task. As an illustration, consider the problem:

> Each gallon of ice cream serves 25 people. How much ice cream will be needed to serve 45 people?

A good estimator will say, "About 2 gallons," because 45 is about 50, or 2×25. Some students feel compelled to use calculators or computational algorithms for problems like this and, on dividing, get 1.8. They then report 1.8 gallons as the amount of ice cream needed to feed 45. They should be asked if they would go the store and ask to buy 1.8 gallons of ice cream.

There is a tendency for children to learn (and for teachers to teach) rules related to estimating rather than to help children make judgments based on common sense about the values being estimated. The *rounding* rule—"round down if the last digit is 4 or smaller"—is an example. When this rule is applied without thoughtful application to the problem situation, incorrect or meaningless results can occur. For example, if each van holds 15 people and 37 people are to use the vans for a trip, 3 vans will be required even though $37 \div 15$ yields 2.47, which is less than 2.5. Some who would apply the *rounding* rule without consideration of the problem's setting would *round* 2.47 down to 2 and state that 2 vans would be required.

A teacher should give students a variety of practical situations such as the one illustrated above to make the point about the practical use of estimates in daily life and the way they ought to be developed.

 ### Estimation Activity

Ask students to list or describe situations where estimates are sufficient to solve problems.

(Include those in which paint or some other product comes only in gallons or other specified quantity and the estimate is a number like $2\frac{1}{4}$ (less than $2\frac{1}{2}$) and the number must be *rounded up* to 3 even though it falls below the $\frac{1}{2}$ mark.)

Summary

It was pointed out that the *Curriculum and Evaluation Standards* (NCTM, 1989) list number sense as one of the standards and that this needs to be developed by students in several ways. Students need to understand the characteristics of numbers and the systems in which they exist. Special attention needs to be given to the base 10 numeration system. The value in studying various special numbers and the use of the number characteristics in calculation and estimation were discussed. Some number theory applications were mentioned and included in activity suggestions.

Exercises

1. Develop a list of divisibility rules for common divisors and illustrate the use of these rules in assisting computation and checking of computation results.
2. Find, describe, and explain three computation tricks in which the tricks depend on some number theory concepts.
3. Read, study, and present to the class some of the history of the development of the base 10 numeration system.
4. Learn the origin of the symbol for *zero*, and describe the development of 0 to the class.
5. Describe the Roman numeral system to the class. Include the origin of the symbols and the subtractive facet of the system.

References

Anno, Mitsumasa (1977). *Anno's Counting Book.* New York: Harper.

Anno, Mitsumasa (1982). *Anno's Math Games.* New York: Harper.

Burns, Marilyn (1993). *Mathematics: Assessing Understanding.* New Rochelle, NY: Cuisenaire.

Carle, Eric (1989). *The Very Busy Spider.* New York: Philomel.

Crew, Donald (1986). *Ten Black Dots.* New York: Greenwillow.

Feelings, Muriel (1994). *Moja Means One.* New York: Puffin Books.

Driscoll, Mark J. (1980). Counting Strategies, in *Research Within Reach: Elementary School Mathematics.* St. Louis: CEM-REL.

Ginsburg, Herbert P. (1977). *Children's Arithmetic: The Learning Process*. New York: D. Van Nostrand.

Hiebert, James (1980). Children's Thinking, in *Research in Mathematics Education*, Ed., Richard J. Shumway. Reston, VA: National Council of Teachers of Mathematics

Jones, Graham A., et al. (1994, September). A model for nurturing and assessing multi-digit number sense among first grade children. *Educational Studies in Mathematics, 27*(2), 117–143.

Kamii, Constance (1990). Constructivism and Beginning Arithmetic (K-2), in *Teaching and Learning Math in the 1990s*, Eds., Thomas J. Cooney and Christian Hirsch. Reston, VA: National Council of Teachers of Mathematics.

Mary, M. (1994, October). Use of manipulative devices: Elementary school cooperating teachers self-report. *School Science and Mathematics, 94*(6), 303–309.

Leodhas, Sorche Nick (1965). *Always Room for One More*. New York: Holt, Rinehart.

Leutzinger, Larry P., Edward C. Rathmell, and Tonya D. Urbalsch. (1986). Developing Estimation Skills in the Primary Grades, in *Estimation and Mental Computation*, National Council of Teachers of Mathematics, 1986 Yearbook. Reston, VA: NCTM.

National Council of Teachers of Mathematics (1989). *Curriculum and Evaluation Standards for School Mathematics*. Reston, VA: Author.

Philomel, Pluckrose H. (1988). *Sorting*. New York: Franklin Watts.

Piaget, Jean (1969). *The Mechanisms of Perception*. London, Routledge and Kegan Paul.

Piaget, J., and B. Inhelder (1969, 1971). *The Psychology of the Child*. New York: Basic Books.

Reys, Robert E., et al. (1980). *Keystrokes: Calculator Activities for Young Students: Counting and Place Value*. Palo Alto, CA: Creative Publications.

Skemp, Richard R. (1987). *The Psychology of Learning Mathematics*. Hillsdale, NJ: Lawrence Erlbaum.

Sowder, Judith, and Bonnie Schappelle. (1994, February). Research into practice: Number sense-making. *Arithmetic Teacher, 41*(6), 342–345.

Thompson, Patrick W., and Diana Lambdin. (1994, May). Research into practice: Concrete materials and teaching for mathematical understanding. *Arithmetic Teacher, 41*(9), 556–558.

Winthrop, Elizabeth (1986). *Shoes*. New York: Harper and Row.

Suggested Readings

Baroody, Arthur J. (November 1986). Basic Counting Principles Used by Mentally Retarded Children. *Journal for Research in Mathematics Education, 17*(5), 382–389.

Dickens, Estelle, and Jeffrey Sellon. (1981). *Cuisenaire Roddles*. New Rochelle, NY: Cuisenaire Co. of America.

Markovits, Zvia, and Judith Sowder (1994, January). Developing number sense: An intervention study in grade 7. *Journal for Research in Mathematics Education, 25*(1), 4–29.

Piaget, Jean. (1965). *The Child's Concept of Number.* New York: W.W. Norton.

Schwartz, David M. (1989). *If You Made a Million.* New York: Lothrop, Lee, and Shepard.

Voigt, Jorg. (1994, March). Negotiation of mathematical meaning and learning mathematics. *Educational Studies in Mathematics,* 26(2–3), 275–298.

Reading Books with Mathematical Themes

Kingsley, Emily P. (1981). *The Sesame Street Circus of Opposites.* New York: Western.

Anno, Mitsumasa (1982). *Anno's Counting House.* New York: Putnam.

Brett, Jan (1974). *The Mitten.* New York: Putnam.

Ginsburg, Mirra (1974). *Mushroom in the Rain.* Palmer, Alaska: Aladdin.

Inkpen, Mick (1988). *One Bear at Bedtime.* New York: Little, Brown.

Lobel, Arnold (1970). *The Lost Button In Frog and Toad are Friends.* New York: Harper and Row.

Pluckrose, H. (1988). *Pattern.* New York, Franklin Watts.

Rees, Mary (1988). *Ten in a Bed.* Boston: Joy Street Books.

Walter, Marion (1985). *The Mirror Puzzle.* New York: Tarquin.

CHAPTER 8

Teaching Mathematical Problem Solving

One of the children's problems: Shelly hates "word problems."

Teacher's problem: Teaching problem solving is difficult because children insist on being told the "way to do it."

Understanding the Problem

Recognizing the difficulty many high school graduates have in coping with the mathematics of everyday life, mathematics educators realize the importance of specifically preparing students to solve problems. This contrasts with a traditional approach which assumed that if the mathematical content and processes were well taught and learned, students would automatically translate them into an ability to solve real life problems. They would thus be able to cope with the current significant need for mathematical knowledge and understanding in everyday life.

In emphasizing the teaching of problem solving, the National Council of Teachers of Mathematics has produced and encouraged the production of significant research and writing on the subject. In particular, the *Curriculum and Evaluation Standards* (NCTM, 1989) give strong emphasis to problem solving, including it in the list of four primary concerns in mathematics education: mathematical knowledge, problem solving, reasoning, and communication.

A related issue is using problem solving settings to teach other mathematical concepts and processes. That is, teaching problem solving can naturally involve teaching other facets of mathematics. Problem solving cannot be taught in isolation, separate from interrelationships with other mathematics. The use of problem solving as a context and motivation for teaching of other mathematics will be considered in related sections of this text.

We begin with an understanding of what mathematical problem solving is all about and a note that there is an ongoing difficulty with the terminology associated with problem solving. Some definitions may help at this point.

> **Problem:** A situation or statement which calls for the use of mathematical content, application, and processes to resolve a blockage or reach a conclusion.
>
> **Solution:** A resolution or conclusion for the problem which meets all the requirements of the problem statement or situation.
>
> **Problem Solving:** The process of using tools, knowledge, problem solving skills, and strategies to find or develop the solution to a problem.

Elementary school students work on two basic types of problems. Those called *problems* are essentially real life in their orientation. They will be problems that take place in students' environments, either pertinent to their daily lives in and out of the classroom or of interest to them for other reasons. The second kind should more properly be called *puzzles*. These typically have no application to real life and sometimes not even to specific mathematical concepts. They are simply challenging and intriguing. *Cryptarithms*, arranging matchsticks, riddles, and math tricks fall into this category. It may be possible to categorize students into two groups: Those who enjoy puzzles and those who avoid working on what seem to them meaningless or impractical. The latter may avoid problem solving because they think it means remembering "the way to do the puzzle."

> **Sub-problem:** *What are the general problem solving teaching methods?*

Basic Principle: To Learn to Solve Problems, One Must Solve Problems

Students who are learning to solve problems need to be presented with many problems to solve. The following section presents criteria and suggestions for finding and presenting appropriate problems. There are several effective ways to establish a problem solving environment that will encourage and reward problem solving in the classroom. Perhaps the most interesting is to arrange for the introduction of a new topic, mathematical principle, or process by posing a problem. A good problem provides motivation for the learning and places the mathematics to be learned in a realistic setting. This can preclude questions such as: "Why do we have to learn this stuff?" and "What use is this stuff, anyway?" Working on the solution of a problem provides opportunities to make helpful connections between the topic at hand and concepts previously learned and to provide an environment for meaningful review. A problem can also help set the stage for learning the subsequent material. When problem solving takes place in cooperative learning settings, the activities generate opportunities for genuine interchange, discussion, and joint decision making among students. Some problems are sufficiently involved and lengthy that they are best placed in a group or class project format.

 ### Examples

A seventh-grade class in Indianapolis used one chalkboard and the entire spring semester to draw a detailed scale model of an Indianapolis 500 race car. This involved careful measurement, scale calculations in fractions, and work with geometrical figures.

A middle-school class used the fall semester to combine math and science in predicting the weather on Thanksgiving day. This involved creating and studying graphs, working with percentages, considering probabilities, and interrelating multiple environmental and media information affecting the solution to the problem. Furthermore, this project had real life connections with the workplace and involved consideration of the jobs of meterologists and weather reporters.

Some teachers experience success on several fronts by having their children keep a *problem solving notebook*. Weekly problems can be worked on at home; in fact, children are encouraged to show their parents the problems they can solve and have solved. The notebook forms a record of a child's progress and success in problem solving and becomes a source of pride. It is also a reference book containing checklists and other helps, and the work done on problems can be referenced for suggestions on solving new problems. A very important skill is emphasized in the process of making the entries: writing about mathematical activity. This involves creating descriptions of what is thought and done. Research indicates what we would expect: *Verbal and written descriptions of mathematical solving processes are the best indications of real problem solving ability and perhaps the best indicators to use for assessing problem solving competence.*

Giving weekly problems for the class or grade, posting the solutions, and giving rewards for success also motivate students to work on problem solving. These problems can be included in grade-wide problem solving contests with prizes given for success with solutions. Problem solving should certainly be included in any Math Day and Math Fair programs. In grades 6, 7, and 8, it is often possible to use current problems in the school or community. Working on this kind of problem and finding solutions warrants publicity and interchange with the school administration, community newspaper, and other media.

 ## Example

The eighth grade class conducts a survey of the status of computer hardware and software in the school, solving the problem of how many students there are per computer, what computers work and with what software, etc. They create graphs, charts, and statistical descriptions of the school's situation.

Closely related to the above could be a survey of student and teacher attitudes and knowledge about computers and software. The number of children with computers at home and what they use them for would be important pieces of information for the school.

Terminology

An astute teacher gives careful attention to terminology as students deal with various problem solving tasks. Teachers and students, and even texts and journals, tend to use inappropriate terminology in mathematics teaching and learning—terminology that gives wrong impressions about problem solving. *Exercises* are called *problems* when the task is really only to recall and use an algorithm properly. Instructions to *answer* a problem are given when no *question* is involved. *Answers* are called *solutions* and *solutions* are called *answers*.

While the term *correct answer* or *correct result* is appropriate in connection with computation, the term *correct solution* is not appropriate for problem solving. *Solution* is sufficient. Having a solution to a problem means the problem has been solved. *Correct solution* implies *incorrect solution*, which is an oxymoron. In problem solving the task is to find solutions. These may be stated or presented in many different formats and styles, none of which is incorrect. Much worse are phrases such as: "Solve this question," "Work this problem," and "Answer this problem." The use of this inaccurate terminology causes two serious difficulties. The misleading impressions students obtain from the wording cause them to deal with problem solving in ways that prevent them from being successful. When the term *answer* is used, the connotation is that there is one correct *answer* (result) as in computation. Thus, when problems with multiple solutions are encountered, students are disconcerted. They may quit after finding the first part of the solution and not realize that there is more to the solution than a single word or number. It will be difficult for them to generalize; that is, write or give general statements that complete the solution. Secondly, the concept of "problem" is poorly understood. *Word problems* are thought of as simply another type of exercise requiring the application of some kind of memorized algorithm or process.

To provide connections with other mathematics learning and to give clear and correct impressions about problem solving, teachers should practice consistent use of good terminology. The term *problem* will be used for those tasks that are actually problems and not *exercises*, *questions*, or *operations*. A student may be having difficulty with computation or applying an algorithm in an exercise, but this does not make that situation into a mathematical problem. Teachers can use the word *difficulty* when this occurs. ("Pat is having difficulty with the exercise.") If an algorithm can be applied to complete an exercise, obtain the result of an operation, etc., then that situation is not a mathematical problem. The term *word problem* should be dropped. Its use suggests that problems expressed in words are the only problems to consider. Students with that impression have difficulty with problems expressed with nonword symbols, geometrical figures, and manipulatives. The word *solutions* should be restricted to discussion about problems, and *answers* used only with questions. When there are questions within the problem statement and even when a question is the major part of the problem statement, it should be made clear to the problem solver that the answers to the question(s) are only a part of the problem solving process and part of the solution. Students sometimes assume that they have solved the problem when they have answered a question which is a part of the problem.

 Example

The tournament problem asks the question:

"How many games will be played if there are 100 players?"

Some solvers stop when they have found 99 as the answer to that question. The solution is completed by generalizing to $n - 1$ where n is the number of players.

Attitudes toward Word Problems

Many texts and worksheets, until recently, followed the format of having explanation and exercises in nonword symbols at the top of the page, then word problems at the bottom of the page. Often, either because the teacher wasn't comfortable with the word problems, there wasn't enough time to get to them, or students had difficulty with the exercises, the word problems were never worked on. This format gives the impression that problem solving should be left to last, is not as important as the exercises, and is the only way problem solving is done. Teachers should reject this formatting, not only in textual materials also but in their own presentation of problems.

Students need to see problems in their natural settings and realize that problem solving is really the essence of mathematics learning. Teachers should often start a lesson with a problem and straightforwardly let the class know that they *can* solve the problem and that they are *expected* to solve the problem. From the beginning, students need to see that the teacher enjoys solving problems and that it is a rewarding activity. When problems occur naturally in the classroom in other subject lessons and classroom activities, the teacher should help children notice the problem, state it clearly, and discuss how it will be solved.

 ## Example

When it comes time for rearranging for cooperative groups in Miss Wilson's room, she poses the question to her fourth graders: "How can we form more than 3 groups with our 24 present today, so that every group will have the same number?" She may add the question: "How many different ways are possible?" and have the students discuss the merits of the various arrangements with regard to the tasks to be done.

It should be made clear that problem solving is a part of real life and that, in solving problems, we actually learn not only how to solve problems in mathematics class, but in other settings as well. The reason we learn to use mathematical tools and processes is so that they will then become tools to be used in other problems. This will put the learning on the basic facts, various algorithms, etc. in the proper perspective. Those who enjoy working with puzzles and solving them should be encouraged to do that, but non-real-life problems should not be pressed on every student. Every student will be faced with daily life problems and needs to acquire mathematical tools for solving them, but not every student has to solve riddles and puzzles or work on contrived problems.

To force puzzle solving on some students will cause them to develop anti-problem-solving attitudes and to avoid all types of problem solving.

Example

The "adding-multiplying" problem mentioned previously is really only a numerical/operations puzzle. There is no clear real life application of the problem or of its solution.

The traditional problems such as: "Keri's aunt is now 3 times as old as she is and in 5 years will be twice as old as she is then. How old is Keri now?" are contrived to fit some type of algebraic process using equations and variables.

Seventh and eighth graders can solve these problems but usually do so only under duress, because they know that the problems are impractical. Problems like this seldom, if ever, occupy the interest of middle schoolers outside the classroom.

Criteria for Evaluating Problems

Since the only way to learn to solve problems is by practice, it is critical that teachers provide ample opportunity for students to solve problems. This means that teachers must create or locate problems that can be used.

Problem selection requires attention to several important criteria. Problems should be:

- Practical and real life related

  a. not contrived.

  b. within the interest range of the children

- Set at the mathematical level of the children

- Ranged across a variety of topics and subject areas

- Varied in the types of skills and strategies likely to be required for solution

- Presented in varying formats

- From *multiple solutions* as well as *singular solution* situations

- Stated in words or symbols children are familiar with or can research.

Practical Problems

Practical problems are directly connected to children's daily lives. The situations described are situations in which children find themselves, and the words used are words that children are familiar with and would use themselves. It is not always easy to find problems that meet these criteria. A teacher should encourage children to bring problems to class (problems they have encountered at home and at play) and be alert to, and use, problems that come up in the context of studying other subjects and in class organization. Problems presented in books and journals, especially the NCTM journals, are usually very good, but may need to be restated to make them really practical. Some of the problems are contrived to fit a particular theme or are simply puzzles and lack realism; children's interest in them is minimal.

Example

The problem: Johnny has three pencils and Mary has five pencils. How many pencils do they have altogether?

This is a poorly stated problem. It is of little interest to children what the total number of pencils is. The total number of pencils is not likely to be a topic of conversation among children.

The problem should be reworked, perhaps along these lines:

> Johnny has three tickets and his sister Mary has five tickets. Do they have enough to take their whole family of eight to the game?

In this problem, the task is the same: To recognize the need to add as part of the solving process. The situation, however is much more interesting and real to children.

A legitimate problem involving Johnny and Mary and pencils might be:

> Johnny has three pencils and Mary has five pencils. How many more pencils does Mary have than Johnny has?

This is a real problem because of the interest among children in who has more regardless of what the objects are or what the situation is.

Who has more? Who is taller? Which car is faster?, and Which team is better? are common topics of conversation among children. These areas of interest are rich sources for problems.

Mathematical Level

The language and the format of the problem statements need to use words that are in the mathematical vocabulary and understanding of the students. If the problems are actually excerpted from real life, the words children actually use should be in the problem statement. For example, if the children use *take away* in their statements describing what is done, then the word *subtract* should not be used in the problem statement.

The mathematical knowledge and processes required for solving the problem must be available to and usable by the students. Obviously, problems involving percentages should not be given to students who haven't yet studied fractions and decimals. The students also must have the mathematical skills and strategies necessary for successful work with the problem. These are discussed later in this chapter. It is essential that the teacher understand the level of the children's mathematical maturity in order to make appropriate decisions concerning the nature and wording of the problems presented.

Problems Over a Range of Topics

Depending on the aspect of mathematics being studied, the problems presented for the students to work on often are restricted to one type or theme. This happens because it is easy to create problems for some topics—such as decimals. Buying and selling situations are convenient and very much a part of daily life; they directly involve decimals and operations with them. There is, however, danger in presenting a very narrow range of problem themes. Students get the impression that those are the only kinds of problems that can be solved and that, when other kinds of situations arise, there is no knowledge or experience to use. The NCTM journals exhibit problems ranging over a wide variety of themes and ideas; these are the most comprehensive and educationally sound sources for an appropriate and educationally sound sources for an appropriate variety in theme and type. The NCTM journal *Mathematics Teaching in the Middle School*, for example, contains a centerfold section entitled "Menu of Problems" in each month's issue.

Problems Requiring Different Skills and Strategies

The appendixes contain checklists of problem solving skills and strategies. As problems are selected, the teacher may consult these or similar check lists to ensure that the problems call for the use of many or most of these skills and strategies. Skills and strategies must be sharpened by repeated use in problem solving. Giving problems which require only one strategy, such as making a table, will, in the long run, be detrimental to learning and to success in problem solving. Additionally, problems should be sought that can involve the use of several skills and strategies within the process of solving the same problem:

 ### Example

The problem: Find all numbers which when added yield the same result as when multiplied.

A typical approach and strategy for this problem involves try-and-modify and classifying skills (among others) and the strategies of making lists; creating, detecting, and extending patterns; solving simpler problems; etc.

$$
\begin{array}{cc|cc}
\underline{\text{Numbers}} & & + & \times \\
2 & 2 & 4 & 4 \\
1 & 1 & 2 & 1 \\
0 & 0 & 0 & 0 \\
\hline
-1 & -1 & -2 & 1 \\
\hline
-1 & 1 & 0 & -1 \\
-2 & 2 & 0 & -4 \\
\hline
3 & 3 & 6 & 9 \\
\hline
\frac{3}{2} & & &
\end{array}
$$

The entries between dashed lines indicate a portion of the solution using classification and deduction (if these patterns are continued no solution will be found . . .), the beginnings of creating a pattern, and modification of a trial.

The $\frac{3}{2}$ represents a significant shift in strategy: To pick a certain number ($\frac{3}{2}$) and, using operations, find out if there is some other number to add to $\frac{3}{2}$ and to multiply by $\frac{3}{2}$ and thus solve part of the problem or learn what type of other trials to make. There is also a shift here as the solver hypothesizes that the numbers may not have to be the same or whole numbers. Note: The finding of two solutions, 0 and 2, initially may condition the solver to search among twin whole numbers only.

Note

Work on this problem will be continued in a later section.

Problems in a Variety of Formats

The traditional text format, placing the dreaded *word problems* at the end of a page of computational exercises, probably did more to discourage problem solving than to help students become problem solvers. Those problems were always in the same format and often both teachers and students never made it to the bottom of the page. The teacher should experiment with the students by placing the problems before the exercises and by using the exercises as a practice field in case, in the process of problem solving, a need is found to review some mathematical facts or procedures. In real life, problems seldom come immediately following practice exercises or in formal problem statements containing all the pertinent information and nothing more. Furthermore, many problems are presented to us visually and tactilely. We see arrangements of objects, visual representations of materials, and situations that present the problems to us. Teachers need to give students problems in a variety of formats. In addition to the usual worded problem statements, we must present problems in:

- Visual diagrams with and without words
- Sets of objects to be manipulated
- Combinations of the above

- Realistic situations, including social situations (as much as possible)
- Subject areas other than mathematics

Example: (visual diagram presentation)

FIGURE 8-1 Visual Representation of a Balance Problem

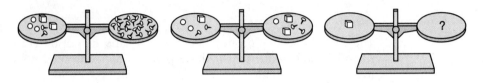

Not only does format variety reinforce the idea that problem solving is a realistic and meaningful activity, but it can encourage students to make connections between mathematics learning, other subject areas, and daily life in general. Teachers have often had the experience of doing problem solving with students in these nonmathematical contexts, only to have the children say, "When are we going to do our math?"

Problems with Multiple Solutions

Unlike operations tasks in which there is one correct result and mathematical questions where there is often one correct answer, problems frequently have a wide variety of solution formats. Sometimes these are called *multiple solutions*, which is actually a misnomer. Usually the solution simply has many parts or, in the case of a problem such as the *added = multiplied* problem mentioned previously, the question has many correct answers when it is presented in question form. In reality a problem has one solution. When there are multiple parts, it is likely that a *complete* solution is in the form of a generalization. In connection with this, the task of the teacher often becomes to help the solver move beyond the first part of the solution discovered. The solver must check to see whether there are any additional possible values or facts which meet the criteria of the problem and, finding those, complete the solution. This may involve discovering a generalization that is a general statement of solution including the individual items as special cases.

Example

Continuing the "added = multiplied" problem:

$$\frac{3}{2} + n = \frac{3}{2} \times n$$
$$\frac{3}{2} = \frac{1}{2} n$$
$$3 = n$$

Checking: $3 + \frac{3}{2} = \frac{6}{2} + \frac{3}{2} = \frac{9}{2}$

$3 \times \frac{3}{2} = \frac{9}{2}$

$$\frac{4}{3} + n = \frac{4}{3} \times n \qquad \text{Checking } 4 + \frac{4}{3} = \frac{12}{3} + \frac{4}{3} = \frac{16}{3}$$
$$\frac{4}{3} = \frac{1}{3} \times n \qquad\qquad\qquad 4 \times \frac{4}{3} = \frac{16}{3}$$
$$4 = n$$

There appears to be a pattern here:

If one number is 3, the other is $\frac{3}{2}$

4, the other is $\frac{4}{3}$

How about 5? $\qquad \frac{5}{4}$ (checks)

6? $\qquad \frac{6}{5}$ (checks)

So perhaps in general: n and $\dfrac{n}{(n-1)}$ are the two numbers.

Checking: $\dfrac{n+n}{(n-1)} = \dfrac{n(n-1)}{(n-1)} + \dfrac{n}{(n-1)} = \dfrac{n^2}{(n-1)}$

$\dfrac{n \times n}{(n-1)} = \dfrac{n^2}{(n-1)}$

Further checking is needed to see whether the 0 and 2 twins, found by inspection or by try-and-modify, fit into the pattern:

$$\frac{0+0}{-1} = 0 \quad \text{and} \quad \frac{0 \times 0}{-1} = 0$$

$$\frac{2+2}{1} = 4 \quad \text{and} \quad \frac{2 \times 2}{1} = 4$$

Additionally, what about negative numbers and 1? Verifying will confirm that 1 is the only integer which cannot be a part of the solution and that an interesting pattern develops in the consideration of negative integers.

In this example the solution is really the generalized form: An integer and the fraction formed by that integer in the numerator and the integer less one in the denominator, or: $\left[n, \dfrac{n}{(n-1)} \right]$.

The reader will note that, in the process of completing the solution of the problem above, there were many opportunities to do different kinds of mathematics. Working with number patterns was interesting and was excellent practice in creating and detecting patterns. Adding and multiplying fractions was practiced. Some elementary algebraic procedures were employed in solving equations. In fact, for more advanced seventh or eighth graders, the type of problems which involve one equation with two unknowns could be investigated and used to understand the nature of a solution. In teaching problem solving, working on problems of this type provides perhaps the best sense of what problem solving is all about. Although it lacks a practical application, the problem's solution involves many strategies and skills, as well as both inductive and deductive reasoning.

An interesting feature of this problem is that it can be solved at many different levels. First graders can find the 2,2 combination, by third grade the 0,0 partial solution can be discussed, and middle schoolers can work with the fractions in the solution. The involved algebra is beyond middle schoolers but can be tackled by algebra students; linear algebra students can examine the ideas in looking at underdetermined systems (sets of equations with more unknowns than equations).

Good Solutions

Good solutions are *complete* and meet all the requirements of the problem statement. Whether a solution is *good* is sometimes open to debate. Problem statements must be interpreted. When a debate over the meaning and requirements of the problem or over the nature of the solutions arises in the classroom, it should be regarded as healthy. When children are interested enough to debate the meaning of words, the strategies to follow, and when and how to apply their skills and knowledge, the teacher has a good opportunity to help build problem solving skills. A skillful teacher will find non-contrived ways to promote discussion and debate about problem solving. A class arranged in cooperative groups can be conducive to this. They might be called *problem solving teams* and modeled after industry's project or troubleshooting work groups. Parents of some students might be in those environments at work and that fact should be capitalized upon. It is best not to allow the children to become accustomed to characterizing solutions as *good* or *bad* in the same way that answers to questions are labeled. The students need to focus on examining the potential solution by checking to see whether it *is* a solution because it meets all the criteria of the problem statement or situation. Teachers must demonstrate this approach and guide children in actual problem solving.

The term *good solution* is also a misnomer. If it is really *a* solution, it is a *good* solution. Often the term *good solution* is applied in making a comment on the method or strategy used in reaching the solution. There are, however, good and poor strategies. In general, strategies which require too many confusing steps are poor and those which are crisp and clear are good. Some mathematicians call the best strategies "elegant."

Subtle Reasons for Difficulties with Problem Solving

Students experience a number of difficulties in dealing with problem solving. Most of these come about from wrong impressions obtained in the process of learning in other aspects of mathematics. A corrective teaching method is suggested for each difficulty. Each of these methods should be enlarged upon by the teacher so that, through class problem solving experiences, these and any other wrong impressions and ideas can be corrected.

Parsimony

Parsimony is an unwillingness to bring anything additional into the problem solving process other than what is given and reluctance to write anything more than a one-numeral symbol *answer*.

> Teacher: Whenever solving a problem, the teacher will call attention to "what we know" and "what we learned before" that can be used here, and will demonstrate the various forms of solutions: (Written explanations, multiple solutions, diagrams, charts, etc.)

 ## Example

Problem: Tommy can buy 20 pogs for $2.10 including sales tax. How many could he buy if he didn't have to pay sales tax?

Some solvers have difficulty starting toward solution because information about sales tax computation or amount is not included in the problem statement. It is difficult for them to estimate to obtain information to use or to input information from their own experiences. There may also be the need to use conditional statements in forming and stating the solution. Such statements might be: If the tax is 5 cents per 1 dollar, then the solution is: . . . ; whereas, if the tax is more than 5 cents per dollar, then Tommy could not buy more . . . , etc.

Imprecision

Imprecision is an unwillingness to be precise and discriminating, or view words or symbols critically. It reflects a view that numbers are inherently precise so that precision will automatically occur no matter how numbers are used, and that estimation is not a part of problem solving.

> Teacher: The teacher will use terminology carefully and require that the students do the same, and demonstrate and discuss appropriate levels of precision. The teacher will present, and solve with the class, problems that involve estimation and which have solutions which are estimates.

 ## Example

Considering Tommy's pog problem from above can be useful here too. For tax rates other than 5 cents per dollar, say 6 cents per dollar, calculations would yield 20 pogs at $1.98 (not a difficulty); i.e., each pog at approximately 10¢. So the conclusion would be 21 pogs, and the cost would be $2.08. However, if the problem is interpreted as requiring $2.10 expended, 21 would not be a solution. The solver has not recognized the need for precision and the relationship between using a discrete number for pogs and a continuous number for cost.

Unitary Solution

Unitary solution designates the view that there is one answer or response for every mathematical task, hence one number will be the nature of the solution to each problem. Some have the impression that each problem is solved by a specific single number or word when, in fact, many solutions are general statements and may actually yield a rule or general algorithm for solving all problems of the same type. (See the tournaments problem below.)

> Teacher: The teacher will present and solve problems for which there are "multiple solutions" and solutions which are in a variety of forms.

 ## Examples

Problem: Two numbers multiplied and added to obtain the same result.

Problem: Edith's age at death was $\frac{1}{31}$ of the number of the year of her birth. How old was Edith in 1940? (A strategy involving hypothesizing is very useful here.)

Unitary Method

The unitary method designates the view that there is only one correct procedure for finding the solution.

> Teacher: The teacher will present and solve problems which admit a variety of methods and strategies for solving.

 ## Example

Problem: How many games are played in a 32-team single-elimination tournament?

Strategies:

1. Create 32 brackets and count.

2. Repeatedly divide by 2 and add.

3. Solve simpler problem and generate patterns.

4. Reason deductively that 31 lose, leaving 1 champion.

One Trial

One trial designates the assumption that one attempt and/or one application of a tool will be sufficient to reach solution. Furthermore, each tool to be applied will be present or indicated in the problem statement.

> Teacher: The teacher will demonstrate the *try-and-modify* (guess and check) strategy and the trials of a variety of approaches and tools.

Example

Problem: Find two numbers which when added yield the same result as when multiplied.

Try matching pairs;   0,0   2,2
Try negative integers
Try 3 + ?

Try n and $\dfrac{n}{(n-1)}$

Transfer

Transfer designates the assumption that memorization of symbolic processes from arithmetic will directly transfer into the problem solving process and yield solution by direct application.

> Teacher: The teacher will demonstrate how the skills and knowledge are applied in a variety of ways in obtaining solutions.

 Examples

Tournament problem
"Added = Multiplied" problem

(No algorithms can be applied for either)

Time

Time designates the assumption that problems require only the quick application of one or two steps and thus must be solvable in a very brief time.

> Teacher: The teacher should pose problems which the class and individuals may work on over several days, doing portions in regular stages. Typically the teacher will give more time for problem solving than for working exercises, and will demonstrate how time can be used effectively and that usually more time is needed for solving problems than for computation.

Keys

Key designates the belief that every problem situation will contain obvious key clues which indicate how to solve the problem.

> Teacher: The teacher will demonstrate and solve problems which have no *keys* in them, showing how one proceeds using translating and try-and-modify techniques and strategies like working backwards to find out how to go about solving.

Example

The tournament problem contains no key words and only one numeral.

Teaching problem solving is often approached by teaching problem solving methods, strategies, and techniques. However, because there is not inherent order or hierarchy in learning to solve problems, such teaching approaches are often ineffective. In an effort to bring some structure to the process, the author has separated discussion on teaching problem solving into two parts: teaching problem solving skills and teaching problem solving strategies. When teachers help students make the distinction between skills and strategies, students have better success with problem solving and also a more complete understanding of what happens in problem solving processes. In addition, this understanding improves their attitudes and confidence in problem solving.

Solving the Problem

Teaching Problem Solving Skills

Following are eight basic problem solving skills with brief definitions: The ability to:

- Classify: Recognize pertinent characteristics and attributes of mathematical problems or expressions and specify the class or classes to which they belong.

- Deduce: Relate a set of statements so that acceptance of the statements and their interrelationships dictates a particular conclusion.

- Estimate: Use available mathematical information to make a judgment of measurement or of a result of a calculation.

- Generate patterns: Place known information or data into systematic arrangements.

- Hypothesize: Recognize or generate conditional relationships between mathematical statements.

- Translate: Substitute for one mathematical representation an equivalent form containing the pertinent information.

- Try-and-Modify: Apply mathematical knowledge or information initially in a random fashion with the intention of changing a subsequent attempt if necessary, according to the knowledge gained in earlier attempts.

- Verify: Apply information to a hypothesis, potential solution, or partial solution to test validity or accuracy.

These are necessary and sufficient skills for mathematical problem solving; that is, all problem solving requires the use of these skills in some application, and no other skills are needed for any problem solving. If this is the case, to enable students to become problem solvers, teachers need to help them acquire these skills or to use the skills they have. The author further believes that most students already possess these skills but that they experience the following difficulties in using them:

- Students have not been made aware that they have the skills.

- Some of the skills have been used so little that they are weak.

- Some students have been taught that the use of some of the skills is inappropriate in mathematics. (Two that are most often regarded in this way are *try-and-modify* and *estimation*.)

- Students are hesitant to apply and reapply more than one of the skills to a given problem or to repeatedly use one of the skills.

The first concern of the teacher in teaching problem solving is to ensure that the students possess the necessary skills. It is critical that the teacher assure the children that they do have these skills. The teacher can be very open with the students in saying that the students have the skills but that they are weak and that one of the class goals is to strengthen those skills that are weak. It is a good idea to list these skills in a prominent place in the mathematics teaching area and to refer to them frequently. This list can be used as a checklist for students as they work on problem solving. The statements, list, and other references should be used in a manner which makes the students aware that they are expected to solve problems; the expectation is that they *can* solve problems using their skills. Teachers should pose problems and guide the solving so that the natural use of skills can be pointed out and praised. Consider the skills that children would naturally apply in solving the following problem.

Example

Problem: Find the number of 1-inch cube blocks (or 1-cm cubes) necessary to fill a shoe box (or smaller box).

Teacher: Guide layering and counting numbers of layers or making units of layers and multiplying.

As the children work on various types of problems, the teacher needs to identify the skills which are being neglected or are weakly applied. These observations will guide the teacher in selecting the next sets of problems. (See Appendix A for problems which are keyed to particular skills). Here the key is to provide multiple problem solving opportunities that give practice in the application of the various abilities. Particular attention should be given to those skills which are weakest.

Typically the weaker skills are:

1. Classifying, especially as it is developed into organization of information

2. Estimating, both in computation and measurement

3. Generating patterns

4. Try-and-modify, especially when children have been taught that *guessing* is not appropriate in mathematics

5. Verifying: Students often feel that, having gone through a process, they have finished—there is no need to check whether what they have found or written is really a solution.

Teaching Classifying

Classifying in problem solving begins in kindergarten with all types of groupings with manipulatives. Starting with categorization by color (of most interest initially to young children), children should be given increasingly complex classification tasks. More complex classification tasks involve classification by two or more criteria or more detailed descriptors.

 Example

- Tennis shoes might be classified according to brand, color and style. (Nike, white, low top; Nike, white, high top; Reebok, white, low top; etc.)

- Children's heights: 42–44 in., 45–47 in., 48–50 in.,

Multiple criteria classifications have useful applications in science and social studies where they are needed to describe reality.

- Leaves are described by: the shade of green, serrations, veining, shape, and size.

- Countries are described by: economy, location, climate, size and topography.

Training in making detailed classifications prepares students for describing sets by graphing and other statistical analysis. Not only should students be asked to perform the groupings, but they should be asked to examine already prepared sets and to state what the classifications are. These settings provide excellent opportunities to incorporate language skills into mathematics lessons. Initial requirements will be to verbalize descriptions, giving justifications for their decisions about which items should fall in which categories. As writing skills develop, students should be asked to write their descriptions and justifications. Students should practice multiple ways to diagram categories. The one technique all children should develop is to place classification information in Venn diagrams.

 ## Illustration

In the parking lot there are Chevys, Fords, and Jeeps. Four of the Chevys are all red, two Chevys are red and black, two Jeeps are all black, one Jeep is black and white, one Ford is black and white, and five Fords are all white.

Many children's reading books have classification themes which provide excellent opportunities for the teacher to work on these skills with the children in the context of reading. (Some of these books are listed in the suggested readings at the end of the chapters.)

In both social studies and science there are many opportunities for students to classify when they describe people, places, objects, materials, plants, and animals. In those settings teachers may call attention to classification tasks and work with the children on the skill while the lesson is actually set in a subject area other than mathematics. This interrelationship should be pointed out to students whenever the opportunity occurs. This will assist the students in making the connections among mathematics, problem solving, and the world around them.

Teaching Deducing

Young children are often already skilled at stringing together two or three cause-and-effect, if-then statements. "If he hits me, then I will hit him back." "If there is too much snow and ice tomorrow, then we will not have school, then we can't have the Christmas program, then . . ." Teachers can capitalize on this ability and help students to refine their chains of thought and show how the first fact can be linked to the conclusion: "If there is too much snow, we won't have the Christmas party." Students could be encouraged to examine the truth of the preliminary statements and the continuity of the argument and should discuss the conclusiveness of the whole. This can be practiced frequently in class discussion in any subject area as well as in class activities.

The important facets of deductive thinking are the:

- Truth of the preliminary statements.

- Linkage and lack of gaps in the chain of statements.

- Specific nature of the preliminary statements.

- General nature of the final statement.

- Conclusiveness of the final statement.

- Equivalence of differently worded deductive arguments.

Examples

If-then form: If the storm continues, there will be over 6 inches of snow.
If there is over 6 inches of snow, school will be canceled.
If school is canceled, we can't practice for the play.
If we can't practice for the play, the play will be postponed.
Therefore, if the storm continues the play will be postponed.

Narrative form: Over 6 inches of snow will accumulate because the storm continues and, when there is over 6 inches of snow, school is canceled. Play practice is not held while school is out. Plays are postponed when practice cannot be held, so this means that the play will be postponed if this storm continues.

Teachers may wish to reference arguments from literature and other sources for the children to consider.

Example

For want of a nail the shoe was lost.
For want of a shoe the horse was lost.
For want of a horse the rider was lost.

The teacher could have children construct similar *if-then* proverbs from their experiences.

Students should be encouraged to analyze the validity of each other's arguments and those they hear on the playground and at home. Discussion about why the team lost the ballgame might be a good source for arguments to analyze. Students should also be encouraged to create deductive arguments which can be discussed and analyzed by the class. Those activities help students develop and strengthen deductive skills which are very helpful in problem solving in a variety of subject areas, but especially in mathematics.

Within a particular problem solving strategy, deductive reasoning should be applied to determine which information in the problem statement is pertinent and useful and which is extraneous and unnecessary. Deductive reasoning can be corrected and strengthened by encouraging children to justify their work, their positions, and their decisions in a wide variety of classroom contexts. As often as is practical, children should write out their chained-together statements in chart or list form so that the lineages and flow are clearly seen. It is also wise to point out the use of deduction as students work in cooperative groups in planning projects and class activities. Ample opportunity should be given for students to critique deductive arguments which classmates develop and those found in advertising.

Activity

Students will collect, bring to class, and analyze advertisement arguments taking special note of *jumping to conclusions*. (Examples: A well-known ball player appears in a commercial for a brand of clothing. A well-known actress is shown drinking cola of a certain brand.)

Teaching Estimating

Some children must first be convinced that estimating is legitimate. Those who were introduced to and practiced estimating as a part of learning to count in the first grade will not have any difficulty at this point. Older children who have come through traditional programs, which focused only on exact computational algorithms, may struggle with any process which admits variation in student responses. Teachers should involve their students in many problems and activities of counting and computing in which estimates are all that are required for solution.

Example

The problem is: How many pizzas should we buy for the party if each pizza is cut into 8 pieces and we have 21 people at the party?

Since the real life situation is that we cannot buy $\frac{5}{8}$ of a pizza, the solution which makes sense is an estimate: 3 pizzas.

The skill of estimating used in computing should also be demonstrated, especially in operating with decimal numbers and fractions.

Example

Problem: Will a 20-dollar bill be sufficient to buy four meals if each meal is $4.79 and tax is at 5%?

Estimation: $4.79 is close to $5.00, and 5% of $5 is 25¢. The tax on $4.79, then, is 23¢ or 24¢ which would put the cost over $5; $20 would not be enough for 4 meals.

(Note: the solution to the problem did not require exact computation. Estimation was sufficient.)

Caution

Some students may go too far with the idea of estimating, beginning to think that there is no place at all for precision. Instruction should help students to understand how one knows when precision, and at what level, is called for.

Example

Problem: Jon made 9 of 14 shots.
Jay made 7 of 11 shots.
Joy made 11 of 17 shots.
Which of them had the best and worst shooting record?

Solution: $\frac{9}{14} = .642$ $\quad$ $\frac{7}{11} = .636$ $\quad$ $\frac{11}{17} = .647$

One-decimal precision is not sufficient.

Two-decimal precision is not sufficient.

The three-decimal numbers are estimates too, but are sufficient to solve the problem.

 Example

Problem: We have 85 kids in the third grade going on a field trip using buses, each of which carries 24 kids. How many buses will be needed?

On the other hand students need to learn that every measurement is an estimate. As units of measure are selected, it must be made clear that a change in the size of the unit will change the level of precision. Again, practice should be given in the choice of units, estimating with them, and in deciding what level of precision is needed.

 Example

Measure the sheet of paper using feet.

Measure the sheet of paper using inches.

Teacher: Which units are better to use in this instance and why?

Measure the distance from the school to the city library in miles and kilometers.

Teacher: Which gives a more precise value?

Why does one give more precision?

Is there a rule of thumb about the kinds of units which give more or less precision? What is it?

Teaching Generating Patterns

Detecting and analyzing patterns is not considered a part of *generating patterns*. It is a more complex skill which is a combination of classification, deduction, hypothesizing, and verifying. Generating patterns includes placing objects and symbols in various orders and arrangements according to specified criteria. Work on this skill also begins very early with manipulatives, as children consider colors and shapes. After these simple beginnings, pattern generation should be made more complex as multiple criteria are considered simultaneously. Teachers should give simple pattern-generating tasks to children beginning in kindergarten, and in subsequent grades make the tasks more and more complex. A number of games children enjoy involve generating patterns. Perhaps the most well known is *Set*. This game can be very effective with third graders and older children. Practice in continuing the pattern someone else has started, changing patterns, and creating patterns within patterns is very helpful. Patterns in geometrical shapes are the most interesting to young children, but they should be encouraged early to develop patterns with other symbols, words, and numbers. Continuing patterns with numbers is obviously an integral part of the skill of counting.

Examples

- Use attribute blocks with angled mirrors.

- Create palindromic numbers.

- Use repeated multiplication by nines.

- Consider odds and evens (for example, consider the page numbers on the left- and righthand pages of open books)

The generating patterns skill is needed by children quite early in their mathematics work. Learning to write counting numerals and to extend the list to the hundreds and the thousands requires generating and continuing patterns. Many problems are solved using this skill. Learning to generate patterns will contribute significantly to a child's problem solving success.

Teaching Hypothesizing

It is important to help children become comfortable asking the question, "What if . . . ?" This question is the beginning of an investigation and experimentation which are essential in much of problem solving. Teachers should ask the question often in efforts to stimulate the students' thinking about problems and to get them started toward the solutions. This is particularly true when children are unsure what route to take or when a particular strategy does not seem to move the solver toward solution.

Example

Problem: Edith's age at death was $\frac{1}{31}$ of the number of the year of her birth. How old was she in 1940?

Teacher asks, "What if you examined multiples of 31?"
"What if you divided 1940 by 31?"

Sufficient practice and a readiness to question in the "what if" manner will lead children to ask this question of their peers in cooperative problem solving activities. The question becomes part of encouraging each other to work toward solution. Finally, it should become natural for children to ask the question of themselves repeatedly. This questioning, whether in a group or to oneself, is often an effective starting point for using try-and-modify techniques (Goos, 1994).

Teaching Translating

Translation is typically the first skill applied in the problem solving process. In fact, many teachers find it very helpful to suggest to students that the first thing they should do is to phrase the problem statements or situation in their own words, either orally (talking through the problem) or in writing. These are essentially translations. Teachers of problem solving should encourage not only rewording but also making diagrams and sketches (translating to graphics) and translating to other kinds of symbols. This restating can involve:

- Identifying variables

- Representing variables with letter symbols

- Making lists of information contained in the problem statement and/or related to the problem

- Arranging concrete objects in some helpful order

Once the translation process is begun, other skills such as deducing, hypothesizing, and try-and-modify quickly are indicated and become usable. Examples of problems that are solved simply through translation in one or two steps should be given to illustrate the power and value of the skill of translation.

 Example

Tournament problem: How many games will be played with 20 players?

(Translating this situation to a bracket diagram immediately shows the solution.)

Teaching Trying and Modifying

Teaching the try-and-modify skill involves mostly demonstration followed by encouragement and practice. Special attention will have to be given to those students who are reluctant to experiment. Teachers should discourage the use of the term *trial and error* because of the connotation of the word *error*. There are many children who want to do *good* work—not to make errors. They are among those who erase a lot. They cannot leave scratch work on their papers but must write and erase, write and erase, until it is *just right*. These students should be helped to understand that these preliminary trials are just that, and not errors. They are not mistakes, but ways of understanding the problem and of learning what steps might help in solving.

Teachers may help children at this point by showing the value of keeping the record of trials and trial results. When a sticking point is encountered, the solver may return to a previous trial and take a different route or perhaps note a valuable piece of information that was previously overlooked.

The second concern is to help the children attempting to solve problems realize that, though the initial trial may be random, subsequent trials are to be modifications, because information is gained and can be used or discarded as appropriate. The subsequent trials are not usually random. It is important that classification be used to organize and arrange information about the trials and results so that the solver is not overwhelmed by a mass of random information. This would lead to confusion rather than to solution. Deduction can also be involved when a student uses a deductive chain such as: "If I list these by number from the smallest to the largest, then I can be sure that I have listed all the possibilities, then the solution must be in this portion of the list, then I can simply check each one . . ."

 ## Example

Problem: What two numbers yield the same result when added as when multiplied?

Working this problem using the try-and-modify skill might include a random choice of numbers at first:

Try	1 and 1	$1 + 1 = 2$	$1 \times 1 = 1$
Modify:	1 and 2	$1 + 2 = 3$	$1 \times 2 = 2$
Modify:	2 and 2	$2 + 2 = 4$	$2 \times 2 = 4$ (solution?)
Modify:	3 and 3	$3 + 3 = 6$	$3 \times 3 = 9$

Generate a pattern showing that larger twin integers will give results farther and farther apart.

Modify:	0 and 0	$0 + 0 = 0$	$0 \times 0 = 0$ (solution?)
Modify:	1 and -1	$1 + -1 = 0$	$1 \times -1 = -1$
Modify:	$\frac{1}{2}$ and $\frac{1}{2}$	$\frac{1}{2} + \frac{1}{2} = 1$	$\frac{1}{2} \times \frac{1}{2} = \frac{1}{4}$
	and so forth.		

Children must be given opportunity, time, and encouragement to conduct their try-and-modify experimentation. This process must not be rushed or made algorithmical, because there are no standardized try-and-modify procedures. Teachers should capitalize on successes children have using try-and-modify processes. They may have children demonstrate or describe try-and-modify work which yielded solution.

Teaching Verifying

Students are usually familiar with checking their computational work when they use a particular algorithm. This involves using a checking algorithm (adding to check subtraction results, for example) or redoing the steps of the algorithms carefully. Teachers can build on these abilities and experience and help students to see the necessity of checking their work in the steps used to solve a problem. But the concept of verifying is more complex than simply checking computational results. Verifying in problem solving includes assessing the compatibility between a solution and the requirements of the problem. Is the solution really *the* solution to the problem presented? Teachers will need to help students to reread or reexamine problems, check the meaning of various aspects of problem statements, and compare aspects of the solutions with the pertinent portions of the problem statements to determine whether a solution has been obtained. Though computation may be involved in problem solving, finding solutions is more than computation. This means that more than accuracy in calculation must be checked in verification.

If the solver is convinced that the strategy employed must lead to solution and the solution has not been reached, then the steps must be carefully examined. This might involve checking computational steps or verifying that various skills had been properly applied. Teachers should "talk through" the problem solving process with students, especially when there is difficulty in verifying a solution. This may help students examine each step for validity. Students should also practice *talking through* in cooperative settings. It will be helpful for the teacher to present groups with solution statements which aren't actually solutions, because they don't meet all the requirements of the problems. Students can then discuss, debate, and decide how to correct the "solution" and attempt to ensure that it is, in fact, a solution. For the second facet, examining the strategies and steps toward solution, a description of a faulty strategy may be presented to the students for them to analyze.

 ## Examples

A teacher might present a problem like this to second graders:

Tim brought three quarters to school for lunch, which cost 60¢. On the way, Tim lost a quarter but found a dime in his desk. Did Tim have enough money for lunch?

The teacher could suggest a statement of solution: "No, because Tim lost a quarter." The children can then debate the validity and reasoning yielding that "solution."

The teacher might describe a set of steps used to solve the problem stated above and include a faulty step (Add 10¢ to 75¢ = 85¢. Yes, Tim has enough money). Allow the children to discuss the steps and this suggested solution.

A strategy can often be thought of as a scheme for applying skills in a certain sequence. When the strategy used for the problem under consideration is identified, then verification would involve checking the order in which the skills comprising the strategy were applied. (For example: Should a further translation have been done before the attempt to draw a conclusion about the nature of these numbers?)

 ## Example

See Edith's age problem again from the perspective of the necessity of checking the various computation results against the requirements of the problem statement.

A solution of: age = 59 would have Edith born in 1829, and she would not have been alive in 1940.

Teaching Problem Solving Strategies

Strategies are plans or schemes that can be used to reach solutions. They may be thought of as road maps to follow. Just as there exist multiple routes on road maps, there are often multiple strategies that can be followed to reach the same solution for a given problem. Some of them are direct, and others may be round-about. Skilled problem solvers develop a strategy creation skill. They seem to know what strategy may lead quickly to solution. This comes with practice rather than by some kind of memorization scheme. Even skilled problem solvers, though, use the try-and-modify skills in order to discover appropriate strategies. Polya is widely regarded as the father of modern problem solving study and teaching. His often-stated strategy was given in four parts or steps (Polya, 1945):

1. Understand the problem

2. Make a plan

3. Carry out the plan

4. Check the solution

This and many other general strategies have been suggested in the literature, and individual teachers often develop their own formats and suggestions for children to help them get started and have success in problem solving. Teachers are encouraged to develop strategies in discussion with the children. The class can make posters listing well-known and useful strategies and hang the posters in the classroom for ready reference and reminders. Some of the strategies commonly listed are very useful:

- Make lists, charts, tables, graphs, etc.

- Work backwards.

- Sketch or diagram the problem information.

- Rewrite the problem in your own words.

- Act out the problem situation.

- Discuss the problem and strategies in a group.

- Model the problem with objects.

- Read over and examine the problem at least three times.

- Solve a simpler problem.

- Solve a related problem.

As was the case with teaching problem solving skills, practice, practice, and more practice are the key. The teacher should give problems for which different strategies will be used. It is best not to suggest strategies at the beginning. When students develop their own strategies, they use those more readily in problem solving. The students should be encouraged to note and explore many different strategies for the same problem. In the process of solving class problems, the teacher should point out and emphasize the different strategies used, and the class should discuss the relative merits of various strategies and how to use them effectively. They may wish to establish some principles, such as:

- Try first working from the beginning, then from the end.

- Start with an organized list of all the information known.

- Start by listing all possible solutions.

- Recall a strategy used on another problem similar to the one under consideration.

- Start by listing *clues* in the problem statement.

- Start by classifying aspects of the problem.

It may help, on occasion, to assign different strategies to different groups, all of which are working on the same problem. The discussion following the group work will help students recognize the viability of different strategies for that particular problem. Students should also be helped to realize that, while one strategy works well with a particular problem, a problem appearing very similar may require a significantly different approach.

Some students who have had success with a particular strategy will try to use the same approach with every problem. This plan will cause serious difficulty. A teacher who notices that students are limiting themselves to only one strategy can illustrate the difficulties this approach presents and guide students to consider multiple strategies.

Example

A student who uses only diagrams and sketches for solving can be shown the following problem:

If one circle separates a plane into 2 regions (inside and outside); two circles into 4 regions; and 3 circles into 8 regions; into how many regions will 6 circles separate a plane? See Figures 8-2, 8-3, and 8-4.

It may be clear now that one way of looking at developing a strategy is to see a strategy as: sequencing the application of problem solving skills. Several of the principles listed above involve classification as a first consideration. This

FIGURE 8-2   The Plane Separated Into 2 Regions, Inside and Outside the Circle

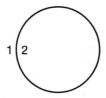

FIGURE 8-3   Two Circles Separating the Plane Into 4 Distinct Regions

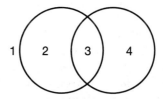

FIGURE 8-4   Three Circles Separating the Plane Into 8 Distinct Regions

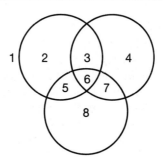

might be followed by hypothesizing, deducing, then trying and modifying. Helping children approach problem solving by realizing the value and necessity of choosing or trying various strategies will help the teacher deal with the often heard statements, "I don't know what to do," "I don't know how to start" (Nesher, 1994).

Caution

Teachers should not try to teach *algorithmic* problem solving. The students will often ask for, and even demand, "Tell us how to do this kind of problem."

A research project with second graders found that when they were not given sample solutions to problems, they were more likely to use higher order thinking, take ownership of strategies, discuss solutions longer, and be more accepting of other views (Buschman, 1994). The wise teacher will not give sample solutions or sample strategy outlines. In reality, giving sample solutions and strategy outlines does not serve as an effective method of teaching problem solving. There are no algorithms for problem solving and there are no standard strategy patterns that will help students to solve any problem of a certain type. As was stated above, if there were an algorithm for a problem, it wouldn't be a problem. The statement or situation would be simply an exercise in using the algorithm.

Those students who have become dependent on memorizing their way through mathematics may look desperately for some rules to memorize to enable them to solve the problems. Such students need to understand that problem solving does not work that way. Problems are sufficiently different from each other that the same strategies may not work on both, and there are innumerable problems to be solved. Teachers should avoid the use of texts that group problems of the same kind together and that give instructions that all these can be done in the same way. These texts give the impression that "Whenever a problem appears to be like these, it can be solved in these ways." Teachers should give suggestions for applying various skills and strategies instead of trying to give *directions* for solving. A Socratic questioning approach will be more conducive to helping students become problem solvers rather than memorized procedure followers.

🔲 Summary

This chapter began with definitions of mathematical problems and problem solutions. Problem solving skills and strategies were detailed. In connection with methods, the importance of care with terminology and in avoiding algorithmic teaching of problem solving was pointed out. Various types of problem settings and solution types with examples were presented, and specific teaching methods for each of the problem solving skills were given.

🔲 Exercises

1. Present a problem to a student at the appropriate level and in a form of interest to the child. Perform a MADS analysis of the solving process the child uses.

2. For a particular grade level, prepare a set of problems to be used with MADS to ensure that all the problem solving skills are examined, or prepare a set of problems which will involve a wide range of the most common strategies.

3. Choose and examine a middle school math text and describe how problem solving is handled by that text.

4. Develop a set of strategies with a suggested hierarchy to assist a solver at a certain level in working with a certain class of problems or puzzles (cryptarithms, rate problems, etc.).

References

Buschman, Larry (1994, March). Sometimes less is more. *Arithmetic Teacher*, 41(7), 378–380.

Cope, Peter, and Malcolm Simmonds. (1994, September). Some effects of limited feedback on performance and problem-solving strategy in a Logo micro world. *Journal of Educational Psychology*, 86(3), 368–379.

Copeland, Richard W. (1984). *How Children Learn Mathematics*. Upper Saddle River, NJ: Merrill/Prentice Hall.

Goos, Merrilyn. (1994, December). Metacognitive decision making and social interactions during paired problem solving. *Mathematics Education Research Journal*, 6(2), 144–165.

National Council of Teachers of Mathematics. (1989). *Curriculum and Evaluation Standards for School Mathematics*. Reston, VA: Author.

Nesher, Pearla, and Sara Hershkovitz. (1994, January). The role of schemes in two-step problems: Analysis and research findings. *Educational Studies in Mathematics*, 26(1), 1–23.

Polya, G. (1957). *How To Solve It*. Garden City, NY: Doubleday.

Suggested Readings

Antonietti, Alessandro, Paola Ceerana, and Laura Scafidi. (1994, February). Mental visualization before and after problem presentation: A comparison. *Perceptual and Motor Skills*, 78, 179–189.

Buschman, Larry. (1994, March). Sometimes less is more. *Arithmetic Teacher*, 41(7), 378–380.

Chandler, Donald G., and Patricia A. Brosnan (1994, Fall). Mathematics textbook changes from before to after 1989. *Focus on Learning Problems in Mathematics*, 16(4), 1–9.

Fernandez, Maria L., et al. (1994, March). Connecting research to teaching: Problem solving: Managing it all. *Mathematics Teacher*, 87(3), 195–199.

Ford, Margaret I. (1994, October). Teachers' beliefs about mathematical problem solving in the elementary school. *School Science and Mathematics*, 94(6), 314–322.

Jaspers, Monique W., and Ernest C. Van Lieshout (1994, Spring). Diagnosing wrong answers of children with learning disorders solving arithmetic word problems. Special issue: Dutch research on knowledge-based instructional systems. *Computers in Human Behavior*, 10(1), 7–19.

Niaz, Mansor (1994, May). The role of insight in problem solving. *Journal of College Science Teaching*, 23(6), 334–337.

Pajares, Frank, and M. David Miller (1994, June). Role of self-efficacy and self-concept beliefs in mathematical problem solving: A path analysis. *Journal of Educational Psychology*, 86(2), 193–203.

Pierce, Karen A., and Barry Gholson (1994, September). Surface similarity and relational similarity in the development of analogical problem solving: Isomorphic and nonisomorphic transfer. *Developmental Psychology*, 30(5), 724–737.

Polya, G. (1945, 1973). *How to Solve It: A New Mathematical Method*. Princeton, NJ: Princeton University Press.

Sigurdson, Sol E., et al. (1994, December). Problem solving and mathematical learning. *The Journal of Mathematical Behavior*, 13(4), 361–388.

Sophian, Catherine, and Patricia McCorgray. (1994). Part-whole knowledge and early arithmetic problem solving. *Cognition and Instruction*, 12(1), 3–33.

Taplin, Margaret (1994, July). Development of a model to enhance managerial strategies in problem solving. *Mathematics Education Research Journal*, 6(1), 79–93.

Verschaffel, Lieven. (1994, March). Using retelling data to study elementary school children's representations and solutions of comparable problems. *Journal for Research in Mathematics Education*, 25(2), 141–165.

Watson, Jane M. (1994, September). A diagrammatic representation for studying problem-solving behavior. *The Journal of Mathematical Behavior*, 13(3), 305–332.

Teaching Mathematical Operations

One of the children's problems: John believes that he "knows" how to divide because he can do the "long division" algorithm.

Teacher's problem: The children have very weak operation concepts. They are satisfied with memorized algorithms.

Understanding Subproblem 1

Much of the mathematics taught in the first eight grades centers around the four basic operations: addition, subtraction, multiplication, and division. From operating with single-digit numbers students move to larger counting numbers, through sets of other types of numbers, and finally, in the introduction to algebra (operating with representatives of numbers). Unfortunately, the operation concepts themselves often receive insufficient attention as algorithmic processes are developed. When studies are limited to a focus on algorithmic processes, they fail to develop understanding of the concepts that underlie the mechanics of computation. This forces students to learn what seem to be abstract and meaningless series of steps. They are then severely inhibited in making corrections and adjustments to processes when something doesn't work. As has been mentioned, students may also be left with a very false impression about what mathematics really is. They have difficulty seeing the practical and useful aspects of mathematics itself and of mathematics learning. When students need to construct their own mathematical ideas, which are dependent on the concepts of the operations, and even to understand the proper working of the algorithms for the operations, there is no basis for construction. Construction cannot take place.

Recall the importance of using correct terminology when teaching operation concepts; for example, it is important to use the word *results* to describe the outcomes of computation. *Answers* are for questions rather than for computation. The requirement that a student perform an operation may not involve a question at all. If students are conditioned to perform an operation only when a question is presented in a problem solving situation and only when the operation or name of the *results* (divided, total, etc.) is overtly stated, effective and successful problem solving is precluded.

Emphases

Recognizing the need to teach the correct understanding of operations and to focus on the operation concepts, the National Council of Teachers of Mathematics, in the *Curriculum and Evaluation Standards*, recommends deemphasizing the following:

- Complex paper-and-pencil computation

- Isolated treatment of paper-and-pencil computations

- Addition and subtraction without renaming

- Long division with and without remainders

- Paper and pencil fraction computation
- Use of rounding to estimate

and giving increased emphasis to:

- Meaning of operations
- Operation sense
- Estimation and reasonableness of results
- Selection of appropriate computational methods and tools (including calculators)
- Thinking strategies using basic facts and algorithms

Operation Concepts

These principles and understandings should guide the teaching of operation concepts:

1. *Operations are tools to help in describing reality and in problem solving.* These operations and the related algorithms are designed to be functional and to work practically. They are used to help us understand the physical world and the cultures in which we live.

2. *Operations are not magical or mystical activities, but are based in reality and reason.* The process used to compute with a given algorithm sometimes appears abstract because the nonessential characteristics of real situations have been removed. The person computing can work with the essentials (the numbers) without the confusion of words and physical variables. The ideas can then be processed efficiently and the results returned to the real world of objects and problem situations. This is all to be done in a logical fashion, with good reasons for each of the steps and processes. Students tend to transfer the "magic" they attach to algorithms to the operation itself. For example, with the long division algorithm, students tend to forget that they are separating a set of objects or a quantity into other equal sets or quantities and determining a number of other sets or quantities. The operation of division is not actually strange or abstract.

3. *Operations build on basic ideas and can be learned progressively.* The abstract operations originate with manipulations of objects and attempts to understand how things work in our world. We learn how to cope with these tasks by starting with symbol manipulation to demonstrate combining and rearranging sets and then building a structure of more complex operations using combinations of simpler processes. We can then teach and students can learn them in the same constructivist fashion.

4. *Operations are not the same things as algorithms.* Operations are abstract mental constructs in the same sense that numbers are abstract. The only way we can work with this abstract characteristic of sets is to form some nonabstraction of the idea, such as a numeral (or other representation), and manipulate that. Algorithms are abstract representations of operations. They enable moving beyond the limited ability to do the operations using only the manipulative based procedures. Computation can be performed because students know the basic facts and other quick tricks, such as adding zero to multiply by 10, and they can link the facts and tricks together to reach the desired operational result.

5. *Operations can be done only with like items and, when done with numbers which refer to certain entities, must have meaning.* Numbers of apples and oranges can be added or subtracted only if both are placed in sets of like objects, such as sets of pieces of fruit. Students should be guided not to label items such as apples and oranges as things. Apples and oranges should be inclusively labeled as fruit. Chevys and Fords should be labeled as cars or trucks, etc. As illustrated below, the numbers of sets of objects can be multiplied or divided only as the operations are understood to be repeated addition or repeated subtraction, respectively. (The exception to this principle occurs with *objects* which are certain units of measurement. It does make sense, for example, to multiply 5 feet by 6 feet and obtain 30 square feet. The resulting unit (square feet, in this case) must have meaning.) Since symbol manipulation is abstract, it is easy to perform manipulation which is meaningless and even counter to understanding the underlying concepts.

This meaninglessness can be illustrated by giving fifth grade students the task of *multiplying* $1.50 × $2.30. Many students will ignore the "$," multiply the numbers 1.5 and 2.3, and write the result as $3.45. A little thought about multiplying dollars by dollars would show us that the results would be "dollars squared" or "square dollars" (being consistent with: A rectangular room 4 yards wide and 6 yards long requires 24 square yards of carpet.) Students will quickly see the meaninglessness of "square dollars." It is not a useful unit of measure. Thus "$²3.45" or "3.45 square dollars" is nonsense, even though 3.45 is the correct result of multiplying 1.5 and 2.3 and 1.5 times $2.3 = $3.45 (2.3 × $1.5 = $3.45). Some may even go so far as to write "$ squared." Part of understanding the concept of multiplication is understanding the meaning of the operation in some real or mathematical context.

🔲 Solving Subproblem 1

Teachers should help students to understand that mathematicians and math teachers are working to find easier and better ways to work with operations. This means that students should not feel that operations are rigid and unvarying in the ways they are understood and applied.

Developing Operation Concepts

To ensure that operation concepts are fully developed, the characteristics and properties of each operation must be presented to students in the context of the basic ideas. Children, even before they come to school, are active manipulators of concrete objects; they count objects in collections, combine two or more groups, recount, take away, and sort according to certain criteria. It is an easy transition to more formally adding and subtracting using the same kinds of manipulatives. Students also gradually add more formal terminology, for example *adding* rather than *putting together*, and *subtracting* rather than *taking away*.

Caution

Teachers should not try to move students too rapidly to abstract terminology such as *subtract. Take away* expresses the nature of the operation more directly and clearly and can be used until the children themselves reject it in favor of the more formal term. Peer influence will take care of this transition—if the teacher uses operation names correctly and repeatedly, students will quickly emulate that behavior. (In other words, it is not necessary to teach the term *subtraction* directly and specifically.) The teacher should help students return to those early expressive terms and descriptors, such as *take away*, when students are struggling with operations in new or different contexts. This return to expressive terminology is also a part of a helpful problem solving strategy.

Operations Characteristics

In keeping with the basic principle in teaching concepts, the teacher must present examples that vary over noncritical attributes and nonexamples that vary over the critical attributes or characteristics of the concept. Students need to understand the following concepts:

Operations Are Binary

As operations are taught and computation techniques developed, teachers should point out and discuss the binary nature of the operations. In the case of some addition formats such as:

$$\begin{array}{r} 34 \\ 59 \\ +76 \\ \hline \end{array} \quad \text{and} \quad 3 + 5 + 9$$

and when children combine three or more sets of objects in one motion and count to obtain the total, they may have the impression that they are adding three or more numbers at once. The same idea could be conveyed when division (top and bottom) is used to simplify the process of multiplying $\frac{1}{3} \times \frac{2}{9} \times \frac{7}{4}$. Teachers should help children to realize that, in an algorithmic process, they are actually stringing together several binary operations. The standard algorithms depend on the knowledge of basic facts, which are binary operations with single-digit numbers. These algorithms are essentially processes that link together a series of binary single-digit operations in a way that produces the desired final computation result.

Algorithms should be understood as simply helpful tools and cunning ways to obtain correct operation results consistently. They must not be thought of as the operations themselves.

Commutativity

Addition and multiplication are commutative while subtraction and division are not.

As students learn the basic facts, it is helpful for them to see that commutativity can be used as a means to shorten the learning process. As they become familiar with various algorithms, begin to experiment with them, and modify them, their use of commutativity should be encouraged. They may want to rearrange numbers, using associativity and commutativity to make work with basic facts and algorithms easier.

 Examples

$$43 + 25 + 31 + 75 =$$
$$43 + 31 + 25 + 75 = \quad \text{(25 + 31, commuted)}$$
$$43 + 31 + 100 =$$
$$74 + 100 = 174$$

If one-fourth of the 50 products with a mean price of \$2.00 is priced at 70 percent, the cost of all the discounted products is:

$$\frac{1}{4} \times 50 \times \$2.00 \times 7/10 =$$
$$\frac{1}{4} \times \$2.00 \times 50 \times 7/10 = \quad \text{(commute \$2.00 and 50.)}$$
$$\frac{1}{2} \times \frac{1}{2} \times \$2.00 \times 5 \times 7 = \quad \text{(un-multiplying of } \frac{1}{4} \text{ to } \frac{1}{2} \times \frac{1}{2}.\text{)}$$
$$\frac{1}{2} \times \$1.00 \times 35 = \frac{1}{2} \times \$35.00 = \$17.50$$

Noncommutativity

In the early grades through middle school, daily activities that are not commutative can be mentioned to help develop the commutativity concept. Starting with the obvious difficulty of taking away 5 marbles from a set of 3 marbles, children quickly get the idea that $5 - 3$ and $3 - 5$ don't work the same way.

 Activity (for K–third Graders)

Teacher asks: When you are getting dressed, does it matter whether you put your shoes on first or your socks on first?

Then the teacher has the children identify other daily operations in which order is critical. They can describe the humorous effects of trying various operations in the wrong order.

Don't emphasize the kind of thinking that leads children to believe, "You can't subtract 5 from 3" or "You can't divide 6 by 9." Students can get that idea early, believe that it is a general rule, and experience difficulty when negative numbers and fractions (as division) are introduced. When they encounter this change in mathematics instruction, they may feel that someone has changed the rules in the middle of the game or that the rules are arbitrary—developed and stated at the whim of the teacher. ("First they tell us you can't do these operations, then they say you can.") It is appropriate to explain, when the issue arises, that, "We don't know how to do this now, but you will learn in the *n*th grade how to do it."

The comparison between commutative and noncommutative operations is between operations that give different results when the order is reversed, not between operations that *can* be done and those that *cannot* be done. It is important to make this distinction in developing the concept of commutativity.

Activity/example

Mr. James gives his class of fourth graders the task of writing all the different expressions for 24. He doesn't specify an operation. Some students write: 1 + 1 + 1 + 1 . . . , 2 + 2 + 2 + . . . , etc. Rick and his partner write: $4 \times 6, 3 \times 8, 2 \times 12$, etc. Rick suddenly notices, "Hey you can turn them around!" They complete their list by adding $6 \times 4, 8 \times 3$, and 12×2, etc.

Associativity

Addition and multiplication are associative while subtraction and division are not.

As children learn the *rules* of manipulating numbers, it soon becomes obvious that numbers can sometimes be rearranged to make computation easier and errors less likely. Associativity can be used, too, in working with basic facts and mental computation where children create their own algorithms. They can also modify the standard algorithms to better suit themselves.

Example/Illustration

In column addition using the standard algorithm, many students naturally adopt a compatible number modification that groups numbers which add to 10. It is not always clear whether they consciously use commutativity and associativity. It is more likely that they simply "know" that they can pick and choose how they wish to add.

$$34$$
$$47$$
$$56$$
$$+23$$
$$160$$

$$4 + 6 = 10$$
$$7 + 3 = 10$$
$$10 + 10 = 20$$
then $5 + 3 + 2 = 10$
or $50 + 30 + 20 = 100$

This sort of *knowing* can be encouraged under the condition that the students realize that this flexibility is possible with addition and multiplication, but that there are likely to be wrong results if rearrangements are tried with subtraction and division. Commutativity allows reordering, and associativity permits regrouping. Children can be taught to use these to take control over computation involving addition and multiplication. It is not necessary (or advisable) to teach children the words *associative* or *commutative*. These terms will be taught more formally after the middle school years.

Caution

Caution: Children will tend to assume that since associativity holds in addition and multiplication, it holds in subtraction and division as well.

 Examples

$8 - 4 - 3 = ?$ Is it $8 - 4$ then -3
or $4 - 3 = 1$ first,   then $8 - (4 - 3) = 8 - 1 = 7$?

$18 \div 9 \div 3 = ?$ Is it $(18 \div 9) \div 3 = 2 \div 3 = 2/3$?
or $18 \div (9 \div 3) = 18 \div 3 = 6$?

Many examples and counter-examples will be necessary to help students understand associativity and when and how it may be used to advantage in computation. These examples need to include work with various manipulatives and directly related number manipulation. Not only should the manipulation of objects and numbers play an important role here, but students should work with as many applications to real life and problem solving as possible.

Nonassociative Operations

What operations in children's daily lives are not associative? The teacher should cite some nonassociative operations and let children present others from their own experiences.

 Examples

Putting on a shirt, a sweater, and a coat.

Putting on socks, putting on shoes, tying shoes.

Taking bread from the package, putting bread in the toaster, spreading butter on toast.

Such illustrations make the idea of nonassociative operations clear so that, when subtraction and division are done with more than two numbers in sequence, children will understand the necessity for appropriate groupings before attempting the string of operations. It is helpful, also, to refer to the binary nature of the operations and to note that the difficulties in obtaining consistently correct results have to do with whether the operator is working from left to right, the reverse, or with some other combination (Boulton-Lewis, 1994).

Operations Interrelationships

Multiplication as Repeated Addition

As students develop ideas of sets and manipulating sets with the same number, they begin to recognize the idea of multiplication as a way to add. This idea can be reinforced with a variety of different manipulative devices which should lead directly to creating paper-and-pencil forms of arrays (rows and columns). In kindergarten through second grade, children should be asked to stack books, arrange sets of pencils, note rows of chairs, examine egg cartons and packs of cola cans, etc. noting the items in equal sized groups. They should experiment with various arrays with the same manipulatives and begin to get a sense of the arrays that come out even and those that leave remainders.

They should create arrays and discuss the sets of equal numbers encountered in everyday life. Part of their counting should include skip-counting up to and including counting by sixes. This should be accompanied by repeated addition, but without reference to multiplication by name and definitely *not* by algorithms. In grades 3, 4, and 5, the foundation developed in skip-counting can be built upon as the concepts of multiplication and division are developed. The algorithms should be presented after the concepts have been studied, not before. This creation of arrays sets the stage for the use of this skill in problem solving. A very powerful tool for problem solving is arrangement of data or objects in charts, lists, or arrays according to some organized scheme.

 Activity

The children will find out the total number of gifts the singer's true love gave him/her during the 12 days of Christmas.

Division as Repeated Subtraction

Our first division tasks are typically of the type, "Share these pieces of candy so that each child has the same amount of candy." Students follow a plan: two for you, two for you, and so on, as two are repeatedly taken away (subtracted) from the original set. Soon children modify the scheme, especially if the taking away of two's doesn't quickly diminish the pile of candy. If this idea does not occur to them after some time even with class discussion, the teacher should encourage thoughtful decisions about how to streamline the process and make it reasonable. At strategic points, the teacher can demonstrate strategies such as estimation, organized recording, and techniques for planning ahead. The teacher should point out that these are being used and are helpful to remember. This will prepare the children for learning the standard long division algorithm or other algorithms for division. The standard long division algorithm is actually a concisely formed procedure to accomplish repeated subtraction. It is difficult for children to learn and remember largely because the connection to repeated subtraction is not immediately evident. Furthermore, teachers often do not overtly teach students the nature of the algorithm. Children cannot develop this understanding on their own. They must have the teacher show them the reason for the algorithm and how it functions. If this does not happen, they are forced to learn it as a highly abstract, even mystical, procedure. More about teaching algorithms will be discussed in the sections to follow.

Helping middle schoolers to remember that division can be thought of as repeated subtraction will provide them with valuable problem solving skills and competence in complex or confusing computation. If students understand division in this way, they may be able to reconstruct an algorithm when they have forgotten the steps but need an algorithm with which to compute.

Inverse Operations

Inverse operations occur in many contexts. Children will be quick to identify many *doing/undoing* operation combinations. Instruction concerning operation inverses can start with reference to opposites and interconnect with reading and word skills where the concepts of opposites and undoing operations are considered. Interesting similar ideas occur in social studies and science as well. Turning the switch turns the light off and turning it again turns the light on. For some locks, turning the key unlocks and turning it again locks. Writing and erasing undo each other. Pushing the computer *Caps Lock* key makes all the letters capitals, and pushing it again returns the letters to lower case.

Both types of inverse operations should be considered. First is the operation in which the operation is its own inverse.

 Examples

- Pushing a button turns the machine off and pushing the button again turns the machine on.

- Turning a shirt inside out and then turning it inside out again returns it to the original state.

- Reversing the order of the digits in a numeral and then reversing the digits again returns the numeral to the original.

- Rotating a rectangle 180°, then rotating it 180° again returns the rectangle to its original position.

The second type of inverse operation is one in which a different operation is required to restore the original number or situation to its original form. Students should be asked to do each of the following tasks and discuss, comment on, and write about the results:

- Add 3 to 5, then subtract 3 from the result. Repeat this with a variety of numbers large and small.

- Subtract 3 from 5, then add 3 to the result. Repeat with a variety of numbers. (Older students should use negative numbers.)

- Multiply 3 times 5, then divide the result by 3. Repeat with a variety of numbers.

- Divide 6 by 3, then multiply the result by 3. Repeat with a variety of numbers. (Older students should use fractions.)

In introducing the idea of inverse operations that are different from each other, a teacher may wish to use some examples from everyday life.

- Fast forward a video/audio cassette, then reverse the cassette.

- Melt ice cubes, then refreeze the water in cubes.

- Get clothes dirty, then wash the clothes.

- Climb a hill, then descend the hill.

- Wreck a bike, then repair the bike.

From mathematics:

- Rotate various polygon shaped objects through multiples of quarter-turns, half-turns, etc. to determine which two operations are inverses of each other (see Fig. 9-1).

Addition and subtraction, as well as multiplication and division, may be thought of as the inverses of each other. These interrelationships are important understandings for children as they develop these operation concepts. In fact the definitions of the operations of subtraction and division can be presented in terms of the inverses. The terminology used here should not be used with second and third graders, but the idea of an inverse underlies the statement, "Six divided by 3 is 2, because 2 times 3 equals 6." The algorithm, *adding the result to the number being subtracted*, to check subtraction, also presents the idea of inverse.

FIGURE 9-1 Rotating Objects

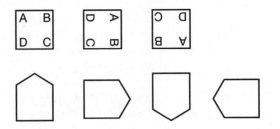

 Examples

$$17 - 9 = 8 \quad \text{because } 8 + 9 = 17$$
$$26 \div 2 = 13 \quad \text{because } 2 \times 13 = 26$$

Reference to the inverse properties in work with basic facts in computation alternatives and in problem solving provides additional tools for students. It allows additional control over the processes of computing, including means for checking computation results and computing by various means. In problem solving, the student can use alternate strategies and also verify computation procedures. Teachers should not only give specific instruction about operation inverse concepts in this context, but also take every opportunity to point out and discuss inverse characteristics when they arise in mathematics teaching and learning as well as in other contexts in the classroom.

 Activity for Second and Third Graders

Children will cite operations and their inverses from their experiences. They will be helped to focus on those in which doing the same action the second time brings one back to the original. Children should consider the following: turning a shirt inside out, then turning it inside out again; turning a book upside down, then upside down again; pushing a button to turn the computer on and pushing it again to turn the computer off. These are all examples of inverse operation where the operation is its own inverse.

The second type of inverse operation is illustrated by the following: tying/untying shoes; opening/closing a door; writing/erasing.

Activities that help students become aware of the concept of inverse operations will prepare them for work with transformations in algebra and geometry.

Counter-examples, illustrating operations that do not have inverses and cannot be undone, should also be given.

Activity

Children will cite and discuss operations (in their lives) that cannot be reversed. Examples include breaking a dish, tearing a piece of paper, burning a match, cooking a potato.

Children should also examine non-reversible numerical operations.

Example

Using calculators, children should find the square root of 3, then multiply the resulting number by itself and note that the result is not 3.0 (on most calculators). Older students should discuss and learn why the result is not 3.0.

Undoing Operations

A distinction should be made between the inverse of an operation and undoing the operation. The author calls this unoperating; unadding, unmultiplying, etc. The ability to rewrite numbers in various forms (as in the example of 24) earlier in this chapter and decompose them into easily used forms is a powerful computational and problem solving tool. Until recently, the only unoperating taught consistently was factoring (unmultiplying). Factoring was needed by students in preparation for developing the algorithms used in reducing and computing with fractions. In recent years, increasing attention has been given to work with the sets of addends for a particular number. Often children are given practice in finding and writing all the combinations of numbers which add to a given number. However, the value of teaching unadding, unsubtracting, and undividing seems to have been largely overlooked. Children should be encouraged to experiment with writing numbers in ways such as the following:

$$8 = 10 - 2 \qquad 7 = 14 \div 2$$
$$8 = 16 \div 2 \qquad 7 = 9 - 2$$

Learning how to create these kinds of expressions also will give students additional control over computation and provide them with useful problem solving skills in algebra (completing the square, for example) and subsequently in calculus.

Distributive Properties

The distributive property relates multiplication and either addition or subtraction and division and either addition or subtraction (if division is from the right). This property of operations also provides students with useful tools in computation and problem solving.

Example: Using Unadding and the Distributive Property

Find the cost of 15 items at $1.30 each.

Unadd $1.30 to $1.00 + $0.30 and distribute:

$$15 \ (\$1.00 + (\$0.30) = 15 \times \$1.00 + 15 \times \$0.30$$
$$= \$15.00 + \$4.50$$
$$= \$19.50$$

Note

Unadding thoughtfully in this example provides numbers that are easier than $1.30 to multiply with.

Since multiplication distributes from either right or left but division does not, the teacher should make sure this is noted by students. Counter-examples are not hard to find and will help students develop this concept.

Example:

$$12 \div (4 + 2) = 12 \div 6 = 2$$
$$12 \div (4 + 2) \neq 12 \div 4 + 12 \div 2 = 3 + 6 = 9$$
$$(12 + 4) \div 4 = 16 \div 4 = 4$$
$$(12 + 4) \div 4 = 12 \div 4 + 4 \div 4 = 3 + 1 = 4$$

The more advanced students should be encouraged to provide counter-examples themselves and to investigate what happens when operations using inappropriate properties such as left distribution of division are attempted. When these examples and counter-examples are developed, it is best to use numbers that allow computation to be done easily and quickly. The students' attention should be on the distributive principle and not on the computation.

Activity

The teacher asks students in groups to find the quickest and easiest way to multiply and divide certain numbers by examining all the possible distributive combinations. Possible tasks could include 5×12 and $15 \div 5$ for third and fourth graders, and 16×245 and $1350 \div 25$ for fifth and sixth graders.

Subproblem 2: *What algorithms should be taught and how?*

Understanding Subproblem 2

Traditionally, mathematics teaching has been focused on the learning and application of algorithms to be used in computation. While mathematics education has shifted significantly away from that to emphases on problem solving, understanding numbers, and practical applications, it is still important to teach algorithms for computing. The algorithms considered in this section are those for the four operations with base 10 numbers, written using the place value system. Algorithms for performing the operations with fractions are discussed in the chapters on teaching fractions. The significant questions are:

- Which algorithms should we teach?
- Should we concentrate on one algorithm only for each of the four operations?
- How much emphasis should be given to teaching algorithms?

Teachers should recall that an algorithm is not the operation. It is simply a scheme, a set of steps (usually a manipulation of numbers) that will consistently yield the correct operation result. From research on algorithm teaching and use, some general principles have been identified.

▣ Solving Subproblem 2

Which Algorithms Should We Teach?

There is general agreement that the four traditional algorithms should be taught (but with limitations) and that, in general, complex paper-and-pencil computation should be de-emphasized in favor of spending more time and effort on other more important aspects of mathematics. The recommended limitations may be expressed as follows, for:

> Addition and subtraction – not more than 3 digits
>
> Multiplication   – not more than 2 digits
>
> Division   – not more than 1 digit in the divisor

For larger numbers, calculators, other tools, or a scheme for breaking the numbers into smaller parts should be used (NCTM, 1989). The algorithms that should be taught are:

> Efficient: There are no extraneous steps.
>
> Accurate: They always give correct results.
>
> General: They apply to a wide range of numbers.

The *standard* (traditional) algorithms meet these requirements but are heavily dependent on place value understanding for both format and for manipulation of numbers in the processes. They also depend heavily on knowledge of basic facts. In fact, these algorithms are designed so that computation with numbers larger than single digit numbers is done by carefully ordered repeated applications of basic facts.

 ## Examples

$$\begin{array}{r} \overset{1\ 11}{345} \\ +657 \\ \hline 1002 \end{array} \qquad \begin{array}{r} \overset{1\ 121}{1234} \\ -\ 698 \\ \hline 536 \end{array} \qquad \begin{array}{r} \overset{1}{\cancel{5}} \\ 37 \\ \times 28 \\ \hline 296 \\ 74 \\ \hline 1036 \end{array}$$

$$\begin{array}{r} 189\ \text{R2} \\ 7\overline{)1325} \\ \underline{7} \\ 62 \\ \underline{56} \\ 65 \\ \underline{63} \\ 2 \end{array} \qquad \begin{array}{l} 7\times 9 = 63 \\ 7 \times 8 = 56 \end{array}$$

(These forms typically indicate or suggest the four standard algorithms.)

To teach these algorithms effectively, the teacher should ensure that the students know basic facts and have a good understanding of the place value system. Then the techniques for teaching processes can be used, as follows:

- Demonstrate the process
- Point out important steps and likely errors
- Guide students through the process
- Correct student errors
- Provide for ample practice experiences

 ## Extension Activity for Seventh and Eighth Graders

Advanced students may investigate and develop algorithms for operations when the numbers are written:

- in different bases
- with Roman numerals
- using other systems such as tallies (tally: ꠵ ꠇꠇꠇ, etc.)

Basic Facts

Opinions differ on which sets of basic facts should be learned by students so that they have the resources necessary for performing algorithms. The author believes that it is sufficient for children to learn the basic addition and multiplication facts, that is, those up to 10. They don't need the extra stress and time used to learn subtraction and division facts. Any single digit subtraction and division can easily be done by reference to the inverse operation with those numbers. To deal with a complete set of division facts comparable to the set of multiplication facts would require learning such facts as $72 \div 8 = 9$ and $63 \div 9 = 7$, etc. This would be extremely cumbersome. Subtraction or division flash cards or other similar devices can still be used effectively, even though the lessons are not focused on teaching basic subtraction and/or division facts. There are advantages to working with the students on such facts as $7 - 4$ and $9 \div 3$, but these can be learned in connection with learning $4 + 3$ and 3×3 and will best be developed naturally rather than in a direct effort to learn them as facts. Recall that many children will initially try to learn the facts by using memorization. If the teacher is teaching basic facts in all four operations and students are attempting to memorize them, the memory load will be too great. In addition, there is a significant difference in the two types of facts. There are facts for every combination of single digit numbers for addition and multiplication, but not for the other two operations. For example, $3 - 5$ and $3 \div 2$ are not part of the basic facts. Those yielding negative or fractional numbers are not needed or really practical to learn. It is more important to spend the time and effort on connections and interrelationships among the operations and underlying operation concepts that become apparent as the addition and multiplication basic facts are learned. (See Chapter 6 on teaching basic facts.)

Place Value Dependency

The use of standard algorithms depends heavily on a user's knowledge of the base 10 place value system. Place value knowledge includes understanding both the meaning of the position of a single digit numeral and trading when moving values from position to position. When teaching these processes initially, it is wise to delay the use of the terms *borrowing* and *carrying*. These sound meaningful to children but may be confusing. How are numbers *carried* or *borrowed*? They are being carried to where and borrowed from where? *Trading* is a better term, especially if it grows out of experience with base 10 manipulative blocks. Dependence on the place value system is expressed in the necessity of working in columns and in keeping columns straight. Some children have difficulty with the degree of discipline and organization required for work with columns. This is especially true for children who are not confident of their knowledge of the place value system (Wearne, 1994).

Caution

Children in kindergarten, first grade, and second grade may not have the fine motor skills necessary for drawing numerals, using straight columns, and creating certain figures. A teacher should consider these aspects when working with a child who is using the algorithmic forms, as the cause of a child's difficulty may not be lack of knowledge of the operations or the basic facts; rather, it may be a problem of mechanics.

FIGURE 9-2 Examples of Mechanical Problems in Computation

$$
\begin{array}{ll}
\text{a.} \quad \overset{1}{78} & \text{b.} \quad \overset{2}{23} \\
\quad \underline{+49} & \quad \underline{\times 17} \\
\quad 127 & \quad 161 \\
& \quad \underline{23} \\
& \quad 364
\end{array}
$$

Figure 9-2 shows examples of the kinds of mechanical problems students may have.

The criteria to be checked when diagnosing performance with algorithms are:

- Is the form/format drawn sufficiently well?

- Are place value columns used properly?

- Is the sequence of steps followed correctly?

- Were basic facts used correctly?

- Was trading done properly?

- Were modifications of the standard algorithms legitimate?

- Was there loss of continuity in repetition of steps?

When a Child Has Difficulty with Standard Algorithms

Two general areas of difficulty have been described above: Knowledge of *basic facts* and knowledge of the *place value* system. Often it is not feasible to hold a child back while waiting until he or she masters basic facts or acquires competence with the place value concept. The rest of the class may be ready to move ahead with problem solving or other mathematics learning using the ability to compute (Cumming, 1994). Remembering that these standard algorithms are not the only ones and, for some students, not even the best, the teacher may wish to help students (especially those having difficulty with the standard algorithms) learn other algorithms or even create their own (Perry, 1994).

Teachers should be aware of common errors students make in working with the standard algorithms. The teacher should not simply mark *right* or *wrong*, but should look for signs of particular errors or error patterns. Typically there are teachable moments involved when computational work is examined carefully. If a child is not given specific assistance regarding the precise nature of his or her difficulty, there is little chance to learn the processes of computation and the related concepts involved. When a teacher gives insight into the specific nature of the error in computation, a child can make the appropriate correction. Appendix B contains lists showing error patterns along with opportunity for analysis of the errors and plans for remediation.

Research and experience has shown that an interesting sequence of transitions occurs as people learn and practice computing. As very young children begin computing, their algorithms are essentially rules for arranging manipulatives (combine the sets and count, for example). With instruction, they move next to the formal algorithms described above. Finally, in middle school and high school many abandon those algorithms in favor of mental computation schemes and "tricks" that do not require pencil and paper or in favor of short-cuts in the processes. These schemes range from modifications of the standard forms to special techniques depending on the nature of the numbers involved. Numbers may be broken into parts, adjusted and compensated, estimated, and reordered in order to make the process easy or quick.

 ## Examples of Nonstandard Algorithms

$$38 + 47 = 30 + 40 + 7 + 8 = 70 + 15 = 85$$

$$45 \times 45 = 40 \times 50 + 25 = 2000 + 25 = 2025$$

$$38 - 29 = 38 - 30 + 1 = 8 + 1 = 9$$

$$16 \times 25 = 16 \times (100 \div 4) = 1600 \div 4 = 400$$

$$6 \times \$7.97 = 6 \times \$8.00 - \$0.18$$
$$= \$48.00 - \$0.18$$
$$= \$47.82$$

$$\$27.72 \div 6 = \$27 \div 6 + \$0.72 \div 6$$
$$= \$24 \div 6 + \$3 \div 6 + \$0.12$$
$$= \$4.00 + \$0.50 + \$0.12$$
$$= \$4.62$$

It may help to solve a child's problem with operating if the child realizes that the goal is to learn to compute successfully rather than to learn a particular algorithm. Finding an algorithm to learn is secondary. Teachers should develop a collection of algorithms for the operations at the level at which they teach. These should be detailed in a notebook or other accessible file so that, as the need arises, the teacher may choose among them for those that will help a student experiencing difficulties. The algorithms should be classified with reference to their likely application.

Example

```
  25
×14
  20
  80
  50
200
350
```

This algorithm would be useful when a student is having difficulty trading in the standard algorithm but does well in adding columns and knows place value.

The Best Algorithms

Students are most likely to understand algorithms that provide direct connections with operations concepts, especially with familiar object manipulation. They prefer those algorithms that do not have too many complex steps. Both of these issues can be illustrated with the long division algorithm:

Consider: 8)7145 and the steps that have to be used.

1. Will 8 *go into* 7? No. How about 8 into 71? Eight into 72 is 9, so I write 8 above the 1. (or the experimentation with multiples of 8)

2. The subtraction of 64 from 71 is not especially easy. Then *bring down* the 4, and repeat the guess and check.

3. Students will often do much erasing and figuring on the side and can easily lose track of the necessary steps in all of this back and forth work.

4. In all these steps there is little connection with reality.

Consider the following scaffold modification of the standard form:

	8)7145	
1. Try taking away five 8s—a known fact	40	5
	7105	
2. Aha! take away 500	4000	500
	3105	
3. Now maybe 200	1600	200
	1505	
4. Now take away 100	800	100
	705	
5. Now take away 50	400	50
	305	
6. Now take away 25	200	25
	105	
7. Now take away 12	96	12
	9	

8. There's one more 8

$$
\begin{array}{r r}
8 & \underline{1} \\
1 & 893 \quad \text{8s with 1 left over}
\end{array}
$$

Note that the scaffold method connects directly and obviously with division as repeated subtraction. It could easily be related to distributing pieces of candy to eight children or some other such real life situation. Furthermore, the steps need not involve a lot of guessing, erasing, rewriting, or sidebar computation. A child doing this computation can design the choices according to well-known basic facts and to the subtractions that will be least difficult (that don't involve trading, for example). In this scaffold approach, place value requires less attention. There is no need to carefully keep the columns *straight* from the number being divided up to where the result is written. Since much of the *borrowing* in the subtraction can be avoided and the adding involves "nice" numbers such as multiples of hundreds and tens, few place value difficulties will develop there either.

A less obvious benefit to using algorithms with these characteristics is that children have more control over decisions made in the processes. The standard algorithms do not provide this; typically, they are cut and dried and must be done exactly correctly. If the order of the steps is violated, errors result, and often a child cannot detect the cause of the difficulty. When the child is more in control and makes decisions along the way, he or she is more likely to be able to do troubleshooting for the process and much more interested in doing it. There may be concern that algorithms such as the scaffold form require more steps. Sometimes that is the case, but the longer form is usually better because the steps are easier, easier to remember, and easier to troubleshoot. Appendix B contains examples of other modifications of the standard algorithms for reference.

Suggestions for Teaching Algorithms

- Present nonstandard algorithms along with the standard algorithms.

  a. This makes it clear to the student that there are multiple ways of getting correct operation results.

  b. If the standard algorithm is place value dependent and a child doesn't have good place value understanding, an alternative may help the child with computation success.

- Teach algorithms that are as close to the way the child thinks and works as is possible, e.g., Use arrays in multiplication and so reference repeated addition, or the scaffold method in division referencing repeated subtraction.

- Avoid teaching algorithms that depend on a complex series of steps.

- Avoid teaching algorithms that are very abstract and thus do not closely relate to hands-on processes.

- Give children opportunities to work in their own ways and to control the computation by allowing them to choose algorithms that work better or more easily for them, with the following provisos:

    a. The algorithm must yield the correct result in the situation for which it is designed.

    b. The algorithm should be simple so that it is easy to remember.

    c. The algorithm should be easy to apply and reasonably efficient.

Motivation

Nonstandard algorithms, especially those that may be presented as magic tricks and those with intriguing results, often motivate enjoyment of mathematics. Students can be taught tricks to pull on their friends and families. These include:

- Squaring numbers which end in 5
- The multiplication 12345679×18, or any multiple of 9
- Creating palindromic numbers

The study of algorithms is an area where students at any level may do interesting inquiry and discovery activities that will not necessarily take them ahead of their class. It provides a rich field of exploration for advanced students and for those who might need something different from the regular class material. The National Council of Teachers of Mathematics journals are good sources for problems, activities, and descriptions related to nonstandard algorithms. Letters to the editor in those journals should not be overlooked—they often contain a teacher's report of student motivation in math processing and discoveries of intriguing algorithms.

Mental Math

Strand 7 in the *Curriculum and Evaluation Standards* (NCTM, 1989) is called "Estimation and Mental Computation." The two concepts are regarded as complementary. When students are out of school and involved in daily life in a highly technical and number-oriented society, mental computation skills are increasingly important. Most people do not carry calculators with them and most situations do not require precise calculating anyway. There are, however, many occasions when the ability to use approximate values in mental calculation and to make sufficiently accurate mental computations is extremely helpful (Koyama, 1994). These occasions occur when buying in various settings, while driving, and while making decisions and judgments about time. Other measurements also often involve some calculation that can be done mentally. With these skills children can be much more flexible in applying their more formal computation skills and are better able to select appropriate computation methods. They are able to explore different combinations of numbers and alternative strategies for obtaining the necessary operation results. Teachers should encourage students to demonstrate mental computation by describing thought patterns for simple computation at the levels of the students' abilities. Students should also be encouraged to develop and attempt to use some of their own mental computation schemes.

Algorithmic Tools

For performing operations, a number of tools and devices exist, ranging from paper-and-pencil procedures similar to the algorithms discussed above to physical objects such as slide rules and calculators. Many of these are intriguing and some can even be created and used effectively by children. The formal use of these tools in the classroom may require inordinate amounts of time to teach, and some have only limited application. However, they are interesting and can be motivational. Two of the most well known and interesting are discussed here. For addition:

 Addition slide rule: Two rulers may be used and laid side by side and one slid along the other to match numbers and read off addition results. Since using two rulers of the same construction would require one to be upside down (forcing one set of numbers to be read upside down), have children construct their own rulers. (This exercise is instructive in other ways too.) Essentially, two number lines are being used so that if children have worked with number lines already, they will have a head start on working with the addition slide rule.

The rulers, as positioned in Figure 9-3, can be used to read off 4 + 5, 4 + 8, etc. If the fractional parts of inches are indicated on the rulers, the same tool can be used in adding with fractions to aid in learning fraction concepts, operating with fractions, and obtaining results quickly. Obvious limitations are that only eighths and tenths might be available. Caution must be exercised in lining up the 0 mark carefully and in noting whether the end of the ruler is at

FIGURE 9-3 Addition Slide Rule

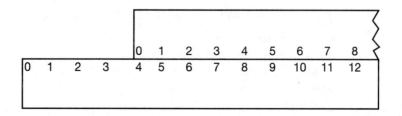

FIGURE 9-4 Napier's Bones

	8	3	5
	0 / 8	0 / 3	0 / 5
	1 / 6	0 / 6	1 / 0
3rd row	2 / 4	0 / 9	1 / 5
	3 / 2	1 / 2	2 / 0
5th row	4 / 0	1 / 5	2 / 5
	4 / 8	1 / 8	3 / 0
	5 / 6	2 / 1	3 / 5
	6 / 4		

the 0 mark. If this exercise is done in connection with learning how to measure with a ruler, it will also help to prepare students to work carefully with a ruler. Figure 9-4 shows an activity for multiplication:

Napier's bones: Another construction children can make is a Napier's bones set on strips of card stock. The strips are about 1 inch wide and 6 to 8 inches long, designed as indicated in Figure 9-4. The teacher should probably mark the horizontal and diagonal lines because they need to be consistently spaced, but the children should write in the multiples to provide practice with the basic multiplication facts. Multiplication is done by placing the strips for the number to be multiplied—835 in this case—side by side and then adding the numbers in the diagonal boxes in the row for the single digit number which is the other factor. Using these bones to find 5 × 835, the multiplier would, starting from the right in the 5th row down, write 5 as the last digit, 5 + 2 or 7 (adding diagonally) as the next digit, then 1 (0 + 1), and finally 4. The result is 4175. The result of 835 × 3 would be found in the third row as 2505. Note that the 9 + 1 results in a two digit number and the 1 is *carried* into the 4 + 0 diagonal and added.

Activities for Seventh and Eighth Graders

- As an extension of this activity, explore connections between this tool and the standard multiplication algorithm. Additionally, research Napier, learn when and where he lived, and learn why these strips are called bones. Is Napier connected with any other aspect of mathematics we do in school today?

- Research and report on the development of calculating machines.

- Create linear or circular slide rules for addition. (Instructions are in Appendix J.) (also for second, third, and fourth grades)

- Find and bring to class an engineering slide rule and explain how it works.

 ## Multiplication by Halving and Doubling

Consider multiplying 52 by 79. There are four steps, as follows:

1. Write 52 × 79 and under either 52 or 79 make a "halving" column by successively dividing by 2. If 52 is chosen, the divisions will result in 26, 13, and so on. (Ignore any remainders.)

2. If 52 heads the halving column, then under the 79 make a column by successive multiplication by 2. This will give 158, 316, and so forth.

3. Identify the numbers in the doubling column that are opposite odd numbers in the halving column. Asterisks are used in the illustration.

4. Add the asterisked numbers for the multiplication result.

$$
\begin{array}{ll}
52 \times & 79 \\
26 & 158 \qquad\quad 316 \\
13 & 316^* \qquad\; 1264 \\
6 & 632 \qquad\;\; \underline{+2528} \\
3 & 1264^* \qquad 4108 = 52 \times 79 \\
1 & 2528^*
\end{array}
$$

In using this process for multiplying 71 × 63, we see that all the numbers in the halving column are odd. This means that all the numbers in the doubling column should be added. Here is the process:

$$
\begin{array}{ll}
71 \times & 63^* \\
142 & 31^* \\
284 & 15^* \qquad 71 \times 63 = 4473 \\
568 & 7^* \\
1136 & 3^* \\
\underline{2272} & 1^* \\
4473 &
\end{array}
$$

There is an opportunity here for an inquiry/discovery activity as children could explore this algorithm to try to learn why it works. A related exploration, connected to number sense, would be to find those numbers which consistently yield odds (or evens) when successively halved.

▣ Summary

General operation concepts were examined carefully, along with specific methods for developing operation concepts. The four operations and their interrelationships were considered individually. Standard and nonstandard algorithms were examined and suggestions given for teaching the understanding and use of algorithms. The concepts of reverse and inverse operations were explained and examples were provided.

▣ Exercises

1. List and analyze the algorithms you are comfortable with. Are you confident with each of the standard algorithms with all sorts of numbers? Have you developed any of your own algorithms? Which algorithms that you were taught have you abandoned? Why did you abandon them?

2. Use one of the Math Activity Diagnosis Schemes (Appendix F) to analyze an aspect of a child's operations/algorithms understanding.

3. Prepare a list of algorithms and algorithmic tools, including those you would like to use with your students. For each, make notes that will enable you to use them easily.

4. Create sets of Napier's bones, slide rules, and other algorithmic devices that you can take with you to teaching internship.

5. Find and bring to class an engineering slide rule and demonstrate and explain how it works.

▣ References

Boulton-Lewis, Gillian M., and Kathleen Tait (1994, June). Young children's representations and strategies for addition. *British Journal of Educational Psychology*, 64(2), 231–242.

Cumming, J. Joy, et al. (1994, Fall). Are any errors careless? *Focus on Learning Problems in Mathematics*, 16(4), 21–30.

Koyama, Masataka (1994, March). Research into relationship between the computational estimation ability and strategy and the mental computation ability: Analysis of a survey of the fourth, fifth and sixth graders in Japan. *Hiroshima Journal of Mathematics Education*, 2, 35–44.

National Council of Teachers of Mathematics (1989). *Curriculum and Evaluation Standards for School Mathematics*. Reston, VA: Author.

Perry, A. D., and Kaye Stacey (1994, Summer). The use of taught and invented methods of subtraction. *Focus on Learning Problems in Mathematics*, 16(3), 12–22.

Wearne, Diana and James Hiebert. (1994, January). Research into practice: Place value and addition and subtraction. *Arithmetic Teacher*, 41(5), 272–274.

🔲 Suggested Readings

Cleary, Beverly (1993). *Dear Mr. Henshaw.* New York: William Morrow.

Fan, Ning, John H. Mueller, and Anthony E. Marini (1994). Solving difference problems: Wording primes coordination. *Cognition and Instruction*, 12(4), 355–369.

Frydman, Olivier, and Peter Bryant. (1994, December). Children's understanding of multiplicative relationships in the construction of quantitative equivalence. *Journal of Experimental Child Psychology*, 58, 489–509.

Saenz-Ludlow, Adalira (1994, January). Michael's fraction schemes. *Journal for Research in Mathematics Education*, 25(1), 50–85.

Thompson, Ian (1994, June). Young children's idiosyncratic written algorithms for addition. *Education Studies in Mathematics*, 26(4), 323–345.

Teaching Geometric Concepts

One of the children's problems: Jeri has memorized many names for geometric fig-ures but cannot use them to solve problems.

Teacher's problem: The terminology in geometry does not follow patterns very closely and the words are difficult for children to remember because they do not have close relationships to the concepts.

Understanding the Problem

The word *geo-metry* comes from the concept of *earth-measure*, an attempt to understand and describe our world and how physical entities interrelate. That is now even more important to children growing up in a high-tech-oriented culture. Geometry still provides a wide variety of real-life connections between and within mathematics topics and between mathematics and other subjects.

Though geometry and measurement cannot be separated from one another, they will be discussed in detail in different chapters in this text.

To many, teaching and learning in geometry seems different from teaching and learning in other mathematics topics. This is because the focus in geometry is on nonnumerical symbols and on manipulation of figures and shapes rather than number symbols. Operations in geometry are also inherently different from numerical operations. This differentiation probably arises from the historical categorization of mathematics into arithmetic, algebra, and geometry and because shapes and measurements are manipulated differently. It was believed that these should be taught and learned separately and that geometry and algebra should be reversed for the high school years. Part of this belief was that algebraic and geometric concepts were too advanced for younger children. Some of the concepts are too advanced, but mathematics educators realize how important it is for younger children to study algebraic and geometric concepts beginning in kindergarten. It has become increasingly evident that high school students have serious difficulty with both algebra and geometry when they have had no exposure to ideas in these two areas before they arrive at high school mathematics (Piaget, 1960).

Mathematics educators have realized that there are important reasons for including geometry at the earliest levels and throughout K–8 mathematics.

- Young children can and do learn geometrical concepts.

- Young children use geometrical ideas in everyday life.

- Integrated learning of geometry with other mathematics benefits learning in both.

- Geometry provides a rich setting for solving problems that are realistic and manipulative based.

- Learning geometry in connection with other topics through the grades prepares students for the more focused and formal study of geometry later.

It is clear that geometry must be taught with ample use of manipulatives. Fortunately, many objects with obvious geometric features can serve as specifically geometric manipulatives. Teachers can take advantage of geometric expressions in the architecture, in packaging, and in commonly used objects. There are also many opportunities found in geometry to teach and practice other mathematics, such as working with fractions and the various operations in realistic settings. The realism inherent in geometrical figures can provide motivation and interest for many mathematics lessons (Cruikshank, 1977).

Topological Considerations

Children begin, as babies, to explore their world. They reach out to touch objects, feel and respond to various textures, and begin to notice shapes. At first the basic topological ideas are foremost: far and near; is a part of and is not a part of; inside and outside; off and on. By the time a child starts kindergarten, he or she has been exposed to a myriad of geometric shapes and has developed, to some degree, a repertoire of geometric concepts. In addition to the basic topological concepts, the child will know a few shape names such as *circle*, *rectangle*, and *triangle*. The concepts to go with these may be fairly well developed even though the child may be unable to articulate them. Early elementary teachers should search for ways to capitalize on these partially complete ideas and help children to build them into more complete structures.

Teachers should not attempt to erase faulty early learning of geometric concepts. Teaching cannot begin with a clean slate. It is, however, difficult to deal with geometric concepts which are inaccurately formed in children's minds. Children bring with them terminology and concepts that may be incorrect in their minds. Some of these are concepts of *square*, *angle*, and *line*. Thus a part of teaching in the early grades is to help children correct misconceptions and build correct constructs. An important starting point is terminology (Burger, 1985). Studying geometry is a good place to begin to understand the importance of precision in language. Learning geometric names and refining the concepts to which they apply helps set the stage for a good deal of learning in mathematics.

Suydam (1984) reports that geometry teaching in the elementary school has traditionally been confined largely to recognizing shapes and learning names for shapes. Children can and should do much more than that. They use geometric concepts in problem solving, in their play, and at home as they manipulate objects and interact with their environments. In fact, some of the games they play depend on understanding geometric ideas and using geometric concepts. They fold paper to make paper airplanes, bounce balls at angles off walls, and draw geometric designs on paper. If they have computers at home or in the classroom, they are likely to have worked with programs with geometric content (paint and drawing programs and design creating programs, for example). This means that we ought to teach geometry in the elementary grades not only to equip children with knowledge basic to further study, but to enhance their functioning in daily life (Suydam, 1984).

Formalizing Known Concepts

Geometric aspects of children's daily lives and interests are excellent starting points for helping them to formalize important geometric concepts. Furthermore, since these concepts are more completely developed through structured experiences, the objects in the children's environments are of direct use.

Throughout teaching in geometry, teachers should provide ample and frequent reference to the physical world. Much of this can be done with manipulatives that can be handled in classroom activities. A math classroom where geometry is taught ought to contain a wide range of manipulatives including drawing tools, geoboards, pattern blocks, C-rods, base-10 blocks, tangram sets, and plenty of paper of different types, including tag board and cardboard. Other construction materials such as toothpicks, popsicle sticks, and straws should be available. The educational materials supply houses have many different attractive posters that illustrate geometric principles and designs. A room decorated tastefully with these and the creations of the children provides an environment conducive to learning in geometry as well as other mathematics.

It is, however, impossible to keep all the manipulatives a teacher would like to have and all the objects children would bring for various geometry lessons in the classroom. It is also impossible to provide manipulatives to illustrate every geometric concept. A computer and software are invaluable here. Where sufficiently powerful computers are available, the teacher should acquire some of the excellent geometry software now available. For older computers, programs such as LOGO can be used effectively. Geometry software enables a student to do much more extensive investigation of shapes, angles, figure properties, and other geometric concepts than would ever be possible with hands-on objects or paper and pencil.

Whatever the tools or devices used, the teacher should begin building the partial concepts the children have from that point. Some topics in geometry follow a simple-to-complex building scheme. The concept of polygon, for example, can be built from triangles to quadrilaterals, to pentagons, etc. But a neat hierarchy from topic to topic does not always exist; therefore, the simple-to-complex mode cannot always be used. Even in the apparently direct progression of polygons from fewer sides to more sides, we have a sequence problem with the terminology. Should we say:

Triangle, quadrangle, pentangle, hexangle, etc., or

Trigon, quadragon, pentagon, hexagon, etc., or

Trilateral, quadrilateral, pentalateral, hexalateral.

Similar difficulties are encountered elsewhere in geometry. Teachers should not try to teach geometry from the standpoint of neat patterns and nice progressions only. Attempting to do so will produce frustration and limited success. Terminology is at the center of much of the difficulty; this is one reason that educators recommend less emphasis on memorization of terminology in mathematics teaching generally and especially in the teaching of geometry. It is more important to teach concepts and applicable processes.

Children learn some facts about one-dimensional, two-dimensional, and three-dimensional shapes and objects simultaneously. Thus it is counterproductive to start with one-dimensional ideas and to build sequentially to three-dimensional concepts. There is no inherent sequence. A child can and does learn about pyramids before he or she knows much about angles, even though an eventual full fledged concept of pyramids necessitates a good understanding of angles (Yusuf, 1994).

Teachers thus have a wide range of viable options regarding when and how to teach various geometric concepts and processes. The *Curriculum and Evaluation Standards* (NCTM, 1989) offer lists of geometric topics recommended for the various grades. One general approach that promises effectiveness is to integrate teaching geometric concepts with the teaching of other mathematical concepts, operations, and processes. For example, when teaching counting and classifying, a teacher might use pattern blocks. Students would count the blue triangle shapes and the red square shapes, etc. Thus, while learning to count, students are also learning about geometric shapes and correct terminology associated with this part of geometry.

Caution

A common but subtle terminology error often occurs here. Teachers and students say *blue triangles* and *red squares* instead of *blue triangle shapes* and *red square shapes* because it's easier and doesn't make much difference at this level. However, this reinforces a misconception, namely that triangles and squares are solid objects.

(It is a good idea to be overt in explaining to children why it is important to call the objects "triangle shapes" and "square shapes." This is part of their concept development too.)

Teaching like this could lead quickly into placing the 8 blue triangle shapes in one set and 7 red triangle shapes in another and combining sets to count (add) 15 triangle shapes.

At all levels, problem solving is enhanced by consideration of geometric problems and by solving nongeometric problems using geometric concepts (Paas, 1994). Children, if allowed and encouraged, can often become more creatively involved in geometry than in other aspects of mathematics. They cannot very well "create" numbers and equations; these are not attractive esthetically in the same way that cut-out shapes are. But in geometry children naturally become creative early. They begin by tracing or outlining their hands, coins, bases of pyramids, or bases of cans, etc. From there they move to paper folding and to creating angles. Then instruments are used to create more and more intricate designs. The obvious interface between geometry and art has already been mentioned. This integration of mathematics and another subject should be exploited in cooperation with other departments and teachers.

Another, perhaps less obvious, connection is with science. Physical objects in biology, earth science, and physical science can be described effectively using geometric terms such as *symmetrical, spiral, circular, spherical, cubical, diagonal,* and *hexagonal.* In a self-contained classroom, this interface can be taken advantage of to enhance learning in both subject areas. The science setting gives meaning and motivation to learning in geometry and the knowledge of geometry strengthens understanding in science.

In the single-subject areas of the middle school, more effort may be needed to make the connections across subject lines. The math teacher should talk to the science, art, and social studies teachers and understand their curricula so that helpful interconnections can be made. When the social studies curriculum considers navigation on the globe and other map skills, students can apply their knowledge of geometry to those issues.

To learn effectively in geometry, students need not only to identify and describe various geometric shapes and entities, but to create these for themselves in a variety of ways. This creation can occur when the children arrange and stack blocks, mold items of clay or dough, or draw figures. All of these should be used as often as feasible.

Subproblem: *Teaching one-, two-, and three-dimensional shapes*

Solving the Subproblem

One-Dimensional Shapes

Children begin early to draw curves; as they develop fine motor skills, they draw line segments. Finally, when they come to school, these skills are further sharpened as they learn to write. At this point linear and curved shapes take on special significance, according to their orientation and interrelationships. Students learn to distinguish between a *b* and a *p*, for example. Another categorization of interest to children is of letters that can be made with one stroke versus those requiring two or more strokes (i.e., without lifting the pencil from the paper). They learn that some letters and numerals such as *5, S, 3,* and *M* are the same in that only one pencil stroke is needed to complete the drawing. The symbols *5, S, 3,* and *M* are said to be topologically equivalent. In this connection, it is helpful for children to classify the various letters and numerals in other ways too; for example, those that are simple, not-closed curves, and those that are simple, closed curves etc. Children enjoy trying to make their bodies into numeral and letter shapes. Which figures require two bodies?

FIGURE 10-1 Goniometer

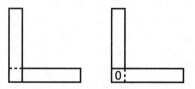

Greeley and Offermar suggest an interesting connection children can make between geometry and people's bodies. They note that in physical therapy, it is important to measure angles made by knees, elbows, and other parts of the body. In connection with this study are activities for middle schoolers both in making an angle measuring device and in measuring body angles for health and fitness purposes.

Activity for Middle Schoolers

Make your own goniometer (Figure 10-1):

1. Form an *L* shape with strips of cardboard with the ends overlapped.

2. Fasten the overlapped ends with a brass fastener.

3. Use the goniometer to measure:

> the smallest angle a knee can make
> the largest angle between thumb and forefinger
> the largest/smallest elbow angle
> the largest/smallest wrist angle
> the largest/smallest ankle angle
>
> (Greeley, 1997)

Activity for Kindergarten, First, and Second Graders

Children will lie on the floor and configure their bodies to make various shapes including numerals, letters, line segments, triangles, quadrilaterals (two students on their sides, bent at the waists) diamonds, and stars. The children should discuss the shapes that are difficult to make and why.

Activities for Fifth Through Eighth Graders

Each student will create figures with rubber bands on geoboards. They will create closed figures; then simple figures; then not-closed, simple figures, then closed, not-simple figures; then not-closed and not-simple figures. With each task seven or eight students will go to the front of the room and display their figures. They will be separated into two groups according to some characteristic common to their figures. The class will attempt to discern the difference between the two groups. Through several rounds of this activity the teacher will bring the class to the point of defining *polygon* or some other geometrical entity.

Following experimentation with drawing shapes with certain criteria attached, children can move on to more formalized consideration of lines and line segments. After drawing *straight* segments with and without tools, children soon have an intuitive idea of what *straight* means, though it will be a long time before they can express the concept of *straightness*. At this time children should be presented the idea of the infinitude of a line and the fact that when we say "line" we usually mean a piece of a line, or a segment. The terminology is not very important here, but the idea is. Again, we are preparing children to accommodate a full concept later on, but if they get the false idea that *line* refers only to a segment at this early stage, it will be difficult for them later in geometry class, where the infinite characteristic of a line is important. The following activity provides for extra practice with line segments as well as the idea of intersection of lines. It is also useful for practice in organized recording of results and the powerful problem solving skill of generating and extending patterns.

 ### Activity for Fourth Through Eighth Graders (Second and Third Graders with Two and Three Lines)

Students will draw all possible intersection arrangements with:

- two lines

- three lines

- four lines

- five lines

(See Figure 10-2.)
Students will then create a chart of the results in terms of numbers of lines, numbers of intersections, and different arrangements yielding the same number of intersections.

Students will conjecture about the numbers for six lines or more.

The concept of parallelism highlights the infinite nature of lines. This is a common feature in our environment and thus in the daily lives of children. The teacher should help the children to work with opposite sides of shapes among the manipulatives in the room and with opposite sides of the chalkboard and other rectangular shapes evident in the school building, and to examine railroad tracks. With reference to railroad tracks, the children should be asked what would happen if the tracks were not parallel at some point.

FIGURE 10-2 Possible Intersection Arrangements for 2 Lines and 3 Lines

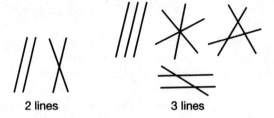

2 lines   3 lines

 Activity for Third Through Eighth Graders

Solving piezels (puzzles with pieces) using pattern blocks

Students will create, using two blocks:

- A shape with two pairs of parallel sides.
- A shape with exactly one pair of parallel sides.

Students will create, using three blocks:

- A shape with exactly three pairs of parallel sides.
- Shapes with two, one, and no parallel sides.
- A shape with a common name using two of the same blocks.
- A shape with a common name using three of the same blocks.
- A square with two blocks.
- An equililateral triangle using two blocks, three blocks.

Two-Dimensional Figures

 Activity for Grades 3 Through 8

In groups of four or five, students will play the game Set.

 Activity for Grades K Through 8

Using geoboards each child will create and show:

- a 4-sided figure with exactly 2 equal sides.
- a 12-sided figure with all sides equal.

- an equal-sided triangle
- a 5-sided figure with 3 equal sides, 4 equal sides.
- a 4-sided figure with 2 pairs of equal sides that is not a parallelogram.
- a 3-sided figure with 2-equal sides.

Activity for Grades 4 Through 8

Using geoboards each child will create and show:

- a 4-sided figure with exactly 2 equal sides.
- a 12-sided figure with all sides equal.
- an equal-sided triangle.
- a 5-sided figure with 3 equal sides, 4 equal sides.
- a 4-sided figure with 2 pairs of equal sides that is not a parallelogram.
- a 3-sided figure with 2 equal sides.
- a 7-sided figure with no equal sides.
- other shapes invented by the teacher or children

The teacher should help children note that the common plane geometric shapes (including lines and curves) are used to describe the shapes of solid objects. The teacher can then guide the children to consider various shapes that occur around them. Just as the terms *edge, side, face, inside, outside, surface, interior*, etc., are used to describe objects, so the plane figure names are used for description. A piece of paper may be described as *rectangular* or a pizza as *circular*. Note that the piece of paper should not be described as a *rectangle*, and a pizza should not be called a *circle*. This type of poor usage of geometric terms is common in our everyday language and causes children to develop incomplete and inaccurate geometric concepts. Again, it is important that students not only be exposed to the ideas and the terminology, but have the hands-on opportunity to *construct* the concepts; when they construct objects themselves the mental construction is further enhanced. This will be true as students trace around and on the Mobius Strip in the following activity:

Activity for Grades 3 Through 8

Give each student three pieces of adding machine tape, scissors, and transparent tape. The instructions are as follows:

1. Tape the ends of one strip together to form a belt. Determine how many edges and faces (sides) this figure has. (Some discussion of terminology may be in order at this point.)

2. Put the first strip aside and tape together the ends of the second strip after making a half-twist in the tape. Determine how many edges and faces this second belt has. Cut the belt down the center. Describe the result again, including numbers of edges and faces.

3. Create another half-twist belt and this time cut all the way around, one-third the distance in from the edge.

4. Describe the results.

5. Create a chart and look for patterns and generalizations.

6. Given time with other strips, experiment with full twists and other configurations.

The next step in developing shape and figure concepts is to formalize some of the specific ideas. The activity using paper folding to create squares and triangles will make clear the necessity of thinking carefully about the critical characteristics of these figures. It is essentially a problem solving activity—and not a particularly easy one (depending on the extent of experience in paper folding). The teacher may need to get the students started and, perhaps, point out the wisdom of solving a simpler problem first. This might be suggested by asking, "How can we create a right angle?" and "How can we measure, exactly, one length on the paper against another?" (This must not involve the use of a ruler or similar measuring device.) Depending on the skills and knowledge about measurement in the class, the teacher might demonstrate the inaccuracy involved in measuring with a ruler and comparing that with the accuracy achievable with paper folding. It would then be appropriate to have a class discussion centering on the reasons for the differences (Thompson, 1985).

Activity for Sixth, Seventh, and Eighth Graders

Students will, given $8\frac{1}{2}$-inch by 11-inch sheets of paper, be instructed to:

1. Fold to create a square and justify their results.

FIGURE 10-3 Beginning Steps for Folding a Square

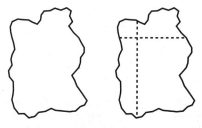

FIGURE 10-4 Figures for Counting Squares and Triangles

2. Fold a sheet to create a square without using an edge or a corner of the sheet and justify their results. (For this part of the task, it is often best to provide irregular sheets of paper. See Fig. 10-3.)

3. Fold a sheet to create an equilateral triangle and justify their results.

 ### Activity for Third Through Eighth Graders

Given figures such as these, children will count the number of squares or triangles in the figure (Figure 10-4). (Olson, 1997)

 ### Activity for Third and Fourth Graders (Steps 1 Through 5) and Fifth Through Eighth Graders (Steps 1 Through 8)

Students will, using two congruent triangles drawn on paper,

1. Cut out the triangle shapes.

For one of the triangle shapes:

2. Find the midpoint of each side by folding.

3. Connect the midpoints by line segments.

4. Cut apart the three smaller triangles.

5. Compare and describe the four triangles, giving reasons for conclusions.

6. Repeat steps 1–5 with another triangle

7. Repeat steps 1–5 with an isosceles triangle

8. Repeat steps 1–5 with an equilateral triangle.

The possibilities for creation of different figures by paper folding seem endless. Children should be encouraged to create their own, to describe and explain what they have done, and to give reasons justifying their results. This is also a good place for incorporating writing in mathematics learning. Students might study origami, which creates geometric figures; learn how to make some of the standard creations; and write instructions for other children to use in repeating them. The process of following instructions carefully and then giving directions clearly and concisely are certainly beneficial in general, as well as in the context of working with mathematical ideas and processes. The next activity moves directly in an intriguing way from plane figures (and an interesting connection between a circle and an equilateral triangle) to solid figures.

Activity for Seventh and Eighth Graders

Provided circular sheets of paper $8\frac{1}{2}$ inches in diameter (the largest circular sheets that can be cut from a sheet of typing paper) students will:

1. Find the center by paper folding (fold in half to create a diameter, then in half again to create a radius and center).

2. Open the folds and refold so that a point on the edge rests on the center.

3. Repeat this fold twice, moving around the circle until a triangle is created.

4. Describe and justify conclusions.

5. Fold vertices of the triangle to the midpoints of the opposite sides.

6. Describe and justify the description of the results.

7. Open the folds and create other folds by folding the vertices to the center.

8. Create a truncated tetrahedron by tucking one vertex into a second over the third.

9. Tape this solid in place.

10. Tape together 20 of these solids to form a class icosahedron. (Students might decorate or sign each of the faces. Many of these could be made for room decorations.)

11. Discuss the reasons why these fit together in this way. (See Fig. 10-5.)

Symmetry

Some feel that symmetry should be studied primarily in art rather than in geometry, but there are many geometric concepts that can be learned and effectively explored in the context of symmetry. Furthermore, symmetry is an integral part of our lives—in the natural world and in the design of many man-made objects. Symmetrical objects are esthetically attractive to most children. Inherent in symmetry is pattern and pattern repetition. This means that there is significant overlap of this field with other mathematics, and that principles learned here can be applied not only in mathematics but in daily life as well. Later, in the study of more advanced mathematics, symmetry is found to be a tool and

FIGURE 10-5 Creating a Tetrahedron

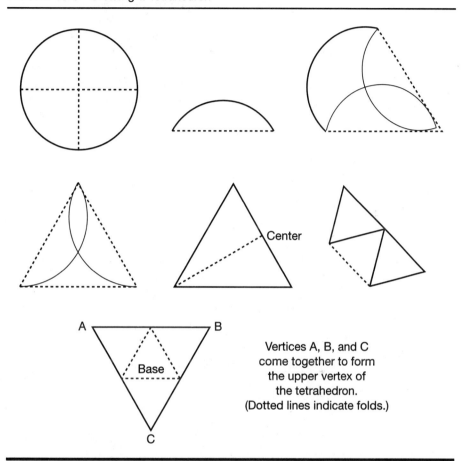

Center

A ——————— B

Base

C

Vertices A, B, and C
come together to form
the upper vertex of
the tetrahedron.
(Dotted lines indicate folds.)

characterization of significant analytical value. An example is in understanding the concept of *congruence* in the formal study of geometry.

Symmetrical patterns in numbers and other symbols provide interesting settings for discovery and exploration. A pattern of particular interest is a palindrome: numbers or words that "read" the same from right to left as they do from left to right. Some palindromic words are: pop, aha, radar, and rotor. ANNA, HANNAH, BOB, and SIRRAH HARRIS (the name of a girl known to the author) are palindromic names.

Palindromic numbers are easy for children to write, and it can be intriguing to experiment with these numbers. Palindromic years children might search for are 1991, 1881, or 2002. They should be asked to write palindromic dates in the form 9/8/89. Do any of them have palindromic birthdates?

In addition to being "read" the same backwards as forward, palindromic symbols in which the first half is the mirror image of the second half should be examined. By this definition, BOB and 404 would not qualify. For these two, the "foldover" equality would require that they be written as BOᗺ and 40⊅. Some palindromic words and numbers that have this additional quality are: OTTO, TOT, 8118, and 101. Children should be asked to find and draw others.

Experimentation with palindromic symbols can enhance problem-solving skills, provide opportunities for discovery, and strengthen the geometric concept of symmetry.

Activity for Fifth Through Eighth Graders

Students will

1. List the numbers of the years since 1800 which were palindromic.

2. Determine what was the last palindromic year and what will be the next.

3. List the next 10 or 20 palindromic years

4. Discuss patterns that seem to be evident.

Activity for Fourth Through Eighth Graders

Students will choose a three-digit number and

1. Write the number.

2. Add, to the original number, a new number which is the original with the digits reversed.

3. Use the result and repeat the process until a palindromic number results.

4. Try a similar process with subtraction, always subtracting the smaller number from the larger.

5. Answer the questions: "Does one of these processes always yield a palindrome?" and "For what kinds of numbers does it not work?"

For seventh and eighth graders,

6. Discuss reasons why the process works.

Activity for Kindergarten, First, and Second Graders

Students will create symmetrical figures using pattern blocks and other manipulatives and, on request, explain or demonstrate why the figures are symmetrical.

In understanding symmetry in figures, students need to learn to identify the *center* line, or *line of symmetry*. From the simplest figures with only one line of symmetry, students should move to considering more complex figures with multiple lines of symmetry.

Activity

Students who are provided with a sheet containing several geometric figures will draw on each figure all the possible lines of symmetry. These drawings are to indicate the location of the line of symmetry only, so they need not be carefully drawn straight line segments.

At the outset, students should not be expected to carefully create the line segments showing the location of the lines of symmetry. Initially it is enough to recognize symmetry, the locations of the lines, and whether there is no line of symmetry. When the idea is well developed, students can explore the different types of symmetry and classify them by type and number. Symmetry can be based on the geometric operations of rotation (circular motion), reflection (flipping over), or translation (sliding) (Dienes, 1967).

Activity for Seventh and Eighth Graders

Students will explore the geometric operations mentioned above and determine whether they are commutative, associative, and whether they have inverses. (It is not necessary to use these terms.)

Figures to use with geometric operations include the regular pentagon, trapezoid, circle, equilateral triangle, isosceles triangle, and square.

Activity for Kindergarten Through Eighth Grades

Students will create symmetrical figures using pattern blocks by:

- placing two or three blocks in the angle made by a folding mirror (folded at about 60°)

- in the foreground of the mirror(s), placing other pattern blocks to duplicate the image seen in the mirror(s).

Three-dimensional as well as two-dimensional designs may be created in this activity.

Activity

Using Miras or similar reflecting devices, children will:

- Draw symmetrical figures with single and multiple lines of symmetry.

- Find lines of symmetry in given geometric figure. (Figures with no lines of symmetry should be included for consideration.)

Tessellations

Another intriguing application of plane geometric figures and certain types of symmetry is in *tessellations*. Tessellations are space-filling curves. Simply put, they are geometrical figures that fit together in repetitious patterns so as to completely fill the plane, leaving no space uncovered. We see them often in architecture and art. Patterns in tiled floor and wall coverings are often tessellations. In art classes and in their own design drawing, students have already made many tessellations, but they may not have recognized the mathematical significance of what they were doing. In this part of the study of geometry, students will have the opportunity to create these designs intentionally, with reference to the geometric properties that allow figures to tessellate.

As always, both examples and nonexamples of tessellating figures should be presented and considered. Obviously equilateral triangles, squares, and some rectangles tessellate. Do all triangles tessellate? What about all rectangles? How can an equilateral triangle or square be modified to make it into a nonregular tessellating figure? Are there classifications of tessellating figures? These questions and many more about tessellations are sources for discovery and inquiry in geometry. (Students often believe that all mathematics has already been discovered long before they came along. This is not true, but hard for students to comprehend as they think of their experiences with arithmetic and algebra. In the fields of symmetry, tessellations, and geometric design, any child can create and invent mathematics that has never been done. This fact should be pointed out to children.)

Some of the pictures of the Dutch painter M.C. Escher that are based on tessellations should be shown to the class. They are fascinating. Children will want to try to duplicate some or at least try to create similar ones. They can explore these and many others using a computer program like Tessellmania. Simple pattern sheets should be provided to children; they can color in portions to make simple tesselations at first and then explore more complex patterns. The computer programs, however, can be used by children to produce tessellations rivaling Escher's. With color software and a color printer, spectacular designs can be created in the classroom. An activity of this kind might well be coordinated with the art department to produce art for a math fair or other community/school event.

Activity for Seventh and Eighth Graders

Students will experiment with creating figures that will tessellate by:

1. Beginning with a square, re-form one of the sides (Fig. 10-6).

2. With care, re-form the opposite side in the same way (Fig. 10-7).

3. Note that multiples of these figures will fit together and cover a surface (tessellate).

4. Continue the process using other parts of the figure (Fig. 10-8).

5. Experiment with other starting figures, equilateral triangles, pentagons, etc.

6. Discuss whether a *regular* polygon must be the starting point.

FIGURE 10-6 Re-form One Side of Square

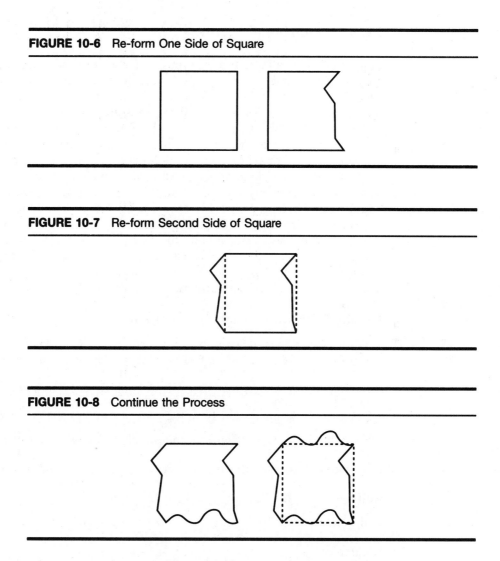

FIGURE 10-7 Re-form Second Side of Square

FIGURE 10-8 Continue the Process

 Activity for Fourth Through Eighth Graders

- Students will use Tessellmania or similar computer program to create and decorate tessellations.

- If the computer program is not available, students will create tessellations by appropriate modifications of equilateral triangles or squares, or by finding other interfacing space filling curves.

- Students will find examples of tessellations in art, advertising, and architecture (Giganti, 1990).

Three-Dimensional Figures

As suggested, it is natural at a number of points to move from two-dimensional to three-dimensional figures. In fact, it is also appropriate to start with three-dimensional figures and shapes for some teaching in geometry. After all, objects in the children's daily environments are three dimensional. It is important that they be able to identify, describe, and interact with many of the objects they encounter. In addition, many common three-dimensional objects can be used to illustrate one- and two-dimensional concepts. Teaching should begin with familiar three-dimensional shapes, including cubical blocks, rectangular blocks, spheres (balls), cones, ellipsoids (footballs), hemispheres, and cylinders; in short, the shapes in a set of blocks. It is assumed that children will have played with blocks, configuring them in various ways and building with them. A teacher should not attempt to classify and name all of them with technical names such as "truncated cones," etc. Only those with common uses and common names should be dealt with formally. Early activities involving classification and patterning are important (Brahier, 1997).

Activity for Kindergarten Through Third Grades

Children will sit in a circle on the floor. Using pattern blocks they will create a circle of pattern blocks, placing them one after another and using such rules as:

- The next block must differ from the previous in one characteristic.

- The next block must differ from the previous in two characteristics.

- The next block must differ from the previous in three characteristics, etc.

(Note: Characteristics include thickness, size, color, two-dimensional shape.)

Activity for Fifth Through Eighth Grades

Children will learn to draw, in perspective, figures representing:

1. Cube

2. Rectangular solid

3. Cylinder

4. Cubes stacked in stair steps

FIGURE 10-9   Two Ways to Draw a Cube

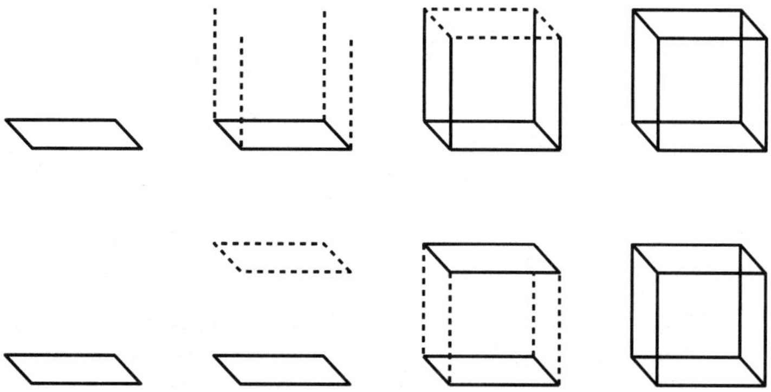

FIGURE 10-10   Stacked Blocks Figures

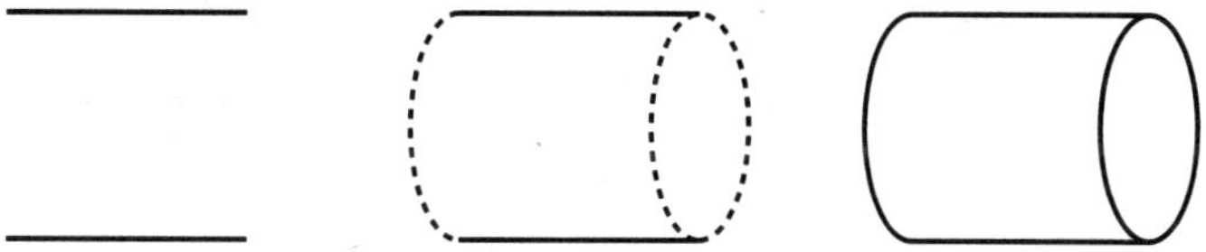

FIGURE 10-11   Drawing Stacked Cubes

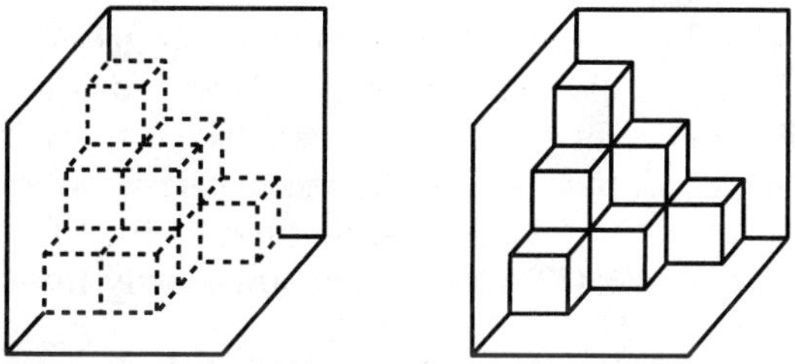

Activity for Kindergarten Through Eighth Grade Students: (Simpler Figures for Younger Children)

Children will construct a variety of rectangular solids and combinations of rectangular solids using Cuisennaire rods or base 10 blocks and duplicating figures such as those shown in Figure 10-12 (a and b).

FIGURE 10-12a Stacked Blocks Figures

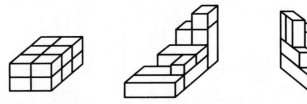

FIGURE 10-12b Figures Combining Geometric Solids

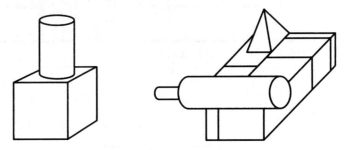

If the activity in Figure 10-12 was not continued into three dimensions, continuing it could be a part of working with three-dimensional concepts. The activity can be extended to illustrate the combination of solid shapes to create others. Of special interest are regular geometric solids—the *regular* polyhedra. These are also known as the *Platonic* solids, named because the philosopher Plato experimented with them. The activity in Figure 10-12 resulted in one of them, an icosahedron (20 faces, each identical to the others). The others are: tetrahedron (4 faces), hexahedron (cube, 6 faces), octahedron (8 faces), and dodecahedron (12 faces). There are exactly five—no more.

Activity for Seventh and Eighth Graders

Students will examine the five regular polyhedra, and:

1. Create charts listing numbers of edges, faces, vertices, and faces at a vertex.

2. Discuss and identify patterns in the chart.

3. Extend the chart to include nonregular polyhedra.

4. Attempt to discover ways to construct each regular polyhedron (including hexaminoes which can be folded to create cubes).

Summary

The interrelationships between geometry and measurement were noted and topological considerations were detailed. It was noted that there is a need to teach beyond names for shapes. The methods of formalizing geometric concepts were shown. Terminology was described as a critical aspect of teaching geometry. Problem solving in geometry and the creation of geometric shapes and ideas by children was given significant attention. Activities involving manipulatives and paper folding were suggested. Finally, symmetry and tessellations and three-dimensional figures were discussed.

Exercises

1. Prepare a report describing symmetry in the daily lives of children. Give examples that can be used with a class to motivate and enable them to grasp the concept.

2. a) Bring to class examples and pictures of Escher's work and other examples of tessellations.
   b) Explain to the class how tessellations may be created by dual modifications on the sides of regular geometric shapes.

3. Prove that there are exactly five regular polyhedra and explain the proof in writing and to the class.

4. Design a lesson to teach topological concepts using the Mobius band and other twisted bands.

5. Design a lesson using *Tangrams* to teach to a specific geometric objective other than creating figures representing animals, etc.

6. Describe to the class the uses of pentaminoes in teaching geometry.

7. Report on the work of Van Hiele and its implications for teaching geometry in elementary and middle school.

References

Brahier, Daniel, and Bill Speer (1997, September 3). Worthwhile tasks: Exploring mathematical connections through geometrical solids. *Mathematics Teaching in the Middle School*, 20–28.

Burger, William F. (1985, February). Geometry. *Arithmetic Teacher*, 32(6), 52–56.

Cruikshank, Douglas E., and John McGovern. (1977, October). Math projects build skills. *Instructor*, 87(3), 194–198.

Dienes, Z. P., and E. W. Golding (1967). *Geometry Through Transformations: 1. Geometry of Distortion*. New York: Herder & Herder.

Giganti, Paul Jr., and Mary Jo Cittadino. (1990, March). The Art of Tessellation. *Arithmetic Teacher*, 37(7), 6–16.

Greeley, Nansee, and Theresa Reardon Offerman (1997, March/April). Now and then: Measuring angles in physical therapy. *Mathematics Teaching in the Middle School*, 2(5), 338–343.

National Council of Teachers of Mathematics. (1989). *Curriculum and Evaluation Standards for School Mathematics*, 210–214.

Paas, Fred G. W. C., and Jeroen J. G. Van Merrienboer (1994, March). Variability of worked examples and transfer of geometrical problem-solving skills: A cognitive-load approach. *Journal of Educational Psychology*, 86(1), 122–133.

Piaget, Jean, Barbel Inhelder, and Alina Szemiuska. (1960). *The Child's Conception of Geometry*. New York: Basic Books.

Olson, Melfried. (1997, December). How many rectangles. *Teaching Children Mathematics*. 4(4).

Suydam, Marilyn N. (1984, November). Attitudes towards mathematics. *Arithmetic Teacher*, 32(3), 12.

Thompson, Charles S., and John Van deWalle (1985, April). Learning about rules and measuring. *Arithmetic Teacher*, 32(8), 8–12.

Yusuf, Mian Muhammad. (1994). Cognition of fundamental concepts in geometry. *Journal of Educational Computing Research*, 10(4), 349–371.

🔲 Suggested Readings

Bearden, Donna, Kathleen Martin, and James H. Muller (1983). *The Turtle's Sourcebook*. Reston, VA: Reston Publishing.

Bennett, Albert, Eugene Maier, and L. Ted (1987). *Math and the Mind's Eye: 1. Seeing Mathematical Relationships*. Salem, OR: Math Learning Center.

———. (1987). *Math and the Mind's Eye: V. Looking at Geometry*. Salem, OR: Math Learning Center.

Burger, William F., and J. Michael Shaughnessy. (1986, January). Characterizing the van Hiele levels of development in geometry. *Journal for Research in Mathematics Education*, 17(1), 31–48.

Copeland, Richard W. (1984). *How Children Learn Mathematics*. Upper Saddle River, NJ: Merrill/Prentice Hall.

Cowan, Richard A. (1977, March). Pentominoes for fun learning. *The Arithmetic Teacher*, 24(3), 188–190.

Fouke, George R. (1974). *A First Book of Space*. San Francisco: Western.

Fuys, David. (1985, August). Van Hiele levels of thinking in geometry. *Education and Urban Society*, 17(4), 447–462.

Johnson-Gentile, Kay, Douglas H. Clements, and Michael T. Batista (1994). Effects of computer and noncomputer environments on students' conceptualizations of geometric motions. *Journal of Educational Computing Research*, 11(2), 121–140.

Schiddell, Betty L., Corinna A. Ethington (1994, Spring). Teaching of geometry in the eighth grade mathematics curriculum: Findings from the Second International Mathematics Study. *Focus on Learning Problems in Mathematics*, 16(2), 51–61.

Shroyer, Janet, and William Fitzgerald (1986). *Mouse and Elephant: Measuring Growth.* Menlo Park, CA: Addison-Wesley.

Sime, Mary. (1973). *A Child's Eye View.* New York: Harper & Row.

Varma, Ved P., and Phillip Williams, Eds. (1976). *Piaget, Psychology and Education.* Itasca, IL: F. E. Peacock.

Zech, Linda, et. al. (1994, November–December). Power on! Bringing geometry into the classroom with videodisc technology. *Mathematics Teaching in the Middle School*, 1(3), 228–233.

Teaching Measurement

One of the children's problems: Natalie can't make a ruler work to measure her math book accurately.

Teacher's problem: There are few area measurement examples in the children's lives. (Measuring the area of the classroom floor seems of little interest.)

🔲 Understanding the Problem

In our technically oriented society, measurement is an integral part of our lives. We measure distance, surface covering, and amounts of substances, and we must do so with some awareness of the accuracy appropriate to the entities being measured. The concept of units of measure must be well established because usually we need to communicate information about that measurement.

In fact, one way of looking at mathematics in a broad sense is to think of it as a system for measurement. The count (census) of a group of people or collection of objects is a measure of that set. The operations can be thought of as shortcuts to counting. Fractions are used to measure parts of wholes; nonrational numbers are needed when the measures of lines of certain lengths (the circumference of a circle of diameter 1 unit, and the length of the diagonal of a square of side 1 unit) are needed. A set of numbers is measured in many different ways, including by computing statistics such as mean, range, and variance.

Many young people leave school with inadequate measurement skills. During their school years they were not impressed with the importance of learning to measure accurately. They did not practice the measuring processes or acquire the measurement concepts they should have been using. One source of difficulty is that children are not engaged in measurement from the beginning of their schooling. Rudimentary measuring must be started in kindergarten, with teachers using the terms *to measure* and *measuring*, and involving children in measurement tasks. Teachers should convey to children that an important goal of mathematics learning (and especially learning to measure) is to understand, describe, and cope competently with the real world of our culture and society. Furthermore, according to Piaget, Inhelder, and Szeminska, "Operations involved in measurement are so concrete that they have their roots in perceptual activity (visual estimates of size, etc.) and at the same time so complex that they are not fully elaborated until sometime between the ages of 8 and 11" (Piaget, Inhelder, & Szeminska, 1960).

🔲 Solving the Problem

Understanding measurement begins with simple concepts that are built on to become more complex. Children's concepts of measurement begin with descriptive comparisons such as, "This is bigger than that," and "That's too heavy." These ideas are tied closely to terminology and discovery as children experiment with language, their bodies, and manipulatives. Small children should be guided to describe real situations with the following terms:

taller—shorter	longer—shorter
wider—narrower	more—less
more—fewer	heavier—lighter
higher—lower	deeper—shallower

Though there is value for young children in knowing the words *bigger*, *smaller*, *larger*, and *littler*, they should gradually replace these ambiguous terms with more precise vocabulary such as that suggested in the preceding list.

Example

A pre-conservation child will say container A is bigger than container B because A is taller than B (Fig. 11-1).

FIGURE 11-1 Cylindrical Containers for Volume Comparison

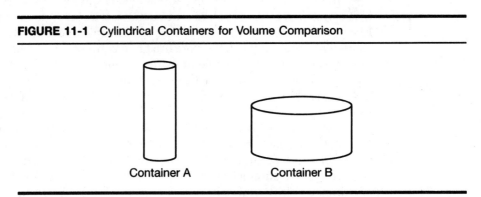

Container A   Container B

Measurement tasks should gradually become more complex so that by grade 3, children are required to consider two and three dimensions and make such statements as, "The red can is taller than the blue can but not as wide as the blue can," or "This box is longer and wider, but not as deep as that one."

Ample experience should be provided children in pouring, filling, and comparing containers using sand, rice, and water. During prekindergarten through the first grade, random experiences like these form the basis for developing measurement concepts. Beginning in the first grade, though, the teacher will help children start to formalize and structure these activities. These experiences should not be left to chance. It is important for the teacher to ask for discussion, description, and answers to questions: "Will this box shape hold more sand than that cylinder?"; "Why do you think so?"; "If you fill this bucket from that box, will you have some left over?"; "A little or a lot left over?" (NCTM, 1989).

Units

Nonstandard units such as "the number of Kelly's shoes it would take to reach across the room," and "The number of Teri's hand-spans to reach across the desk," can and should be used by young children. They can be encouraged to invent their own measuring units by using objects readily at hand. These might be pencils, books, finger-widths, etc. In the process of these informal measurements, children should be further encouraged to note and discuss the variability in the count of units when different sized units are used. It is especially important for children to see that smaller units result in larger counts and vice versa. Discussion and debate should also lead the students toward reasons for using standard units.

The *formal* use of standard units should be delayed until the third or fourth grade. Prior to that time, children will have heard and may even use, with fair accuracy, the terms *centimeter, inch, foot, meter, yard, gallon,* and *liter.* When they are to be learned formally, attention will have to be given to making them precise and uniform in the child's mental construction of the ideas. Experiments with nonstandard units (different children's feet, for example) and with standard units (feet) to measure the width of the classroom and other objects will help to illustrate the value of standard units. A teacher should set up a variety of sets of circumstances (as closely related to children's lives as possible) which illustrate misunderstanding or the difficulty of communicating a description to someone else when units are not standard.

The approach to teaching the standard units mentioned above should not be through memorization of the terms. Conversions (relationships such as 12 inches equal 1 foot, 3 feet equals 1 yard, etc.) should not be mentioned too early. Unit interrelationships should be studied later. To introduce interrelationships before the idea of a measuring unit is well established will cause confusion and make both difficult to construct. Teachers should incorporate, in lessons on measurement, multiple examples of children using the units under consideration in their daily lives (Kaster, 1989).

Examples

- Children should classify their bicycles as 20", 24", or 27" and see that this is a measure of the wheel diameter.

- Children should know some distances in miles: home to town, home to school, etc. They should make understandable comparisons with an obvious distance such as 1 mile from school to the highway.

- By comparison with 2-liter cola bottles or 12-ounce cola cans, children should state whether quantities of liquid in other containers are more or less than in the cola container.

- Gallon, half-gallon, quart, pint, and half-pint containers for milk should be used for comparisons also. "Does a half-pint container for milk hold more than a pop can?"

The teacher should help each child identify some part of his or her body or some familiar object to represent particular units. A part of a finger might be very close to an inch long. Wrist to elbow might closely approximate 1 foot. Two 2-liter bottles would contain about 1 gallon of liquid, etc. Initially, only these few units should be taught. These occur in children's daily lives, while others do not and should be left until they are a more direct part of the children's lives or are required for science classes or more advanced mathematics.

In the process of describing lengths, areas, and volumes, it will be helpful to work on the correct use of the general words *number* and *amount*. Thus, we don't say, ". . . the amount of people in the room . . ."; we say, ". . . the number of people in the room. . . ." *Amount* is usually used for quantities of non-discrete substances such as sand, water, and flour while *number* is used for discrete objects. Children will learn, by appropriate and repetitive use, to say, "amount of sand" and "number of crayons," etc.

A crucial aspect of teaching measuring units is making clear that a unit does not vary because of position or environment. An inch is always an inch. This is not obvious to young children because they are not yet conservers. The reasons for having standard units for various measuring tasks should be explained. Children may not wholly grasp the meaning and significance of being able to make consistent, accurate measurements and to communicate precise information to others, but these aspects of the concept will begin to be part of their construct of unit. The operative method continues to be providing as many real-life experiences as possible in measuring with units, both standard and nonstandard. Teachers should make opportunities to discuss with students the use of standard and nonstandard units. When is it best to use nonstandard units and when is it best to use only standard units?

Measurement

Through experiences with different types of measurement activities involving measuring certain dimensions of different objects and making different measures on a given object, children begin to develop the concept of measurement if they are guided by the teacher. Critical aspects of the concept are:

- Solid objects of rigid material do not change in measurement.

- Measurement is comparison of a characteristic of an object with a single specified unit.

- Measurement results can be found by direct or indirect comparison of the measured object and the measuring units.

- Measuring may be done by measuring a small part and using computation to learn the desired measure.

- Measuring tools may be used, in place of unit-sized objects, for comparison purposes.

- Measurement of non-discrete objects and materials involves approximation.

- The level of accuracy is determined by the measurer and depends on the instrument being used.

- Different units may be used to measure a given dimension of an object.

- Units are chosen for convenience, precision, personal preference, or ease of communication.

The first measuring that makes sense to children are measurements of length, volume, and weight. These should involve only the units mentioned above; volume measure units should *not* include cubic inches, cubic centimeters, etc. until sixth grade. Area is also not measured until later when it is possible to use square inches, square meters, and other similar units. An exception to this might be in farming communities where many children know about acres and sections of land.

Activity for Kindergarten and First Grade

1. Students will examine two unmarked sticks of the same length, which are positioned as shown (Fig. 11-2).

2. They will be asked if they are the same length. The answer will likely be that they are.

3. The sticks will then be placed successively in different orientations and the question asked again. If the answer is no for one of the positions, the question should be posed in other ways, such as, "Could you place them next to each other and see if they are the same length?"

4. The teacher asks why they are different.

FIGURE 11-2 Comparing Lengths

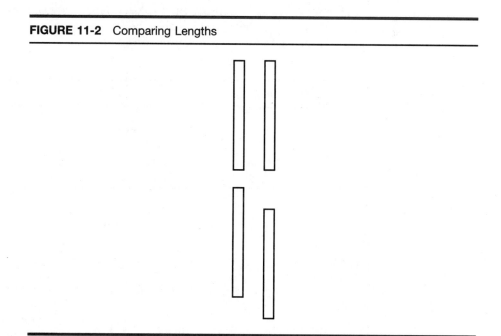

Activities such as that above should be done repeatedly with different rigid objects until it is clear that a child is developing conservation. In transitional stages, children will believe that some types of objects, maybe certain colored objects, have invariant measure while others don't. Conservation is a developmental stage that can't be forced through practice or memorization. It comes only as a child matures psychologically. Teachers should not force measurement learning on children who are not conservers. Measurement is meaningless for nonconservers, and they will resort to random guessing or memorization to try to cope with measurement tasks.

Comparison Using Units

Activity for Grades 4 Through 8

Teachers and students in two classrooms will arrange to create a poster or design on a poster board, each class working from written instructions sent from the other class. Each class will first design a not-too-complex geometrical figure covering most of a piece of tag board, then measure using nonstandard units (objects, children's hands) and exchange communication of those measures with the other class, who will, using the instructions, recreate the design without having seen it. (The differences between the original and copy may be striking and should be discussed along with the reasons for them.)

To give further emphasis to measurement skills and the importance of precision in the use of units and in communication, the activity should be repeated using standard units. This should enable the creation of a reasonably accurate copy to contrast with the first. A sample design is shown in Figure 11-3.

FIGURE 11-3 Sample Design

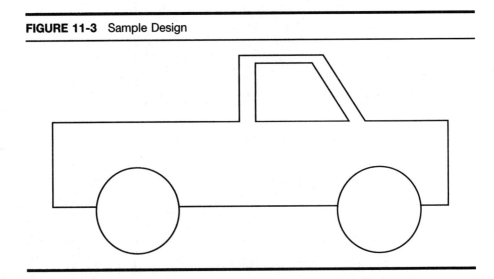

Direct and Indirect Measurement

Direct measurement means applying a measuring instrument to the object to be measured.

Examples

- Using a tape measure by applying it to the edge of a chalkboard

- Counting the number of square foot tiles on a floor

- Noting the quart markings and the level of water poured into a pitcher

Indirect measurement is accomplished by comparing a dimension of an object with an object of known measurement, when the object to be measured is inaccessible in some way.

Examples Include

- Measuring the height of a tree by measuring comparable shadow length and using a ratio

- Measuring a shoe size by trying it on and noting the feel in comparison with the feel of a shoe of known size

- Measuring the distance between two places by noting the time taken to drive between them when traveling at 50 mph

- Measuring temperature by noting the height of a column of mercury

Both direct and indirect measurement should be practiced and the benefits and drawbacks of each discussed, along with the advantages of each and sets of circumstances which would preclude one or the other being used. If children are given examples of indirect measurement, they will be able to think of many other indirect measurement instances.

Activity

Students will:

- Measure the length and width of a classroom directly, comparing length and width to marks on a 50-foot tape measure. (direct)

- Measure the length and width of a classroom by measuring one of the tiles (9″ × 9″, or 12″ × 12″ typically) or parts of the floor design and use multiplication and/or adding to obtain a measure. (indirect)

- Compare results from the first activity and the second activity.

- Discuss reasons for discrepancies.

- Decide how to measure length and width of the classroom ceiling. (indirect)

- Discuss how to apply the method to find the length of the block if the divisions in the sidewalk are uniform (or another real-life measurement where the 50-foot tape could not be directly applied, such as the height of an antenna tower or of a two- or three-story building made of a number of uniform small sections). (indirect)

The teacher should help children understand that these are not magical processes. We do what is feasible and what makes sense. For example, when we need to know measurements of certain objects and cannot measure directly, we find ways to use measures of other objects and/or mathematical computation to make comparisons and to estimate.

Measuring Tools

The process of measuring often involves using a measuring tool. The tool is an object (like a rod or container) with markings on it, each of which indicates a number or fraction of units. The design of the tool is dependent on the nature of the objects typically requiring measurement. For example, a ruler or a meter stick is not easily used to measure the diameter or circumference of a circular object, but Vernier calipers are very useful for measuring diameter, and a flexible tape measure can be used to measure circumference.

Children need experience with various measuring instruments and the opportunity to choose appropriate devices. The decision about which device to use should not be based on memorization but rather on what makes sense and what works. To accomplish this a teacher should plan activities such as the following:

Activities for Fourth Through Sixth Graders

Children will measure their waist sizes (or head circumferences) and record their results by using:

- Rulers or meter sticks.

- Cubic centimeter blocks and/or C-rods.

- A shoe.

- A cloth tape measure.

- Children will discuss the different results and state reasons for using the cloth tape.

As with any tool, proper use must be learned. Children do not automatically know how to use devices, even as simple as a ruler, correctly. Among the tool-use skills children must be taught specifically are:

1. Choosing the correct tool with respect to application and units.

2. Knowing how to apply the tool and read scales.

3. Knowing how to modify the use of a tool to fit indirect application.

Choosing appropriate tools with regard to application has already been mentioned. With experimentation students will discover (through experience with some guidance) that some manipulatives may be used helpfully in a number of different measurement tasks. The cubic centimeter blocks from a C-rod set, for example, can be neatly used for length measure (up to 20 cm) and for area and volume measures as well. One reason they are so convenient is that the cubes contain all three units: cm, cm², and cm³, and can be directly applied to many measurement situations (Lindquist, 1989).

Difficulties with Tools

Rulers

1. Children do not line up rulers with the *0* point at the measurement beginning point.

2. Old rulers have the *0* point indented 1/8-inch from the end, and children line up the end of the ruler.

3. Children sometimes line up with *1* on the ruler, thinking they should begin with *1*, not *0*. (Counting always begins with 1.)

4. Many rulers have no *0* on them if the ends of the rulers themselves are at *0*, and children are reluctant to line up with a nonnumbered point.

5. For numbers of units children often count the whole number marks on the ruler rather than the unit spacing between whole number markings.

6. Children are uncertain which of the whole number marks to cite when the point on the object does not fall on or very near the whole number mark on the ruler.

Containers

1. Children may not keep the container level or may read the scale at an angle.

2. Children read only the whole number scale markings not recognizing the starting point.

3. Children assume that the top of the container is a measurement point when the scale may end below that.

4. Children are uncertain when the substance level falls between whole number scale marks.

5. Children do not compensate or modify the method when the substance is in irregular chunks and will not "fit" the container.

As children practice measuring, the teacher should look for these or other difficulties. When errors are observed, they can be corrected for the individual student; the teacher can explain to the class how those errors can be prevented. It is advisable for the teacher to measure the objects in advance so that student errors are more easily detected. For individual students experiencing many difficulties, and when the nature of the difficulties is not immediately apparent, an application of the Math Assessment and Diagnosis Scheme (MADS) may assist the teacher in analysis.

Teachers should schedule many measurement activities, preferably in the context of lessons in science, fractions, problem solving, and social studies. All of these contain activities in which these various facets of measurement difficulties will be encountered and can be corrected so that proper methods can be practiced.

Estimation

Because much of children's experience in mathematics is with exactly correct computation results (one exact result exists), students frequently come to measurement tasks believing that measurement results must be exact. This belief can cause bewilderment when *reading points* do not coincide exactly. Part of measurement teaching is to build the concept of measurement as an estimation and an approximation. There are actually two different uses of the word *estimation* in connection with measurement.

- Accuracy: Each measurement is an estimation which is based on a level of accuracy required by the object being measured and the units being used.

- Judgment: In the absence of knowledge of a measurement and/or of a measuring instrument, a measurer makes an educated judgment about a measurement value.

Accurate estimation is an integral part of each measurement. Students must learn that measurement values are relative to some standard or other measure. A measurement value statement must be accompanied by a statement such as "to the nearest inch" or "to the nearest cubic centimeter" in order for the measurement to have real value. The student must decide how close the measurement needs to be and which units will enable the necessary precision. Examples and tasks should be given to the students to encourage and demonstrate the necessity of making these decisions.

Examples and Activities for Grades 4 Through 8

- Students in pairs, will, in each group (the As or the Bs), measure items in the classroom. The As will use the units feet or meters, and the Bs will use inches or centimeters. Each student pair will record results on a record sheet.

- In pairs the students will compare their results, discuss any differences, decide on which measurements are most accurate, and write the reasons for their conclusions. (Comparable tasks could use other units and measure area or volume.)

Judgement Estimation

In life outside school, a person is called upon to make measurement estimates as frequently as to make direct measurement. Estimating should be given as much attention as is given to direct measurement. Drivers of cars must estimate distance between cars in traffic and lengths of parking spaces. Persons who make crafts, do creative hobby work, or cook all profit from the ability to estimate. People who engage in sports or work in art also must estimate effectively. On the playground, children learn to judge how far the ball is hit or how high a ball will bounce.

Activity for Third Through Eighth Graders

Students will illustrate and discuss judgment estimations they make while playing ball, riding bikes, and doing other activities. The discussion should include statements describing how they arrive at those judgments and what units they use.

This sort of estimation involves making an educated guess about a measurement based on visualizing comparisons, sometimes with items in the environment and sometimes with mental images alone. Practice makes perfect here, too. Those who are good at making measurement estimates have practiced extensively. There are a few estimates that all children should learn to make; the rest may be relegated to areas where there is repeated need for the particular kinds of estimates. For example, a golfer should become an expert at estimating distances in yards between points on a course from under 10 yards to 500 or 600 yards. A carpenter must estimate board lengths and widths, usually in inches from 1/16 of an inch to 20 or 30 feet.

A student should learn to estimate lengths and distances from a fraction of an inch (e.g., $1/4$-, $1/2$-, and $3/4$-inch) to about 10 feet; 1 cm, 1 mm, $1/4$-mile, $1/2$-mile, and 1 mile; square foot, square yard, square centimeter; cubic centimeter, cubic inch, cubic foot, cubic yard; cup, gallon, liter, quart ($1/4$ gallon), pint. To learn these (and perhaps others in certain communities such as rural farm communities where students might learn to estimate acre and section), the students must be provided many activities both in math class and in the context of other studies to make, to check, and to refine estimates.

Relative Measures

Before they develop a full understanding of the relationships among measures in one-, two-, and three-dimensional settings, students typically have wrong impressions which lead to inadequate measuring. A familiar example is the child who believes that a square yard is equivalent to three square feet since a yard is equivalent to three feet. Figures and manipulatives should be used generously to correct these wrong ideas and establish the concepts.

 Example

(1 square yard is equivalent to $3 \times 3 = 9$ square feet.)

FIGURE 11-4 One Square Yard

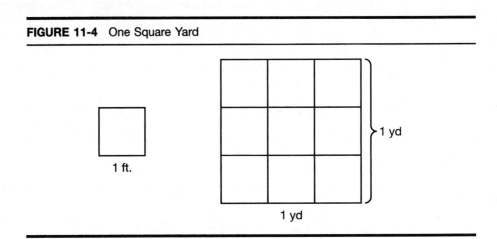

1 ft.

1 yd

1 yd

It is perhaps more difficult to counter the idea that two distances containing the same length would surround different areas or that two surfaces of the same area could enclose different volumes.

 Activities for Grades 5 through 8

Students will create and measure different areas using given numbers of cc blocks to measure a given perimeter.

FIGURE 11-5 Same Perimeter, Different Areas

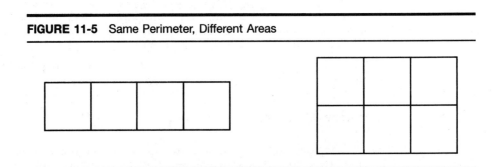

Example

Perimeter = 10 cm

Area 4 sq. cm   Area 6 sq. cm

Students will reverse the process and consider given area configurations and the related perimeters.

FIGURE 11-6 Same Area, Different Perimeters

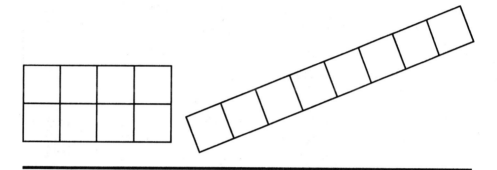

 Example

Area 8 sq. cm

Perimeter 12 cm   Perimeter 18 cm

 Advanced Activity for Seventh and Eighth Graders

By explaining area-perimeter combinations, students will discover the nature of shapes with maximum area, with fixed perimeters. They will discuss the implications for cost in producing products, fencing areas, or creating borders such as picture frames.

 Activity for Grades 6 through 8

Students will:

1. Cut standard sheets (8 $1/2$" × 11") in half (creating 8 $1/2$" × 5$1/2$" sheets).

2. With one-half sheet, create a cylinder 8 $1/2$" tall and with the other a cylinder 5 $1/2$" tall.

3. Note the equal surface areas and discuss whether the volumes are equal.

4. Stand the taller cylinder on end and fill it with rice.

5. Slide the wider cylinder down over the other, resting it on the table, too.

6. Lift out the narrower cylinder, allowing the rice to flow into the wider cylinder.

7. Discuss the difference in volumes and record the reasons for differences.

Activity for Grades 5 Through 8

Students will:

- Create rectangular solids using C-rods, chart for each length, width, height, surface area, and volume.

- Repeat the process after doubling each of the three measurements (length, width, height) in creating another rectangular solid.

- Repeat with other configurations.

- Draw conclusions and give reasons in writing.

These activities, variations on them, and many others (detailed in various activity books and the teacher's handbooks) are necessary to provide children with the material for building full concepts of measuring in one, two, and three dimensions and of the interrelationships among the units and techniques for each of the three.

Advanced Activity for Seventh and Eighth Graders

Students will measure the thickness of a piece of notebook paper by measuring the thickness of a stack of notebook papers and dividing (using calculators). Students will discuss the technique and how to determine accuracy.

Time Measurement

Two aspects of time measurement to be taught are telling time and noting time duration. Children begin to catch on to the idea of telling time using a moving-hands clock in kindergarten and first and second grades. This gradually forming understanding is built on repeated reference to the clock, using the positions of the hands for hours and minutes. Although children may be able to say the numbers they see on a digital clock before this time, they are usually not telling time. There is general agreement that moving-hands clocks should be used to teach telling time and that when that has been learned, digital clocks and watches can be used. Having learned to tell time on moving-hands clocks, children will have no difficulty using digital clocks.

Among the reasons for using the circular clock to help in teaching time measurement are:

- Children can see movement of the hands and connect that with elapsed time.

- The hour values are indicated and can be seen in relation to each other.

- The 5-minute divisions can be seen and time accurate to 5 minutes can be measured.

- Counting by 5s can be used.

- The base 12 or mod-12 nature of telling time can be seen on the clock face as the hands move past 12 to 1.

These facets of telling time and evaluating elapsed time and time duration cannot be easily detected on a digital clock.

Difficulties with Time Measurement

The preceding list suggests some aspects of time measure which make it difficult to learn. Among them are:

- Time is measured using a mixture of base 12 and base 60 systems (and when extended to days, months, and years, it uses base 4, 7, 365 and 28, 29, 30 and 31 systems).

- Time is measured indirectly—the movement of the sun, hands on a clock face, digits changing in a display, changing seasons, etc.

- Time is an abstract concept.

- A person's understanding of elapsed time is greatly influenced by concurrent events and changes in situations.

- Clocks come in all sorts of styles and designs—some with all 12 numerals (some Roman numerals), others with only 12, 3, 6, and 9 numerals, and still others with no numerals at all.

- Different phrases can be used for the same time (6:45, a quarter to 7).

- Fraction terminology is used early (quarter after).

Teaching Time Measurement

As with teaching other measurement, teaching time measurement requires hands-on repetitive experimentation. Catalogs offer multiple clock-face manipulatives to use in the classroom. The better ones (and more expensive models) have the hands geared together so that rotating the minute hand one full revolution causes the hour hand to move from one hour to the next. This is more realistic than a model with independent hands, but for kindergarten, first, and second grade children, not necessary. Children should answer questions about the time indicated on the clock, record their responses, and starting with hour values, move to the identification of *quarter to, quarter after, half past*, etc. and use these common phrases. They should also be taught to *set* the clocks according to given instructions.

Activity for Fourth Through Eighth Grades

Students will learn to set the time on a VCR or other digital clock device.

Opportunities during the school day to tell time and to measure length of time should be used to help in learning time measure. The teacher should often ask questions such as, "It's now 10:30; we go to recess at 10:45; where will the clock hands be then?" "How many minutes is it until then? How would you describe how long that is?" "If you ride in a car in town how far could you get in 15 minutes?" The questions need to be correlated to the grade level and knowledge of the children.

Time Duration

Time duration is difficult to teach because circumstances vary so much from situation to situation. There are, however, several aspects of children's lives at school and at home in which elapsed time is important. Among events that will help children begin to understand time duration are:

Elapsed time for:

- eating (a hamburger, pizza, full meal)
- the school bus ride
- a movie/video/tv show
- a ball game (including quarters in a basketball game)
- walking a mile, running a mile (and other distances)
- sleep
- various classes at school
- recess

Longer times:

- a baby to be born
- a chicken to hatch
- bean plants to grow 6" high
- winter
- growing an inch

Activity for Third Through Eighth Grades

Students will make charts or graphs showing events requiring various lengths lengths of elapsed time.

Again, the teacher must incorporate practice in using these concepts until the students know how to measure elapsed time in a variety of practical settings.

Activity for Sixth Through Eighth Graders

Students will sit quietly with their eyes closed and hold up their hands when a second (5 seconds, 10 seconds, $\frac{1}{2}$-minute, and a minute) has passed.

Activity for Sixth Through Eighth Grades

1. Students will discuss in groups and record their ideas of how much time is required to:

   - Drive between two familiar cities, 1 hour to 2 hours apart.

   - Run a mile; run a marathon.

   - Walk a mile.

   - Run 100 yards.

   - Fly in an airplane from New York to Los Angeles; drive from New York to Los Angeles.

   - Other events (fly to the moon, Venus, etc.)

2. Students will research using books, the Internet (if available), or knowledgeable adults and discover reasonably accurate times for the events listed above.

3. Students will use stopwatches to time themselves running 100 yards (or other distances) and project those values to running or walking a mile.

Obviously there are many significant connections between this part of mathematical learning and science and social studies classes. These connections should be capitalized upon to make this topic very practical and real to students at all levels.

Measuring Weight

Weight is also an abstract idea and must be measured indirectly by comparison with known weights or by reading the scale on a weighing device. The attribute of weight is an important descriptive characteristic. Our groceries, produce, and other objects are mostly in containers with weight labels attached. Nowadays, very few homes contain weighing devices other than bathroom scales for weighing members of the family. This means that, other than as preparation for working in science classes (chemistry and physics), there is no need to emphasize learning to weigh objects using weight-measuring devices. In fact, teaching the use of weight-measuring devices is better left to science classes where the equipment is available and specific instruction can be provided. The use of beam balances and other weighing devices should be part of the process of learning weight measurement concepts rather than the focus of the teaching in mathematics.

Teaching about weight in mathematics class should focus not on weighing things but on the ideas of weight units and the mathematical aspects of weight measure, such as numerical comparisons, estimation, and the multiplicative nature of weight and distance on beam balances. Initially, weight measurement also should not focus on numerical values but rather on comparisons, the critical attributes of *heavy* versus *light* objects. Children's development of weight measurement concepts depends upon their being conservers (Shroyer, 1986).

 ## Activity for Kindergarten Through 3rd Grade

Children will be given balls of clay which are about the same size and a two-pan balance beam. They will:

1. Be asked to say which ball is heavier.

2. Take clay off the heavier one until they think they're about the same weight.

3. Flatten one ball to a pancake and roll the other into a long cylinder.

4. Be asked if one is heavier or if they weigh the same.

5. Be asked to check their answers.

Preconservers believe that shape, color, and orientation can change weight. In the minds of young children texture and appearance are also important factors to consider when weighing.

The use of a balance for weighing is not as simple as one might think, because of the multiplicative relationship between distance from the fulcrum and weight at that position. Using a balance beam (recommended manipulative for each math classroom), a teacher can readily integrate practice with multiplication ideas in a practical setting.

 ## Example

Using a balance beam, with pans that are moveable along the beam, and uniform objects such as pennies, counters, markers, etc., students will demonstrate that equal weights at equal distances balance; two weights at half the distance balance one weight at a given distance, and four at one-quarter the distance balance one at the full distance, etc.

Units of Weight

After experimentation, the concept of weight units needs to be formally constructed. It must be remembered that children (and many adults), although they use the terms for units (pounds, ounces, kilograms, grams, ton), frequently may not have a fully developed unit concept. They may be confused by such riddle questions as: "Which weighs more, a pound of feathers or a pound of lead?" Multiple experiences and examination of weights of different kinds of objects with different measuring devices (balance beam, two-pan balance, one-pan scale, and spring scale) must be a part of learning unit concepts. Part of this experimentation should focus on estimating weights of entities common in the lives of children.

Advanced Activity

Students will construct and calibrate their own weighing devices, capable of weighing up to 2 pounds (or kg).

Weighing Techniques

Techniques such as those involved in dimensional measurement can also be used, and should be taught in connection with weighing. Among them are:

- Comparison with known weight using a balance

- Consideration of environmental factors.

- Weighing parts and adding or multiplying

- Using appropriate or available tools

Activities

Students will "weigh" the following:

- A small brick building's walls by considering the weight of one brick and using computation

- An object by suspending it from a spring scale

- The same object suspended from the spring scale but with the object submerged in water

- Another object of the same weight, but larger or smaller in volume, submerged in water

  Students will discuss, record, and report their findings.

Estimation in Weighing

Estimation in weighing is also used in two contexts. We recognize that, since weight is a measurement of a continuous quantity, every weight result is an estimate. It is approximate. A weight which appears as exactly 120 pounds on a bathroom scale would be seen, with a weighing instrument which measured accurately to 1/100 of an ounce, perhaps as 119 pounds, 15 and 79/100 ounces; that is, not *exactly* 120 pounds. A student learning the concept of weight understands that there is no need to express a person's weight to the nearest 1/100 ounce—the *estimate* of 120 pounds is quite adequate for most purposes. Knowing something of body weight, the student might record "120 pounds" on a personal information record sheet even though the measurement that morning indicated almost 119 pounds. Weight changes during the day with ingestion of food and changing clothing. However, if the student is a competing wrestler it might be important that the weight be recorded as 119 rather than 120 pounds if that means wrestling in another class.

The other aspect of estimation is the ability to make close educated guesses concerning weight. For children, this skill is not frequently needed or used and may not ever be used extensively. Farmers, for example, become adept (and need to be) at estimating the weight of a load of grain, a piece of equipment, or an animal. Laboratory scientists, through experience, become skilled in estimating a variety of measurements including weight because good estimates help them reduce time and labor. A fairly accurate preliminary estimate saves effort necessary to develop a more precise measurement (Hiebert, 1984). Children can profit from practice in estimating common weight measures at least to the extent that it helps them communicate meaningfully in describing objects and situations. Among these should be weights of:

- Persons

- Things carried: books, book bags

- Sports objects, balls, discus, shot, exercise equipment

- Food items and groceries

- Items carried in cars and trucks

Advanced Activity for Seventh and Eighth Graders

Students will estimate the weight of the earth in tons using rocks and water as starting points, then research through the Internet or library resources for the best scientific estimate to compare with the class's result, arrived at through calculation, discussion, and justification.

Special Considerations

As with other unit and measurement concepts, students have to correct wrong impressions and terminology seen and heard in everyday life. Stores advertise a special price on a *Big Quarter Pounder* and give the impression that there are heavier and lighter quarter pounds of hamburger. People talk about "tons of stuff," meaning only that there is lots of it, and having no real reference to a weight measure. Others refer to lead as heavy and popcorn as light—which is not necessarily the case. What they are really saying is that a container of a given volume of lead will weigh more than the container with the same volume of popcorn. At this point teachers should make the students aware of the need to understand the importance of measurements which are rates, or a relationship between two measures. Here the measure is density, a combination of weight and volume measures.

Measuring Temperature

Temperature measurement is uniquely different from other measurement. Two major differences are that it is usually a two-stage indirect measure and that measurement values include negative numbers. Most temperature measuring devices use a substance such as mercury that expands or contracts according to temperature changes, and the scale marking the amount of length change is calibrated to be read in degrees. In other measurements, negative values are used to indicate direction and are not really a part of the specific measurement. Instead, in temperature measurement, negative numbers are used for actual measurements. (Teachers should discuss with the students the meaninglessness of talking about negative length, negative volume, negative time, etc. A student may mention negative yards in football; it should be pointed out that the *negative 5 yards* run or pass is actually 5 yards measured in the usual way and that the "negative" refers to the direction.)

Students and teachers may struggle with everyday terminology here, too. The words warm and cold are relative in their application. In midwinter, when the temperatures are usually around 30°F during the day, a day with temperatures in the 60s would be called very warm, while in the summer, a day with temperatures in the 60s would be called cold or cool. Discussion of *warm* and *cold* temperatures may be inaccurate and misleading. Temperatures are numbers indicating the amount of heat present. Numbers cannot be hot or cold. Thus we should say the wind is cold; the air is warm; the temperature of the air is 75°F. Temperatures can be referred to as high or low in the sense that the numbers are high or low on a vertical scale.

Added to the terminology difficulties of temperature measure is the fact that there are two different scales in common use. Although both the Celsius and Fahrenheit scales are based on the freezing and boiling points of pure water at standard pressure, they have different points as their bases. The conversion formula is not particularly easy to remember (Thompson, 1985).

 Examples

Fahrenheit scale: Water freezes at 32°; boils at 212°

Celsius scale: Water freezes at 0°; boils at 100°

Conversion formula: C° = 9/5F° + 32°

Advanced Activity for Seventh and Eighth Graders

Students will:

1. Derive the formula for F° as a function of C°.

2. Derive the conversion formula.

(These are useful problems with real application value for pre-algebra and algebra students.)

Activity for Fourth Through Eighth Graders

Students will:

1. Choose a month during school and keep a running record and graph of high and low temperatures for each day (24 hours).

2. At the end of the month create a report on the temperature reading for the month, including highs, lows, low highs and high lows.

Measuring temperature is probably the least complex of the measurements. Computation and comparisons are typically not necessary. Usually the only task is to read a scale, avoiding inaccuracy because of parallax (error in reading a measurement scale because the scale and measured objects are viewed from a nonperpendicular perspective).

Interrelated Measures

We correlate two measures and describe aspects of our environments by using rates. Measuring these is more complex, but still a part of our daily lives and thus important for school children to learn. Among the more common forms and examples used by children are relations such as mi./hr. (distance per time), and cost/lb. (cost per weight) and cost/hr. (cost per time). The most familiar are miles per hour, cents per ounce, dollars per pound, dollars per hour, and the weight per volume mentioned in the section on weight. The measuring device for miles per hour is a car speedometer, a policeman's radar gun, or a ball speed counter at a baseball game or tennis match. For cost per weight we rely on the grocery store's scales, machines, and labels for unit pricing or we use a calculator to do the necessary division. In these instances we are measuring rates (two interrelated measures).

Creative pricing techniques in grocery stores may cause difficulty. In the same cheese display, one many find some packages labeled in cents per ounce and other packages labeled in cents per pound. Some companies make boxes containing slightly different weights of the same product. One raisin bran box contains 14.5 ounces and the next, 20 ounces. Without a calculator and understanding of unit prices, a student cannot measure the differences in actual product cost.

Activity for Fifth to Eighth Graders

Students will, given real prices and volumes (or weights), calculate and compare unit prices on some of their favorite foods: different brands of peanut butter, candy, colas, etc. (Students could go to the store, collect the information, and bring it to class.)

Examples

Which is the "better buy"—the store's brand of peanut butter at $2.98 for a $2^1/_2$-lb. jar or the national brand for $2.09 for a $1^1/_2$-lb. jar? (Note: Here's a good opportunity for practical problem solving using fractions.)

Which is the "better buy" (more pizza for the money) at the Pizza Place? A 10" round pizza for $6.59 or a 14" round pizza with the same topping for $8.99? (Note: This problem requires use of knowledge about circle area from geometry.)

Further Advanced Activity for Seventh and Eighth Graders

Students will fold a square piece of paper twice, forming a $1/_4$-sized square four times as thick.

Then students will solve the problems:

How many folds would be needed to create a 1" thick paper stack?

What would be the cross-sectional area when the 1" height is reached?

Is there a maximum height?

(In this problem solving setting it is assumed that students will use good problem solving skills and strategies.)

Summary

Forms of measurement children use and need to learn for future use are outlined and suggestions are given for teaching both concepts and processes critical for understanding and performing measurement. Emphasized are critical underlying concepts and understandings. Each type of measurement—length, area, volume, weight, time, temperature, and related measure—is described and attention is given to the special difficulties which students and teachers may encounter in learning and teaching that aspect of measurement. Throughout, emphasis is given to the necessity of using manipulatives, measuring instruments and objects in the context of repeated practice and experience. For this reason, numerous real life activities are suggested and teachers are encouraged to engage students in as wide a variety of hands-on experimentation and discovery activities as is possible. Children learn to measure and understand measurement by multiple, guided experiences in measuring.

Exercises

1. Using only a narrow piece of tag board (about 1″ wide and more than 12″ long) and a 3″ × 5″ card, make a ruler with the whole inch marks and the fractions of inches marks also. Include at least halves, fourths, eighths, and sixteenths.

2. Bring to class price and volume and price and weight information for grocery store items of interest to kids; compute unit prices and describe effective methods for teaching children how to compute and use unit prices. Especially important are estimating and adjusting techniques when calculators are not available.

3. Bring to class and demonstrate various measuring devices, including Vernier calipers.

4. Demonstrate the use of similar triangles in measuring in inaccessible situations such as measuring across a lake or measuring the height of a tree or building.

References

Hiebert, James (1984, March). Why do some children have trouble learning measurement concepts? *Arithmetic Teacher*, 31(7), 19–24.

Kaster, Bernice (1989, February). The role of measurement applications. *Arithmetic Teacher*, 35(6), 40–46.

Lindquist, Mary Montgomery (1989, October). The measurement standards. *Arithmetic Teacher*, 36(2), 22–26.

National Council of Teachers of Mathematics (1989). *Curriculum and Evaluation Standards for School Mathematics*. Reston, VA: Author.

Piaget, Jean, Barbel Inhelder, and Alina Szemiuska (1960). *The Child's Conception of Geometry*. New York: Basic Books.

Shroyer, Janet, and William Fitzgerald (1986). *Mouse and Elephant: Measuring Growth*. Menlo Park, CA: Addison-Wesley.

Thompson, Charles S., and John Van deWalle. (1985, April). Learning about rules and measuring. *Arithmetic Teacher*, 32(8), 8–12.

▣ Suggested Readings

Barson, Alan (1971). *Geoboard Activity Cards (Intermediate)*. Fort Collins, CO: Scott Scientific.

———— (1972). *Geoboard Activity Cards (Primary)*. Fort Collins, CO: Scott Scientific.

Bitter, Gary G., Jerald L. Mikesell, and Kathryn Maurdeff (1976). *Activities Handbook for Teaching the Metric System*. Boston: Allyn & Bacon.

Hallamore, Elisabeth (1974). *The Metric Book . . . of Amusing Things to Do*. Woodbury, NY: Barron's Educational Series.

McWhirter, Ross (1990). *The Guinness Book of World Records*. New York: Sterling.

National Council of Teachers of Mathematics (1989). *Curriculum and Evaluation Standards for School Mathematics*. Reston, VA: Author.

Sime, Mary (1973). *A Child's Eye View*. New York: Harper & Row.

Varma, Ved P., and Phillip Williams, Eds. (1976). *Piaget, Psychology and Education*. Itasca, IL: F. E. Peacock.

Teaching Rational Number Concepts

One of the children's problems: Shawan does not know the difference between decimals and percents and cannot change from one to the other.

Teacher's problem: Children read all the decimal values on the calculator screen and believe that they all indicate great precision.

Understanding the Problem

Even before they come to school, children begin to work with the ideas underlying fractions. At the kindergarten and first grade levels, children are already very conscious of breaking wholes into parts and sharing equally from a set of toys, pieces of candy, or a cake cut into roughly equal-sized pieces. Along with these partially formed fraction ideas they hear and use such terms as *one-half*, *one-third*, *one-fourth*, and perhaps *three-fourths* and *one-and-a-half*. These concepts are not well developed; for example, *one-half* may refer to one of two parts regardless of their relative sizes. Even after a child recognizes that one of the parts is larger than the other, he or she may persist in calling it one-half. Remember that young children are not conservers and consequently have difficulty thinking of equal value or quantity when appearances are different. They also experience difficulty in keeping two interrelated variables in mind simultaneously. This means that children cannot consider the whole at the same time as a part of the whole, and that when a whole is split into parts, children may believe that quantity has changed. Wentworth (1995) states that defining the unit or the whole is often confusing to students because of the example being considered and/or the representations used by the teacher.

As children grow older and begin to refine and formalize the ideas of fractions, they are confronted with the necessity of attaching specific meanings to terminology and the realization that there are multiple concepts under the label *fraction*. Some educators have listed as many as 20 different meanings for the word *fraction*. Among them are:

- Part of a whole

- Rational number

- Division

- Ratio

- Proportion

- Rate

Each term relates to a different aspect of the concept of fraction. In fact, some of these terms refer to special concepts in their own right. The difficulty is further compounded by the fact that some of the words above and related terms are used loosely or incorrectly in everyday language. Ratio, rate, proportion, and odds are used interchangeably, for example, though the concepts they represent are not interchangeable. The statement, "He did only a fraction of the work," usually means, "He did a very small part of the work," giving the impression that *fraction* means small. In reference to a fast moving car, some say, "It was traveling at a high rate of speed." This statement contains redundancy, since speed is a rate. In addition, there is a large variety of symbols used to represent fractional numbers. When the term *fraction* is used, the usual symbol is a/b, where a and b are integers. In reality, decimal numbers such as 3.45 are one form of this concept. It may also be assumed that a is less than b and that a and b have no common factors. Other symbol forms for fractional numbers are as follows:

 Examples

$$\frac{3}{4}, \qquad 1.23, \qquad 23\%, \qquad \text{3 to 4 ratio (3:4)},$$

$$\frac{9.85}{5}, \qquad 1\tfrac{1}{2}/7$$

Khoury and Zazkis (1994) found that even as late in the study of mathematics as when preservice teachers are preparing for teaching, most of the students in the study believed that fractions changed their numerical value under different symbolic representations.

Because there are so many interrelated concepts, different terminologies, and symbol forms, students are confronted with a difficult learning task and teachers with a difficult teaching task. Several factors add to the difficulty:

- Ambiguity of terms and forms.
- Lack of inherent order.
- Lack of direct connections with integer concepts.
- Lack of continuity in teaching fraction concepts.
- Lack of emphasis on concept construction.

The ambiguity of terms and the wide variety of concepts, terms, and forms has been mentioned. Since the study of fractions and the development of concepts come in no particular order, it is difficult for teachers and students to base their learning plan on some kind of hierarchical structure. It doesn't make sense to try to learn about fractions starting with small fractions and working toward larger ones, just as it doesn't help to focus on fractions with top numbers of 1, then those with 2 on top, and so forth. The first fractions children encounter are scattered along the 0–1 interval and follow no particular pattern. First, children experience difficulty because of conservation limitations. Then, with fractions, they encounter a transition from integers (which have obvious order) to the apparently nonordered system of fractions. It is difficult for children to see whether one fraction is larger than another by looking at the symbols.

The characteristics of counting numbers that helped a student determine larger and smaller cannot be applied to fractions. More digits does not mean a larger number; large digits may actually mean smaller numbers.

Examples

$$\frac{23}{30} \text{ is not larger than } \frac{7}{8}.$$

$$\frac{3}{8} \text{ is smaller than } \frac{3}{4}$$

Note also the difficulties students have with the form. Both the upper and lower numbers have to be considered together. The relationship *is* the number. A more subtle difficulty is that students have progressed from working hard to accept the idea that 23 is a number composed of 2 single-digit numbers adjacent to one another and that the positioning tells the reader of an abstraction called place value. Now students are presented not only with two integer numbers placed in a different position, but also with a bar (which may be horizontal or slanted— 5/8 or $\frac{5}{8}$) and with another abstraction in which the bar can mean many different ideas.

At this point the student encounters another dilemma: fractions that look different but that have the same value. The student is expected to understand that two fractions are the *same*. This is another point where students may experience difficulty with terminology. Two fractions, that may not contain any common numerals, are called the *same*. The teacher may say that 2/3 is the same as 6/9. Any child can see that none of the numbers match. The figures do not look the same at all. Teachers could really help their students by using better terminology at this point. These fractions should be called "same valued," or "equal value," or "equal size." Terminology, diagrams, and positions on a number line or ruler that have meaning to students should be used. It is better to avoid the terms *numerator* and *denominator* as long as possible. These terms are abstract and are easily mixed up since, for most people, they have no obvious meaningful literal connections to fraction symbols or the fraction concept. For this reason, most students memorize them, thus adding to their increasingly heavy memory load as they attempt to memorize their way through mathematics.

Students encounter prejudicial terms used to describe fractions, such as *improper fraction*. The negative connotation of this term leads children to believe that there is something wrong with fractions with larger top numbers than bottom numbers. They may believe that when such a fraction shows up as a result, the process must have been flawed; they have a wrong result. Other terms such as *mixed numbers* and *unreduced fractions* may also carry negative conceptual baggage.

Another hampering factor in teaching and learning fractions is the off-and-on use of fractions in typical curricula. First graders may draw circles showing halves and quarters and use manipulatives with the more common fractions at their level for a week or two; then they may not see fractions again until second grade. Attention to, and opportunities to work with, fractions are scattered and inconsistent throughout the curriculum. In some cases, fraction work is left to the end of the chapter or to the harder problems. This erratic and delayed attention to fractions, coupled with comments from peers and parents ("Just wait until you start doing fractions, then you'll have big trouble!") can give students the idea that fractions are difficult and best avoided.

These difficulties have prompted considerable research by mathematics educators and developmental psychologists on the learning of concepts basic to understanding fractional numbers. (see Suggested Readings at the end of this chapter)

Decimal Forms

Children must come to understand that the integers they have studied are really just a subset of all the decimal numbers and that decimal numbers may be thought of as an extension of the numbering system. The digits to the right of the decimal point are also place holders for powers of 10. When decimal forms of rational numbers are presented, there are again several forms.

 ### Examples

Terminating, nonrepeating	1.25
Repeating, nonterminating	0.3333
Nonrepeating, nonterminating	$\pi = 3.14159625.\ldots$

This understanding can start from the place value concept of the integer numbers but requires students who are relatively mature in their thinking. The concept of negative powers of 10 should be reserved for the late middle school and high school. This is not an easy transition for children, but older students may quickly pick up the pattern of the increasing and decreasing powers of 10. Younger children may be taught simply that the 3 in 2.345 is in the tenths place, 4 is in the hundredths place, and 5 is in the thousandths place. No reference to powers of 10 is necessary or advisable until the fifth grade or later.

Students often experience difficulty with the idea of percentages. It may be that the logical flow of the reasoning (that we consider those decimal numbers or fractions which are related to a whole of 100 and place them in a class of numbers with a new name) is itself the difficulty. If students are unsure of the decimal number concept and are moved too quickly to work with percentages, they may never be able to cope adequately with the concept. Pointing out the equivalent values of the various forms is not likely to be sufficient. Additionally, some students may bring underdeveloped conservation abilities to a study of these different forms. Certainly their experience with percentage numbers in a variety of applications (which is so critical in developing conservation) is limited. At the same time, children at middle school grade levels are bombarded in their daily lives with advertising and store signs containing percentage information about things they buy and are interested in (Kindig, 1986).

One major problem students (and many adults) have with percentages is the lack of consideration given to the base on which the percentage is calculated. They take a percentage as a fixed number and do not realize that it is

FIGURE 12-1 Graph of Percentage Increases

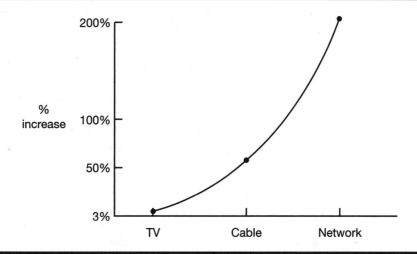

relative to some base. They believe, for example, that if a price is increased by 25%, then decreased by 25%, the overall result will be an unchanged price. There also is difficulty with considering percentage increases as quantities increase. Consider the graph in Figure 12-1:

At first glance, the appearance suggests that network media use is much larger than that of TV. The graph, however, really shows only that network media increased more proportionally. Teachers may need to use particular numbers in order to give conceptual meaning in situations like this:

 Example

	1994	*1995*	*% Increase*
TV	858 units	891 units	3%
Cable	400	600	50%
Network	150	450	200%

Note

Although Networking showed a very large increase, the total of units for networking is still only about half the number of units for TV.

Percentage numbers can be part decimal, as illustrated by the number 12.5%. This mixture of the percentage concept and the decimal concept can also be confusing to students. The decimal point now represents two different ideas. It can be the point between the units and the tens positions in a percentage number and the point between the units and the tens positions in equivalent decimal numbers (12.5% = 0.125). This ambiguity is difficult for children who are uncertain about decimal concepts to begin with. Prospective teachers may need to work on their own ideas of decimals and percentages in order to be sure they understand decimal concepts sufficiently to be able to teach them effectively (Lembke & Reys, 1994).

Operations with Fractions

Operating with fractional numbers presents another set of difficulties; difficulties with the a/b forms are different from those with the decimal or percentage forms. When operating with the a/b forms (which in this section will be called fractions), students are confronted with algorithms that are very different from the algorithms for the integers with which they have developed some operating skills.

Because of repeated experience with integer operations, students believe that:

- Adding results in a larger number than either of the addends.

- Subtracting results in a number smaller than the number being taken away from.

- Multiplying results in a much larger number than either of the factors.

- Dividing results in a number much smaller than the number being divided.

When faced with rational number operations for which these notions are contradicted, students may feel at a total loss. Math anxiety often develops in students confronted with destruction of some of these closely held notions. Teachers should note that there are none of the obvious signals in these numbers to help students know whether the numbers are smaller or larger.

The shift from integers to rational numbers also includes a transition from counting numbers to noncounting numbers. Children with ample manipulative experience in connection with operations readily (and appropriately) rely on counting as a basis for understanding the operations. They have combined two sets of objects by physically rearranging them and counted the objects in the combined set to obtain an addition result. They have distributed objects in a set into smaller equal-sized sets and counted either the sets or the items in the small sets to obtain a division result. Essentially, the ability to count formed the basis for operating and for understanding the operation concept. Counting, however, cannot be the sole basis either for operating with fractions or for understanding the concepts. (Note: It is possible to arrange manipulatives and reformulate the operations ideas to assist in understanding an operation with fractions. This should be suggested to a student who is experiencing difficulty with operations with fractions.) (Payne, 1990)

It is not always possible to find manipulatives to help directly with fraction operations.

If the concepts of division and multiplication have not been fully taught and conceptually understood, even with the counting numbers, students will have difficulty with these operation concepts when using rational numbers. These are two ways of understanding each of these operations:

Twelve objects can be arrayed as 4 objects in each of 3 rows or 3 objects in each of 4 rows. This fact is pointed out to young children and they are asked to work with both arrangements and helped to understand that the total is the same whether one has 4 sets of 3 or 3 sets of 4. That is, $3 \times 4 = 4 \times 3 = 12$.

Unfortunately, many teachers and students do not proceed beyond that to realize that 4 sets of 3 each and 3 sets of 4 each are not necessarily equivalent in other respects. In a group of 12 children with 8 girls and 4 boys, for example, placing them in groups of 4 each could yield groups with all boys and all girls; however, all-girl and all-boy groups could not be achieved using 4 groups of 3. The two scenarios are different along dimensions other than total number.

This distinction is even more critical with respect to division. When division is introduced and studied by young children, sometimes only one facet of the division concept is emphasized, and this emphasis likely grows out of the sharing model. It often has this form: "There are 12 pieces of candy to be shared equally among three children. How many pieces will each get?" The model is: *divide* the set of 12 into 3 equal sets and the result is a count of the *equal* share in each of the 3 sets. Copeland (1984) calls this "partitive division" and the other form "measurement division." The second model is less emphasized or perhaps even ignored. If we *divide* 12 pieces of candy so that each child gets 3 pieces, how many children will have 3 pieces each? Now the number in each set is pre-assigned, and the number of sets is counted to determine the 12 ÷ 3 result.

Either of these scenarios (especially using manipulatives) is adequate for obtaining division results by children. Students use either or both, but teachers seldom point out both to their students, have them discuss each and their differences, and ask children which is better and under what circumstances. There is a significant difficulty, however, when it comes to operating with fractions—again because of the counting aspect of operating.

 Examples

Consider $\frac{1}{2} \div 3$

1. It makes sense to split 1/2 into 3 different equal sized sets and determine what part of the whole (a fraction) is in each set (Fig. 12-2).

FIGURE 12-2 One-half Divided into 3 Equal-sized Sets

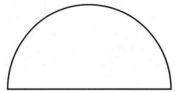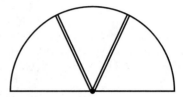

2. It is difficult even to say that we would take 1/2 and *divide* it into sets containing 3 each and then determine how many sets there are. The terminology doesn't help at all. The situation can be reasoned through and can be worded in such a way that we realize that there is 1/6 of a set of 3 when 1/2 is divided, but that is cumbersome and may not be not helpful to children.

In Figure 12-3, the 1/2 is *not divided;* that is, broken down in some way. This contradicts a child's sense of *division*. The situation changes when we consider $3 \div 1/2$.

FIGURE 12-3 Half a Rectangle in Three Equal Parts

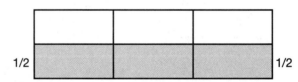

 Example

$$3 \div \tfrac{1}{2} =$$

1. Recall that in the first instance our plan was to separate the first number (3, in this instance) into a given number (the divisor) of sets and count how many were in each set.

   The student's task is to separate 3 objects into $\frac{1}{2}$ the number of sets. This is obviously difficult even to think about. The language doesn't make sense. What is $\frac{1}{2}$ set? On the other hand, the second scenario does make sense.

2. Separating 3 wholes into sets, each containing half of a whole, can be neatly and easily demonstrated (Fig. 12-5).

   If we had 3 pizzas, each of 6 children could have half a pizza each.

FIGURE 12-4 Separating Three Wholes Into Six Equal-Size Pieces

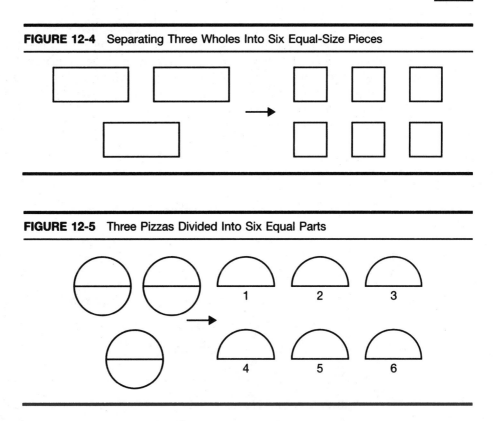

FIGURE 12-5 Three Pizzas Divided Into Six Equal Parts

A challenge is $\frac{1}{2} \div \frac{3}{5}$. Which of the aspects of the division concept should be used?

🔲 Solving the Problem

Successful teaching rational number facts, concepts, and processes requires attention to the developmental stages of the children and to providing ample experiential exposure to the ideas. Extensive use must be made of manipulative devices created specifically to aid with certain rational number concepts, experiential connections with objects and situations in the children's environments, and practice in writing, computing and reforming rational number expressions. It is critical, also, to pay close attention to the underlying concepts of conservation and the impressions and half-formed ideas of numbers and operations that are brought by children to the study of the concept of fraction. Teachers should capitalize on the ideas that are sound though only partially complete, take note of the wrong impressions, and plan instruction and activities that will correct wrong concepts (Mack, 1990).

Children whose stage of development makes them unable to consider two dimensions simultaneously or to understand an interrelationship of two numbers, one representing part of the whole represented by the other, cannot understand fractions. Teachers need to structure the environment for these children so that their developmental progress will be enhanced through varied experiences until sufficient to enable them to think of two entities simultaneously and to view the number as a relationship rather than as a single entity.

In developing the idea of fractions, teachers should provide variety in the examples and counter-examples, using objects that children are familiar with.

 ## Examples

Pizzas: 1/3's, 1/6's, 1/2's, 1/4's, 1/8's

Ball games: 1/2's, 1/4's (quarters)

Gallon measures: 1/2's, 1/4's

Shoe sizes and clothing sizes: 1/2

Money: 1/4's (quarters)

Diagrams and pictures of sets: Separated into equal sized subsets

Labeled manipulative devices

Oranges: broken into segments

Ages: $7\frac{1}{2}$, $8\frac{1}{2}$, etc.

Students should be required not only to examine wholes and identify the various parts by name and mathematical symbol—$\frac{3}{4}$, $\frac{1}{2}$, etc., but also to draw their own wholes and fractional parts with labels.

 ## Activity for Second Through Fifth Graders

1. Students will peel and segment oranges into halves, then break one half into all its segments. (Use navel oranges, which peel and break easily.)

2. Students will determine what fraction one segment represents by counting.

3. Students will note the equivalence of 1/2 to 5/10 or 6/12.

4. Students will compare oranges to see if each yields the same fraction for one segment.

5. Students will be instructed to eat one tenth or two eighths, etc. and at each stage comment on what fraction is left.

 ## Activity for Fourth Through Eighth Graders

1. Students bring to class a newspaper or magazine clipping or container of some sort that contains a fraction number.

2. Students point out the fraction numbers out to the class and explain what they know about their meaning.

From the above, it should be clear that before children can be expected to operate with fractions from a conceptual base, the concepts of the operations must extend beyond the superficial and abstract manipulation of symbols. Furthermore, if students learn only the algorithmic manipulation of symbols, they may not fully develop rational number operation concepts. If the algorithmic steps are forgotten, the ability to operate or to understand the operations will then be lost. However, when students construct concepts of operations through experience and practice through all the dimensions of the concepts, they will not easily forget, and they will be more able to reconstruct forgotten material.

Operation Processes

The algorithms for operations with integers are supported by basic facts and place value; however, the algorithms for operating with fractions have neither, nor do they have comparable supporting ideas or concepts. The algorithms for operations with integers are, in fact, schemes that are designed to use basic facts to break large numbers and complex forms into easily manageable quantities about which operation facts are known. Since integers are written in decimal (base 10) place value format, the operator is enabled to deal with any numbers using only the 10 digits.

When working with fractions, students quickly realize that there are no basic fractions into which every other fraction can be broken. There is no place significance except the position below or above. In an attempt to standardize procedures, teachers typically resort to presenting the standard algorithms for fraction operations too early in the teaching/learning process. Standard algorithms are shown in the following examples:

Examples

For Addition: *Cross multiply*

$\frac{3}{4} + \frac{5}{6}$ yields $3 \times 6 + 4 \times 5 = 38$ for the numerator and $4 \times 6 = 24$ for the denominator, so that $\frac{3}{4} + \frac{5}{6} = \frac{38}{24}$. (The conditioned response is that this fraction is *improper* and must be *reduced* to a mixed number; or it is not in its *reduced* form and so must be *reduced* for that reason. Thus, either $\frac{38}{24} = \frac{19}{12} = 1\frac{7}{12}$, or $\frac{38}{24} = 1\frac{14}{24} = 1\frac{7}{12}$.)

For Subtraction: *Cross multiply*

$\frac{5}{6} - \frac{3}{4}$ yields $5 \times 4 - 6 \times 3 = 2$ for the numerator and $6 \times 4 = 24$ for the denominator or $\frac{2}{24}$. (Again, the *reduction* issue must be dealt with.)

Note: This algorithm, if well known, can provide a means for checking relative size of two fractions.

For Multiplication: *Multiply across*

$\dfrac{5}{6} \times \dfrac{3}{4}$ yields $\dfrac{15}{24}$; or *cancel* first, then multiply across: $\dfrac{5}{6} \times \dfrac{3}{4} = \dfrac{5}{2} \times \dfrac{1}{4} = \dfrac{5}{8}$

For Division: *Invert and multiply*

$\dfrac{5}{6} \div \dfrac{3}{4} = \dfrac{5}{6} \times \dfrac{4}{3} = \dfrac{20}{18}$. Here it must be remembered that the divisor $\left(\dfrac{3}{4}\text{ in this}\right.$ instance$\left.\right)$ is to be inverted, not the number divided or both.

Each of these is clearly abstract and not closely related to possible manipulative arrangements to do the operation or to the operation concepts. There are several steps that must be in correct order and, in the case of division, an algorithm which is from multiplication is to be used among the steps. If that multiplication algorithm is not secure, the division algorithm cannot be either (Thompson, 1979).

In order to connect addition and subtraction of fractions more closely to concepts, teachers should not teach the *cross multiply algorithm* but instead should approach the task from the perspective of adding or subtracting fractions from the same equivalence classes. By some means, 5/6 and 3/4 are replaced by equivalents in 24ths or other common multiples of 4 and 6. The fraction 5/6 is identified as equivalent to 20/24 and 3/4 to 18/24. Adding and subtracting can then proceed on the basis of well-known and clearly understood addition and subtraction of integers. The obvious value of this process is its close connection with the concept of fractions and understandable addition and subtraction. The teacher should use clearly descriptive language with the children to ensure that they understand what is happening in an instance like this. It should be made clear that this task has been broken down so that 24ths are the items in the two sets. One set contains 20 of these and the other contains 18. There are items of the same kind in the two sets so that addition or subtraction can take place. That is, 20/24 + 18/24 = 38/24 and 20/24 − 18/24 = 2/24. Other helps are found with specially designed manipulatives and/or diagrams.

Other thoughtful attempts to teach operations with fractions center around the use of special manipulatives that illustrate the fraction values and that can be manipulated to demonstrate the operations clearly. Figure 12-6 shows diagrams of parts of circular objects. Some of these, however, have use limited to particular operations or to particular fractions.

The marketing of inexpensive fraction calculators has provided new tools for operating with fractions. As with the use of calculators for other computation, there are inherent dangers. Students using these without a background of number sense (the meaning and value of fractions) and understanding of operations concepts will often do meaningless computation. They tend to take at face value what they read on the calculator screen, and if they haven't understood the process and the numbers used, may produce meaningless results because of having pushed the wrong buttons or pushed the buttons in the wrong order.

FIGURE 12-6 Fractions Expressed on a Circular Graph

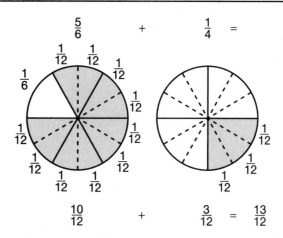

Fraction calculators can be used very helpfully to develop fraction concepts of order, equivalence, and what it means to multiply or divide by numbers close to zero, less than 1, greater than 1, or very large. As with other tools and manipulatives, the teacher must be very sure of the lesson's objective. If the objective is to teach computation, the calculator should not be used. If the objective is to teach problem solving where computation is involved, that may be a good place for a calculator to be used. If the objective is to teach number sense, with fractions, the calculator is a powerful and useful tool. In children's daily lives fractions play a limited role, but where they are used and expressed properly, they can be helpful to children as they develop the concepts. Some sources are:

- Games divided into halves and quarters.
- Dollars divided into halves and quarters.
- Gallons divided into halves and quarts (quarters).
- Length, volume, and weight measurements shown on grocery store packaging.
- Sports data and statistics.
- Clothing and shoe sizes.
- Age values.

Operations with decimal numbers and percentages are not as problematic as with fractions. Since the numbers are in decimal form (base 10 place value forms), the standard place-value-based algorithms for integers can be used effectively as processes for obtaining correct operation results. The major difference occurs in the necessity for adding rules about decimal placement to the algorithms. As is the case with many other algorithms, the usual rules, though based in the concept of decimals and the operations, are presented abstractly. The tendency is for students to memorize them and then to apply the rules without reference to the concept of the operation and without reference to the sizes of the numbers involved. When students attempt to recall these rules from memory, especially when there has been a long period between their uses, they may confuse the rules and thus be prevented from working out multiplication and division results with confidence (Hiebert, 1987).

There are basically two forms of standard algorithm rules for dealing with decimal points:

1. Columns: For addition and subtraction, maintain vertical columns for the place values and keep the decimal point between the units and tenths places in the columns also.

2. Counting: (a) For multiplication, add the numbers of digits after the decimal places in the factors and use that sum to determine the placing of the decimal that many spaces to the left of the rightmost digit. (Count the decimal places and add.)
   (b) For division, move the decimal point in the divisor a sufficient number of places to make the divisor a whole number. Move the decimal point in the number being divided the same number of places (to the right). Place the decimal in the result directly above the new decimal point position in the number being divided. (Essentially, this creates place value columns.) Divide using the new numbers. The number of digits following the decimal point in the result is dependent on the desire or need of the operator. (Count the decimal places in the two numbers and subtract.)

Examples

i.
$$\begin{array}{r} \overset{1\ 1}{2.35} \\ +3.896 \\ \hline 6.246 \end{array}$$

ii.
$$\begin{array}{r} \overset{6\ \ 10\,11\,1}{\cancel{7}.\cancel{1}\cancel{2}3} \\ -4.978 \\ \hline 2.145 \end{array}$$

iii.
$$\begin{array}{r} 75.83 \\ 47.905 \\ \hline 123.735 \end{array}$$

iv. 2.135 + 4.9781 =

v. 98.25% − 2.58 =

vi.
$$\begin{array}{r} 3.52 \\ \times\ 7.4 \\ \hline 1408 \\ 2464 \\ \hline 26048 \end{array}$$

1. Note 2 decimal places in 3.52.

2. Note 1 decimal place in 7.4.

3. Add: 1 plus 2 = 3.

4. Place the decimal between 6 and 0, yielding 26.048

$$
\begin{array}{r}
1.03 \\
3.6\overline{)4.72} \\
\underline{36} \\
120 \\
\underline{108} \\
12
\end{array}
$$

1. Place numbers in the standard form.

2. Move both decimal points to the right, one place.

3. Maintain columns yielding 1.03.

These rules, especially in the cases of division and multiplication, can be rather complex, with many contingencies. Such rules are too involved for a middle schooler to follow and remember. The case of the addition or subtraction computation requires orderly and organized drawings of the forms. Middle schoolers often work with situations like the one pictured in *iii* above. When this is further cluttered with carrying marks, obtaining correct results is very unlikely. The nonstandard formats of *iv* and *v* would present difficulties to those who had been taught only the standard column arrangement. Example iv could be placed easily in standard format, but example v presents another difficulty, potential confusion about working with a percentage number, and a nonpercentage decimal. Does the percentage number have to be converted to a decimal number in order to divide? Would one of the numbers have to be converted to the other's form in order to add, subtract, or multiply (Carpenter, 1981)?

The potential confusion in decimal placement should be taken care of by abandoning the *count-and-add, count-and-subtract,* and *move-the-decimal-point* rules. Another, more reliable approach should be constructed by the person computing. This approach depends on number sense and understanding of the operations and can be reconstructed easily whenever needed.

 Illustrations

Multiply: 2.13 × 5.89

1. Without regard to decimal points, multiply 213 × 589 = 125457

2. Since the original numbers are near 2 and 6, the product will be near 12. Place the decimal between the 2 and 5. The result is 12.5457.

Divide: 175.5 ÷ 3.81

1. Disregard the decimals and divide 1755 by 381, yielding 4.606.

2. Noting that 175 is in the vicinity of 160 and 3.8 is near 4, recognize that the result should be in the vicinity of 40. Thus, 46.06 to two decimal places.

Add: 28.392 + 23.03

1. Rough estimating places these numbers near 30 and 20 so the resulting sum should be about 50. One could also add 28 and 23.

2. Add 28 and 23 (perhaps 40 + 11 = 51)

3. The decimal point will follow the 1. The result is 51.

4. The remainder can be broken into 39 hundredths plus 3 hundredths, or 42 hundredths and 2 thousandths or 51.422.

Subtraction: Follows addition similarly.

Because many students will be using nonstandard algorithms for their decimal (integer) operations, they should not be taught only the standard rules for decimal placement. To teach these exclusively is to create a defacto requirement to learn and use the four standard algorithms. A calculator was used for the multiplication and division above. A calculator is not necessary; however, students must learn how to use the calculator effectively as a tool. The danger is that using a calculator without number sense and operations concepts causes students to rely unquestioningly on what they read on the screen. They push buttons and read results but may not understand whether what they read is correct. Approaching decimal computation through the use of nonstandard algorithms provides the calculator user with confidence in results and with an understanding of the proper and best use of the calculator.

Other Processes

When dealing with fractions, three other processes are important: reducing and unreducing (changing a reduced form to an equivalent form which is not reduced) fractions, checking order, and converting from one rational number form to another.

In traditional arithmetic, a fraction not in its most reduced form is called *improper*, as if there were something wrong with it. Unfortunately, this practice persists in many classrooms today. It may have developed partially from the need to obtain only one right result (*answer*). As a result, more attention is devoted to reducing fractions than is really necessary. In many texts, no attention is given to unreducing fractions even though this skill (finding an appropriate unreduced form for a particular task) is very useful and needed in advanced mathematics studies (algebra and calculus).

Actually, it should be recognized that there is no need to emphasize reducing fractions. There should be more emphasis on changing a fraction to an equivalent one, either reduced or not, as a means of simplifying one's computation or expressing more clearly the situation under consideration. In fact, math educators should probably do away with the term *reduce* and the reduction processes entirely and approach the whole idea from the basic understanding of equivalence classes.

Examples

Add: $1/3 + 1/2$

1. Note that $1/3$ represents the equivalence class:

FIGURE 12-7   Equivalence Class for $1/3$

$$\left\{\frac{1}{3} \quad \frac{2}{6} \quad \frac{3}{9} \quad \frac{4}{12} \quad \frac{5}{15} \quad \frac{6}{18} \quad \frac{7}{21} \quad \frac{8}{24} \quad \frac{9}{27}\right\}$$

---

and $1/2$, the class:

FIGURE 12-8   Equivalence Class for $1/2$

$$\frac{1}{2} \quad \frac{2}{4} \quad \frac{3}{6} \quad \frac{4}{8} \quad \frac{5}{10} \quad \frac{6}{12} \quad \frac{7}{14} \quad \frac{8}{16} \quad \frac{9}{18}$$

---

2. Select like terms (in terms of the bottom numbers), one from each class:

$$\frac{2}{6} \text{ and } \frac{3}{6} : \quad \frac{2}{6} + \frac{3}{6} = \frac{5}{6}, \text{ or}$$

$$\frac{4}{12} + \frac{6}{12} = \frac{10}{12}, \text{ and so forth.}$$

Divide: $1/2 \div 1/3$

1. Using the equivalence classes above, select like terms:

$$2/6 \text{ and } 3/6 \text{ or } 4/12 \text{ and } 6/12$$

2. $3 = (1 + 1/2) \times 2 \qquad 6 = (1 + 1/2) \times 4$

3. Thus, $3/6 = 1\frac{1}{2} \times 2/6$, etc.

4. Or $1/2 \div \frac{1}{3} = 1\frac{1}{2}$

Teaching the terminology and the standard algorithms for these operations is necessary only because of their required use on proficiency tests and in future mathematics.

The practice of reducing fractions has spawned algorithms that are taught to students as part of what must be learned about fractions. In addition to the fact that they are really unnecessary, the typical algorithm contains further misleading terminology and additional abstract terminology.

Example

Reduce 60/126 to its lowest terms.

As it is often taught:

1. Completely factor (to prime factors) numerator and denominator, obtaining:

$$\frac{2 \cdot 2 \cdot 3 \cdot 5}{2 \cdot 3 \cdot 3 \cdot 7}$$

2. *Cancel* common factors in numerator and denominator:

$$\frac{\cancel{2} \cdot 2 \cdot \cancel{3} \cdot 5}{\cancel{2} \cdot 3 \cdot \cancel{3} \cdot 7}$$

3. Multiply remaining *uncanceled* numbers top and bottom:

$$\frac{2 \cdot 5}{3 \cdot 7} = \frac{10}{21}$$

The difficulties with this algorithm are clear. First, obtaining prime factorization is sometimes a difficult task in itself. Students are usually not very clear on primes and factorization, which involve a separate algorithm for some. Often, students will account for the presence of a factor of 2 and omit the second factor of 2. Second, the term *cancel* has a misleading connotation. Because of its use in everyday language, many students believe that it means to erase or to remove. That appears to be happening although, in fact, it is not. What is actually supposed to be happening is division of both numbers by a common factor. Some teachers have students indicate that by writing *1's* in place of the divided factors; however, that may not help very much because the students may not understand why they are using 1's.

Example

$$\frac{60}{126} = \frac{2 \cdot 2 \cdot 3 \cdot 5}{2 \cdot 3 \cdot 3 \cdot 7} = \frac{\cancel{2}^1 \cdot 2 \cdot \cancel{3}^1 \cdot 5}{\cancel{2}^1 \cdot 3 \cdot \cancel{3}^1 \cdot 7} = \frac{1 \cdot 2 \cdot 1 \cdot 5}{1 \cdot 3 \cdot 1 \cdot 7} = \frac{10}{21}$$

A further danger with the idea of *canceling* is expressed when students do the following:

$$\frac{\cancel{2}3}{5\cancel{2}} = \frac{3}{5}, \qquad \frac{\cancel{5} + 8}{\cancel{5}} = \frac{8}{0},$$

or

$$\frac{\cancel{5} + 8}{\underset{1}{\cancel{5}}} = \frac{9}{1} = 9$$

The latter becomes especially critical when students are in algebra class. Some, who would not calculate $(\cancel{5} + 8)/\cancel{5}_1 = \frac{8}{0}$ (possibly because they would first add the 5 and 8 in the numerator), would not hesitate to calculate

$$\frac{\cancel{a} + \cancel{2b} + 3c}{\cancel{a} + \cancel{2b}} = 3c.$$

Such action results from the wrong impression of the term *cancel* and a lack of understanding of the nature of fractions.

Activity for Sixth Through Eighth Graders (With Calculator)

Have students examine the numbers less than 100 (for numerator and denominator) for which this strange type of *cancellation* actually works, for example:

$$\frac{1\cancel{6}}{\cancel{6}4} = \frac{1}{4}$$

How many such are there?

(This is a kind of counter-example which helps with concept construction.)

The algorithm for unreducing is usually stated "Multiply the top and bottom by the same number." This algorithm is much more straightforward and more directly connected to the basic understanding of equivalent fractions.

If the top and bottom numbers are relatively small, an examination of equivalence classes may suffice for finding particular reduced or unreduced forms. For others, the simple expedient of dividing or multiplying by common factors will be effective.

Example

$$\frac{60}{126}$$

1. Note that 6 is a factor top and bottom

2. $(60 \div 6)/(126 \div 6) = 10/21$

3. Or note that 3 is a factor top and bottom.

4. $(60 \div 3)/(126 \div 3) = 20/42$

Students need to be given examples and shown that in their daily lives, it isn't always convenient or meaningful to reduce fractions to their lowest terms. For example:

Kelly's playing time, in three basketball games, was 2 quarters, 1 quarter, and 3 quarters respectively. How much playing time does she have to her credit for the three games? Response: 6 quarters (since playing time for her is measured in quarters)—that is, (6/4 not 3/2).

Teachers should develop a repertoire of similar examples and real life problems in which unreduced fractions should remain unreduced and/or unreducing fractions is advisable. As always, students should be taught that fractions and other numbers are to be manipulated and used to make computation easy, understandable, and less error prone. These processes must not be approached from the perspective of always using a particular rule or process regardless of the task or situation.

Checking for Relative Size of Fractions

Another *cross-multiply* algorithm is taught for determining which of two fractions is larger. In general terms, it goes like this:

Consider a/b and c/d

Cross-multiply a/b and c/d, obtaining ad and bc.

1. If ad < bc, then a/b < c/d
2. If ad > bc, then a/b > c/d
3. If ad = bc, then a/b = c/d

Example

$$\frac{3}{4} \ ? \ \frac{5}{6} \qquad 3 \times 6 = 18 < 20 = 4 \times 5.$$

 Therefore, $\frac{3}{4} < \frac{5}{6}$.

The attractiveness of this algorithm may be that it works so easily if the numbers aren't too large and the conditional statements 1, 2, and 3 are distinctly remembered. However, this *cross-multiply* algorithm might be confused with the *addition cross-multiply* algorithm. To avoid confusion and to work closely to the underlying concepts, students should return to equivalence classes or use the multiplication/division technique. This comparison algorithm can be presented to high school students or very advanced middle school students, but generally not to middle school students.

Example

Is 5 shots made in 8 attempts better shooting than 2 shots in 3 attempts?

- Compare equivalence classes:
  15/24 < 16/24 Therefore, 5/8 < 2/3; two successes in three attempts is a better rate (see Fig. 12-9).

- By what factor can I multiply 5/8 top and bottom so that after multiplying 2/3 top and bottom similarly, the bottom numbers are the same? The re-

---

FIGURE 12-9 Identification of Like Terms (Denominators) in Equivalence Classes

$$\left\{ \frac{5}{8} \; \frac{10}{16} \; \frac{15}{24} \; \frac{20}{32} \; \frac{25}{40} \; \frac{30}{48} - - - \right\} \left\{ \frac{2}{3} \; \frac{4}{6} \; \frac{6}{9} \; \frac{8}{12} \; \frac{10}{15} \; \frac{12}{18} \; \frac{14}{21} \; \frac{16}{24} \; \frac{18}{27} \right\}$$

---

sulting equivalent fractions are 15/24 = 3·5/3·8 and 16/24 = 8·2/8·3; this gives the answer to the original question.

Note that, in the example above, the term *least common denominator* was avoided. For this work with equivalent fractions, this term is unnecessary and only compounds difficulties for children. A common denominator is being found, true, but any common denominator will do. So the *least* part is unnecessary. Furthermore, the big words *common denominator* should be replaced with the much more understandable *same bottom numbers*. The terms *numerator* and *denominator* can be taught after the concepts and operations are reasonably well understood. There is danger that children will learn the words without the conceptual backing and begin to believe that they have the concepts simply because they know the words. Efforts to teach the terminology, per se, should be restricted to when it is needed for examinations or future classes.

Conversions

Algorithms for converting fractions to decimals, decimals to fractions, decimals to percentages, and percentages to decimals are also available. Fortunately, some of these are closely related to concepts and thus are meaningful and easily constructed. This is true of the processes for converting fractions to decimals and terminating decimals to fractions. Both of these should be taught well, for they assist children in developing the concepts of fractions and decimals fully.

Since one understanding of a fraction is that it represents a division, it is natural to divide the bottom number into the top. (Note that some students can't remember which divides into which.)

Those students should experiment with and compare results with the approximate values (estimates) of the fractions; for example, $8 \div 3 = 2 + 2/3$, which is not less than 1).

Examples

Convert $\dfrac{3}{8}$ to a decimal.

1. Note that the number is less than 1.

2.
$$
\begin{array}{r}
375 \\
8{\overline{\smash{\big)}\,3000}} \\
24 \\
\hline
60 \\
56 \\
\hline
40 \\
\end{array}
$$

3. To place the decimal so that 375 forms a number between 0 and 1, write 0.375.

4. $\dfrac{3}{8} = 0.375$

Convert 0.432 to a fraction.

1. Examine the place value holders and note: 4/10, 3/100, and 2/1000.

2. Consider the equivalent fractions in 1/1000's and add.

3. $400/1000 + 30/1000 + 2/1000 = 432/1000$.

The process of converting terminating decimals to fractions obviously involves an understanding of the meaning of the place value positions to the right of the decimal.

Activity for Fifth Through Eighth Graders (With Calculators)

1. Students will examine those fractions of the form 1/a and list, in orderly fashion, their decimal equivalents.

2. Students will identify and write descriptions of the patterns seen.

3. Students will attempt to discover a means for converting repeating deci-

mals to fractions (A helpful hint is to think about how many digits there are after the decimal in a repeating decimal.)

The usual algorithm about moving the decimal point two places to the right or left when converting decimals to percents, or the reverse, is not a particularly good algorithm. Some children are not really sure about right and left, and it's difficult to remember which process requires *left* and which requires *right*. In short, teaching this algorithm is not recommended. It is much better to approach the process by reference to the meaning of *percentage*. As the word indicates, it means "per 100." Thus, 85% is 85/100 or 0.85 and 0.435 is 43.5 100ths or 43.5%.

▣ Summary

The difficulties students and teachers have with fractions were explored. These difficulties include the trauma of transition from whole numbers to a new kind of numbers and the fact that operations with these numbers do not follow the patterns common to working with whole numbers. Ordering fractions was also pointed out as a problem area. The different forms for fractional numbers—a/b, decimals and percentages, the equivalence transfers from one to the other, and operations with each were discussed. Typical difficulties and teaching methods for each of the areas were also described. The traditional methods were described along with methods using equivalence classes and other non-problematic approaches. Many examples and activities were detailed. These can be used with students to provide interest and models which will promote understanding rather than attempts to memorize.

▣ Exercises

1. Prepare a sample set of fraction bars which can be made from construction paper by students or by the teacher for the students.
2. Demonstrate the use of Cuisenaire rods to illustrate division by fractions. Include fractions divided by fractions.
3. Provide a list of examples and counter-examples to demonstrate clearly the difficulties with the idea of *cancellation*.
4. Make a list of the manipulative devices available for teaching fraction concepts. Rank them according to their effectiveness and applicability.
5. Bring to class a wide ranging display of clippings, ads, etc. showing the practical use of percentages in daily life. Include examples of poor and/or inaccurate uses.

🔳 References

Carpenter, Thomas P., et al. (1981). Decimals: Results and implications from national assessment. *Arithmetic Teacher*, 28(8), 34–37.

Copeland, Richard W. (1984). *How Children Learn Mathematics*. Upper Saddle River, NJ: Prentice Hall/Merrill.

Hiebert, James (1987). Research report: Decimal fractions. *Arithmetic Teacher*, 34(7), 22–23.

Khoury, Helen A, and Zazkis, Rina (1994, September). On fractions and nonstandard representations: Pre-service teachers' concepts. *Educational Studies in Mathematics*, 27(2), 191–204.

Kindig, Ann C. (1986). Using money to develop estimation skills with decimals, in *Estimation and Mental Computation*, National Council of Teachers of Mathematics, Yearbook. Reston, VA: NCTM.

Lembke, Linda O., and Barbara J. Reys (1994). The development of and interaction between intuitive and school-taught ideas about percent. *Journal for Research in Mathematics*, 25(3), 237–239. Reston, VA: NCTM.

Mack, Nancy K. (1990). Learning fractions with understanding: Building on informal knowledge. *Journal for Research in Mathematics Education*, 21(1), 16–32.

Payne, Joseph N., and Ann E. Towsley. (1990). Implications of NCTM's standards for teaching fractions and decimals. *Arithmetic Teacher*, 37(8), 23–26.

Thompson, Charles (1979). Teaching division of fractions with understanding. *Arithmetic Teacher*, 26(5), 24–27.

Wentworth, Nancy (1995) A Factor Analysis of Parent Perceptions Concerning Role of Education, Mathematics, and Teachers in the Implementation of Technology. University of Utah. DAI, 54A, 2546.

🔳 Suggested Readings

Bennett, Albert B., Jr. (1982). *Decimal Squares*. Fort Collins, CO: Scott Resources.

Bennett, Albert., Jr., and Patricia A. Davidson (1973). *Fraction Bars*. Fort Collins, CO: Scott Resources.

Bezuk, Nadine, and Kathleen Cramer (1989). Teaching about fractions: What, when and how? in *New Directions for Elementary School Mathematics*, Ed., Paul R. Trafton and Albert P. Shulte. Reston, VA: NCTM

Bradford, John (1981). *Everything's Coming Up Fractions with Cuisenaire Rods*. New Rochelle, NY: Cuisenaire Co. of America.

Dorgan, Karen (1994). What textbooks offer for instruction in fraction concept. *Teaching Children Mathematics*, 1(3), 150–155.

Hutchins, Pat (1986). *The Doorbell Rang*. New York: Greenwillow Books.

Jenkin, Lee, and Peggy McLean (1972). *Fractions Tiles: A Manipulative Fraction Program*. Hayward, CA: Activity Resources.

Lichtenberg, Betty K., and Donovan R. Lichtenberg (1982). Decimals deserve distinction, in *Mathematics for the Middle Grades (5–9)*. Reston, VA: National Council of Teachers of Mathematics.

National Council of Teachers of Mathematics (1989). *Curriculcum and Evaluation Standards for School Mathematics*. Reston, VA: Author.

Post, Thomas R. (1981) Fractions: Results and implications from national assessment. *Arithmetic Teacher*, 28(8), 26–31.

Rational Numbers (Focus Issue). (1984). *Arithmetic Teacher*, 31(6).

Sheffield, Linda Jensen (1993). *More Math Manipulatives for the Overhead.* Greensboro, NC: Carson-Dellosa.

Vance, James H. (1986). Estimating decimal products: An instructional sequence, in *Estimation and Mental Computation*, National Council of Teachers of Mathematics, Yearbook. Reston, VA: NCTM.

Vance, James (1986). Ordering decimals and fractions: A diagnostic study. *Focus on Learning Problems in Mathematics*, 8(2), 51–59.

Woodcock, Gary (1986). Estimating fractions: A picture is worth a thousand fractions, National Council of Teachers of Mathematics, Yearbook. Reston, VA.

Yeager, David Clark (1983). *Story Problems: Fraction, Decimal, Percent.* Palo Alto, CA: Creative Publications.

Teaching Interpretation and Manipulation of Data

One of the children's problems: Terry gets mode, mean, and median all mixed up and is not clear on whether any of them is the typical number of the set.

Teacher's problem: Children come to class with a collection of statistical terms that they use in every day life but which do not seem to convey clear conceptual ideas.

Understanding the Problem

Today's children are growing up in a society that is becoming increasingly number oriented. Advertising aimed at children describes products using numbers and data to make their points. Children interested in professional sports are given abundant numerical information by sports commentators and on the sports cards they collect. As adults, people are inundated with numerical data in advertising, buying and selling, government reports on the economy, election and political news, and descriptions of almost every object and situation. We try to understand our social status in almost every arena by analyzing data we acquire, and we make many personal decisions based on our understanding of that data. Business people, especially, make significant decisions based on what they believe can be learned from data about consumers, the nature of their products, and the means of production. Educators depend heavily on analysis of demographic data as well as data on test results, and even on the tests themselves.

Many people do not understand how to make sense of all this numerical data. Education for this part of their lives must help children learn:

- How to collect data in order to understand situations.

- How to organize data.

- How to calculate measures on a data set.

- How to display and communicate information about a data set.

- How to interpret reports and information based on data.

Many of the misunderstandings about data sets and data-based descriptions of situations involve terminology. The most common difficulty is with the word *average*. Most students and adults understand that it has to do with the center of a set but may not distinguish among *mean*, *median*, and *mode*. Another frequently misused and misunderstood phrase is of the type: "One out of 10 Americans will contract a particular disease." People, accepting this statement as truth, may believe that in any group of 10 Americans, one of the group will contract the disease. They may also misunderstand the predictive nature of the statement, not realizing that any prediction of future events is made on the basis of assumptions that trends will continue as they have in the past.

Meaningless statements such as: "Every 18 seconds an American turns 50," and "Every 4 minutes a child drops out of school," may sound informative, but they are actually presented in isolation, without explanation of how the statement was generated. A context is needed so that comparisons can be made and the value of the fact understood.

Misunderstandings about percentages find their way into statistics and contribute to the difficulties experienced by students. Percentages and probabilities are important in describing data measures so that expressions such as

"110 percent effort" cause confusion. Many students also do not know the difference between *200 percent of last year's value* and *200 percent more than last year's value.* Others lose track of the base and believe that if a price is increased by 30%, then reduced 30%, the overall result is no change (NCTM, 1989).

Dealing with Data

Students first must realize that much of our understanding about the world comes about as we process sets of data and that most of that data is numerical. Children understand their own classes at school according to how many are in the class, its size relative to other classes, how many are girls or boys, how many ride the bus, etc. As they grow older, age information, proportions of the class participating in certain activities, scoring averages of team members, and many other pieces of numerical information are added to the mix.

Good and Bad Data

Children need to be taught early to distinguish between appropriate and useful (good) data and irrelevant, confusing, or useless (bad) data. In describing their class to parents or others, for example, there is value in giving data about the number of students, the number of boys and girls, and the number of computers in the room. There is, however, no value in reciting the number of fingers and toes present in the room when all the children are there. Some data suggest great accuracy when accuracy is not possible or the data are meaningless. This kind of information usually comes from calculated measurements, such as when a student reads the calculator display after dividing and reports that a block weighs 47.0329765 grams. All the digits after the 3 are irrelevant; the .03 is probably unnecessary, as it conveys no useful information. Mixing different forms of data presents problems, too. The mixture might be from different scales or different number types:

 Examples

The proportion of people involved dropped from 85% to one in four.

The temperatures were: 25°F, 0°C, 25°C, and 75°F.

The lengths of the races were: 1 mi., 400 yd., 1500 meters (the "metric mile"), 1 furlong, and 10K.

These cans contain 12 oz., and the others 300 ml.

The set is: 0.5, 0.70, 1.32, 4.785, .007, .2.

The set is: many, 3.95, a few, over 4, 6.28.

Describing discrete data with decimal numbers (There are 23.0 chairs in the room. The mean family size is 2.3 children).

Describing continuous data with only whole numbers.

Stating very large numbers with impossible precision (The number of people traveling to Europe in 1996 was 3,479,682).

Children must also realize that there is great variety in measurements that we might make on objects and situations. This means taking multiple readings and looking analytically at a data set so that we know the characteristics of the numbers and the set and how to describe them (Shulte, 1981).

Collecting Data

Not only is it important for students to recognize good and bad data, but they must learn to put together a data set in order to understand a situation or to learn the nature of the data and set. This needs to be done to describe objects and situations accurately. To collect data that will be useful requires attention to several details:

- The data should come from as many samples as it is feasible to collect.

- The data should be appropriate to the situation.

- The data should be collected systematically.

- Recording and displaying should be organized.

Example/Activity for Grades 3 and 4

When determining the number of candy M & M's of a particular color in a bag of M & M's, students will sample from several bags (all of the same size) and chart or graph in order to look for patterns.

It should be pointed out that we can make errors, sometimes very serious ones, when we try to make a decision, draw a conclusion, or describe something on the basis of one exposure to a situation or one piece of data.

Activity for Grades 4 Through 8

The students will discuss and list wrong ideas that people have formed and that they form on the basis of exposure to only one piece of data. For example, they may realize that judging all persons in a certain category as alike, based on one individual, can be a big mistake.

To be useful, type of data collected must match the situation or object being studied and must be the best data obtainable under the circumstances.

Examples

When surveying in the school regarding what cafeteria foods are most liked, data that came from students who checked both pizza and macaroni and cheese as most liked could not be used compatibly with data from those who checked only one food.

Opinion-based data should not be collected when facts are being assessed and vice versa.

Measurement data should not be listed using a level of accuracy greater than that of the measuring instrument.

Data should be collected in a systematic fashion, so that no items or responders will be overlooked and omitted and to prevent duplication of measurements or responses. Teachers should help students create and use checklists or other devices to ensure that the data come from the intended source and accurately represent that set or situation.

Recorded data should be organized systematically. This is best done by establishing categories of responses or numerical data in advance and preparing sheets so that the data can be listed categorically when obtained. Children need to be guided in this preliminary task by the teacher so that this becomes standard practice as they prepare to display data. It should be pointed out to the students that a data collector does not always know in advance what the categories should be. The collector's best judgment should be used at the start but the collector may want to modify the categories as needed or start over with different categories if necessary (Hopkins, 1997).

The different types of data are: *nominal, ordinal, interval,* and *ratio.*

Nominal Data

This type of data includes primarily the names of categories such as yes or no, colors, and classifications. In the early grades, this is the type of data that children understand as they first learn to collect and to use data. In the M & M's example, children would be determining the usual number of red, brown, orange, and other color M & M's in a bag and charting or graphing.

Caution

It is common for teachers to say something like, "Today we are going to graph M & M's (or the colors of the M & M's)." This is poor wording and may leave a wrong impression with the students. We graph numbers, not colors, not M & M's. The teacher should say, "Today we are going to graph the numbers of M & M's of different colors."

Ordinal Data

Some sets of numbers come to us in a data set from a setting where order is the most precise measurement we can glean from the analysis of that data. Ordinal data typically comes from descriptive, but nonmeasurement, sources. Consider the rating scales often used:

Examples for Fourth Through Eighth Grades

Students are asked to rate election candidates or professional teams on a scale such as:

Excellent

Very good

Good

Average

Fair

Poor

Very Poor

Students are asked to give their opinions about some change in school policy on a Likert scale:

Strongly Disagree	Disagree	Neutral	Agree	Strongly Agree
1	2	3	4	5

We can agree on order in data collected from these sources—that is, *Good* ranks above *Average* and *Average* above *Poor*. *Agree* can be thought of as above or below *Disagree* depending on the perspective of the survey taker. Even if numbers are assigned to the Strongly Disagree–Strongly Agree scale as in the example above, all that can be known from the numbers is that a score of 4 is to the right of 3 on the scale. It is not justifiable or appropriate to draw any conclusions based on the fact that the intervals between 2 and 4 and 3 and 5 are equal. Neither can one conclude that a score of 4 is twice as high or twice as good as a score of 2.

Interval Data

Interval data comes from situations or descriptors where an interval between values on a scale has meaning, but ratios may not. The most common scale of this kind may be the temperature scale. We read temperatures from the weather reports and science experiments and note comparable increases and decreases in temperature. It is meaningful to discuss and to note that, for example, the daytime high temperature and the nighttime low temperature difference (an interval) in a certain location is typically the same as that in another location. But it does not make sense to talk about the air at 60° being twice as warm as it is at 30°. Here a meaningful ratio is being improperly assumed. This is not ratio data.

Activity for Fourth Through Eighth Grades

Students will collect daytime high/nighttime low temperatures for a month and graph the differences. They will then compute the mean difference and the range of these differences and note how these measures relate to each other by examining the graph.

Extension

Students will do a similar collection and graph for another location chosen by individual students or the class (perhaps interfaced with social studies or science lessons).

Ratio Data

Students need to learn that measurements such as length, area, volume, weight, angles, and rates provide ratio data. Conclusions and decisions that involve order, intervals, and ratios can be made using this data. It makes sense to talk about the distance to school being twice the distance to the video shop or the cost of a CD being $1^1/_2$ times the cost of a cassette.

Activity for Fourth Through Eighth Grades

Students will use toy cars, a strip of rigid cardboard, base 10 blocks (or C-rods), and a measuring tape to perform experiments, collect data, and draw conclusions about ramp height/distance traveled relationships. The cardboard is used as a ramp resting on the floor on one end and on successively raised heights using the blocks on the other end.

For example, the ramp is made using a 1 cm height on one end, the car is released from the top of the ramp, and the distance traveled is measured and recorded. The ramp height on one end is raised to 2 cm and another measurement is obtained. The process is repeated for 8 to 10 readings. The ordered pairs (height, distance) are graphed, and discussion and drawing conclusions follows. This activity is neatly done in cooperative groups. (Each person of the team of three or four has a specific assignment: ramp adjustor, car releaser, distance measurer, etc.)

In any data collection-graphing-analysis activity, the major emphasis should be on care with the data, both in the collection and analysis aspects of working with it. Less emphasis should be given to graphing. The reason is that graphing is not difficult because it is basically mechanical, and it is possible to have variety among appropriate graphs. Furthermore, graphing is always possible even if the data is poor or improper. On the other hand, significant problem solving skills are involved in ensuring that the data is good, appropriate, and in forms from which data can be read and interpretations can be made. Analysis also requires thought and reasoning in order for the ideas and information contained in the data set to be presented and communicated well.

Note and Caution

Teachers often give adequate attention to, and practice on, creating graphs (which require only low order thinking skills) and very little to interpreting graphs (which require higher order thinking skills). In daily life, people very seldom *create* graphs but are called upon to *interpret* graphs very often. TV news programs, newspapers, and sales brochures often include graphs intended to influence adult thinking. Thus, if we are preparing students for life outside of school, our emphasis needs to be on what they will actually encounter in daily life. Some graph creating obviously will help students with graph interpretation, but teachers should not assume that all the skills necessary for interpreting graphs can be obtained through graph creating exercises only. Related to this is the fact that most computers are equipped with graphing software. Increasing amounts of graphing will be done by students and adults on computers. When computer graphing programs are used, it is usually easier for the graph creator to set scales by try-and-modify approaches rather than to spend the time making appropriate calculations. This is because the computer can immediately show the graph form chosen; if it is not the best form, the operator can delete that graph and modify the scale selections so that the computer can graph another trial form (Nuffield Foundation, 1967).

回 Solving the Problem

Organizing Data Sets

Students should be made aware that data come to us in disorganized and sometimes confusing forms. Usually it needs to be organized so that it will be easier to make measurements. Students will have practice in various science and math contexts in placing numbers in increasing or decreasing order. This is the easiest and usually the first organization of data to be done. However, if the data is in fraction form or decimal form, ordering in this way can be difficult. In any case, students should be given practice in placing data sets of random numbers in numerical order. Students should not be given large data sets because they make the task of organizing busy work and a source of frustration rather than learning (Hopkins, 1997).

Activity for Kindergarten Through Third Grades

Students will, in playing with various manipulatives such as counters and attribute blocks, organize them in different ways. The teacher will give very little direction—simply that as individuals or in small groups, they are to arrange the objects in sets of their own design.

Ideally, the teacher will give students objects to work with so that organization along certain lines is likely. The teacher will ask for explanations and reasons for the arrangements chosen.

The teacher will highlight those arrangements that are precursors of the more advanced organizational processes to be learned later. (An example would be a side-by-side column arrangement for multiple categories.)

Extension Activity

The teacher will present sets of numbers or counters, with numerals on them, for organization. Some numerals might be single digit and others in various decades. The items should not be presented in sequence.

Note

It should be pointed out to students that we do, on occasion, have to deal with very large sets of numbers. When that is the case, it can be very difficult to simply put them in order, or even to find the largest or smallest number in the set. It should then be pointed out that we have various tricks and techniques for coping with large and confusing sets of data and that these all begin with some kind of organization.

The other basic organizational technique is to group and categorize parts of the data set. Students in fifth through eighth grades should be encouraged to create charts and tables starting with gross separation of the larger numbers from smaller numbers (without necessarily referencing the median) and then to use finer classifying such as stem-and-leaf graphing (Fig. 13-1). Practice in doing this with various kinds of numbers will strengthen children's abilities with organizing data.

Example

Data Set
25, 36, 47, 56, 41, 38, 33, 26, 32, 51, 49
43, 40, 28, 27, 33, 34, 41, 24, 22, 23

Some quick conclusions can be drawn by noting that nearly the same amounts of data are found in the 20's, 30's and 40's, but significantly less in the 50's, etc.

FIGURE 13-1   Stem-and-Leaf Plot for the Data Set

Stem-and-Leaf

20	2, 3, 4, 5, 6, 7, 8
30	2, 3, 3, 4, 6, 8
40	0, 1, 1, 3, 7, 9
50	1, 6

Measuring a Set of Data

Range

In the early grades, children, as part of their acquisition of number sense, naturally explore the ideas of largest numbers and smallest numbers. By the time they are collecting data and analyzing it, these ideas are quite well established. Thus, not much time is needed to help children formalize the concept of *range*. Perhaps it is important to help students note that this is a formal name for a concept (the difference between the largest and smallest number in the data set) that they already understand well, and that this is one of the descriptors of a set. Range is one of the *measures* of a set.

As is the case with constructing any concept, varied examples as well as nonexamples should be given, and the examples should vary over noncritical attributes of the range concept such as dispersion and type of numbers in the set.

Examples

The sets contain the numbers of points scored by three different players in 12 games.

Alice (A):   7, 6, 6, 5, 6, 8, 12, 20, 19, 18, 19, 20

Betty (B):   6, 5, 12, 13, 11, 12, 15, 13, 20, 14, 12, 13

Cheryl (C):   2, 3, 6, 3, 17, 3, 3, 3, 8, 3, 2, 4

Each player has a range of 15, yet:

- Set A has two items at the top of the range.

- Sets A & B have the same values at top and bottom but are very different sets.

- Set C has the same range but it is located differently. The top and bottom numbers are lower than for sets A and B.

Centers of Sets

As children examine range in sets of data, it should be pointed out to them that the range and upper and lower data points are not sufficient to explain and describe differences among sets. Examples such as the comparison of sets B and C above should be discussed. The ranges are the same, but the sets are very different. Those trying to understand or describe the set need to have another *measure* (a number which is in some way descriptive of the whole set) of the set. This will be coupled with the students' already acquired partial concepts of a typical or likely value in the set and begin to be formalized by considering measures of the centers of sets. We have helped students examine the extent of a set (range); if we can position the whole set by considering an additional descriptor we are better able to understand the situation described by the data.

Note and Caution

It is important, throughout the study of data and statistics, to maintain the direct connection of this study with real life. We are developing tools to aid us in solving problems and in understanding the world and culture in which we live. This is *not* an abstract and academic exercise that should result in the memorization of formulas and definitions. We are describing and understanding real life situations, using data from them and working with the data in such a way as to obtain the most complete description possible.

Again, there are difficulties with everyday language as we try to understand statistics and data management. The term *average* is probably the worst. It has three different technical meanings and various shades of general meanings as it is used very loosely in daily language. In general usage, *average* means that is typical or most frequently seen in a data set. It is also used in contexts such as "average person," where it is difficult to know what the term means. It is even used to make predictions such as: "In the year 2000, the average car will get 35 miles per gallon," leaving the reader with more questions than information. A reworded statement such as, "In the year 2000, the mean miles per gallon will be 35 for all cars," will convey the intended information more accurately.

Mode

Though we can (and should) leave the term *mode* out of the children's vocabulary until high school, we can and should point out and discuss the fact that some sets contain repeated data items. We then note that in describing sets it is helpful to state whether some items appear more often than others. The mode is the item appearing most often in the set. In set C in the example of points scored, 3 points was scored more often than any other; thus 3 is the mode for the set. Students should be asked, "After looking at these scores for the player Cheryl in 12 games, what would you expect to be scored in the 13th game?

Graphs of single-mode and bi-modal (2 equal height bumps) sets should be presented or acquired by the students and discussed. Students may be asked to look for this characteristic of a data set and describe the real situation using phrases such as: "Cheryl has scored 3 points in most of the games so, unless something changes, she will probably score 3 points in other games, too." These questions and comments can be worded to illustrate that *mode* is sometimes what is meant by the word *average*. This occurs when the *typical* or *most likely* idea is being discussed as a set is described. Note that the mode is an item in the set (Shulte, 1981).

Median

For small sets, of the size students would be likely to be work with, it may be helpful to identify the middle of the set. This is the center of the set in the sense that there are as many numbers of the set larger than the *median* (the middle value) as there are less than this number.

The connection should be made here with the number sense idea of midpoint or halfway-between.

When there is an even number of items in the data set, there is no middle number. In order to identify all the numbers above and below the middle, it is necessary to find the two middle numbers and the number halfway between those two. That value is the *median*. It is also at the 50th percentile. It may be one of the numbers of the set, but not necessarily. It should be noted that the median is not affected by outliers or their distance from the median. (An outlier is a number in the set that is much higher or lower than numbers in the rest of the set. In the second set in the example below, 30 could be considered to be an outlier.) A variety of sets, some with outliers and others without, should be examined by students to help them develop the concept of median.

 Examples

Set: 4, 5, 5, 6, 8, 8, 9, 10, 10, 10, 14, 16, 16
(mode 10, median 9, mean 9.3)

Set: 4, 5, 5, 6, 8, 8, 9, 10, 10, 10, 14, 16, 30
(mode 10, median 9, mean 10.4)

Mean

The third formal measure of the center of the set is the *mean* (the sum of all the numbers divided by the number of the items in the set). This is the value often intended when the word "average" is used. Piaget's research indicates that children cannot comprehend the concept of the mean until about age 12, when they become conservers and can consider two or more interrelated values simultaneously (Piaget, 1975).

For small sets with whole numbers, children can perform the necessary computation to find the mean. It should soon become obvious that, for most sets, the mean is not a number in the set. (See the sets in the example above.) It should also be made clear that all elements of the set must be used in the calculation.

Some students will be aware of certain scoring arrangements for sporting events in which the highest and lowest numbers are omitted from the calculation. Students should be asked why this does not give a true mean.)

Sports scores and situations in which performances are evaluated using means provide good motivating examples. Students may also calculate means for their grades on quizzes and exams; these values are usually discussed with real interest. Experimentation with various sets of grade scores will be instructive and of interest to students, especially when these are set in problem solving formats.

Example

A grade of B requires a mean score of 90. Jake's scores are 95, 80, 92, and 88. What will he have to score on the next assignment to qualify for a B?

If an A requires a mean of 95, can Jake get an A?

Note

Unfortunately, grades are nearly always discussed using the word *average*. Teachers should take the opportunity to discuss the meaning of *average* as it applies to grades and to ensure that students understand that in this context it signifies *mean*.

Students should find the value of each of the measures—mode, median, and mean—on the same sets, then graph and record the information, looking for patterns and comparisons. At the grade 6 to 8 levels, students can analyze graphs and learn to interpret them by noting the relative positions of these three values. "What does a data set look like when the mean, mode, and median are nearly the same?" "How does the graph of a set appear when the mode is below the mean and median?" are among the questions to be considered.

Activity (for Sixth Through Eighth Graders)

Students will create and examine data sets with *outliers* and answer the questions:

How does the existence or absence of outliers affect the mode?

How does the existence or absence of outliers affect the median?

How does the existence of absence of outliers affect the mean?

When the concepts of range and mean have been developed, they should be connected with the graphs that students draw when they began recording data. These graphs are essentially frequency distributions. Students must learn how to examine frequency distribution graphs to get estimates for the range and mean for a set of data.

Activity for Sixth Through Eighth Grades

Students will graph the frequencies for a set using a line graph as shown in Figure 13-2. Students will then cut out the graph from the paper cutting where the dotted lines are and along the graph curve.

FIGURE 13-2 Frequency Distribution Graph for a Set

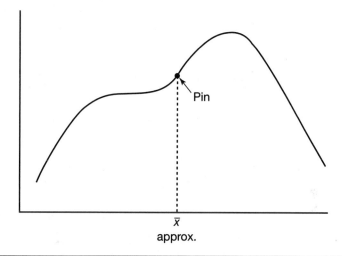

The students will use a push pin, sticking it through the paper just below the graph line, attempting to find the balance point so that the paper hangs horizontally. The value below the balance pinhole on the horizontal axis will be noted. If the graph has been carefully constructed, the balance pinpoint should be very near the vertical line on the mean value.

The mean is really a balance point in the data and it may help students understand more fully if this exercise is connected with weighing with a balance beam. Balance is dependent on both quantity and distance from the balance point. The same concept defines the mean. This balance concept should be emphasized, rather than the computation or a formula.

Frequency Distributions

Older students can create frequency distributions by creating classes within the data set. This requires the following:

- Between 6 and 15 classes.
- Each class the same width.
- A class for every data item.
- No class overlap.

These rules ensure that graphs can be read and understood and that the graph will accurately communicate information about the data set. The process of creating a frequency distribution should emphasize the characteristics that make a graph clear and accurate in conveying the pertinent information. Understanding these characteristics also enables students to interpret graphed information effectively.

Example

In graphing a frequency distribution for the following set, this class configuration is one which may be used:

20, 32, 43, 21, 28, 35, 40, 25, 45, 24, 31, 26, 32, 33, 47
25, 35, 38, 46, 23, 39, 47, 32, 39, 29, 46, 38, 32, 37, 38

The range is $47 - 20 = 27$, and a convenient 7 classes would yield $28/7 = 4$, for class width. (Twenty-eight is an approximation [estimate] for the range.)

FIGURE 13-3

	Class	Frequency
I	20-23	3
II	24-27	4
III	38-31	3
IV	32-35	7
V	36-39	6
VI	40-43	2
VI	44-47	<u>5</u>

The totaling of the frequency values provides a quick check of the count for frequencies. The vertical axis for the frequencies should extend to allow the largest frequency to be near the top of the graph and the seven class values should be evenly spaced and on the horizontal axis.

Caution

Students must resist the temptation to connect the end points of the graph down to the horizontal axis. That connection would give a wrong impression of the nature of the data. Another point to make is that a vertical scale that does not begin with zero may be misleading and that the intervals on the horizontal scale *must* be *equal*. The horizontal scale usually does not start at zero.

Normal Distributions

Seventh and eighth grade students should be introduced to the concept of normal distributions and given the general facts about them. Unless an advanced student wishes to explore the idea in some depth, though, the concept of standard deviation and probabilities related to the normal distribution would not be

---

FIGURE 13-4 Pascal's Triangle through the Sixth Row

```
                    1
                1       1
            1       2       1
        1       3       3       1
    1       4       6       4       1
1       5       10      10      5       1
```

---

studied until high school. At the middle school level the shape of the normal distribution should be noted, especially in connection with *shake-and-spill* probability activities and with sets which yield near-normal distributions. From algebra, the binomial coefficients can be examined from this perspective, too, and Pascal's triangle may be used to generate these values for graphing (Figure 13-4).

It should be pointed out that each of the normal frequency distribution graphs has features in common with the others and all normal distributions. They are symmetrical; the mode, mean and median coincide; and the ends (tails) are low (near the horizontal axis), indicating very few items at the high and low ends. Incorrect attention to these important characteristics should be noted in graphs presented in the media as attempts to describe data sets and real life situations.

Creating Graphs

In activities preliminary to learning to graph formally, kindergarten through second graders should be given opportunities to place symbols, markers, or objects in adjacent columns or rows according to some classification scheme. Students can then count the items in the various categories and discuss the relative sizes of the categories.

Activity for Kindergarten Through Second Grades

Students, in groups of four or five, will open bags of M & M's, place the M & M's in the color-appropriate columns on a prepared sheet, count, and record the number for each column.

The results for all the groups can then be recorded in a similar format on the chalkboard so that they can be viewed as children discuss their findings and draw conclusions regarding the most likely numbers of the various colors of M & M's found in a bag.

Among the most common graphs students in grades 5 through 8 will learn to create are: circle graphs (pie charts), line graphs, histograms, box-and-whisker graphs, stem-and-leaf plots, Cartesian plots, and pictographs. Third and fourth graders may create circle graphs using halves, quarters, and possibly thirds or eighths. The line graphs, histograms, and Cartesian plots are based on the same principles but may appear to be different. Each of these requires plotting of two dimensions—one related to another by the use of vertical and horizontal axes. Each has a scale for one of the variables and ordered pairs to identify the points for the positioning of the bars or lines. Creating graphs of this type must be left to sixth, seventh, and eighth graders because the concepts of interrelated data sets and variation in one variable, dependent on variation in another, are late-developing mental abilities. Developing coordinated pairs and understanding their significance depends on these abilities (Nuffield Foundation, 1967).

The following must be attended to in the creation of line graphs, histograms and Cartesian plots:

- The vertical axis must usually begin with 0.

- Both scales should occupy nearly the full axis length in the graph.

- The horizontal and vertical scales must be uniform but are usually not the same scales (the histogram bars must all be the same width).

- The number of points plotted should be between 6 and 15.

- For a few points to be plotted, bars may be preferable to broken or smooth line graphs.

- Bars may be horizontal or vertical, though vertical is more common and usually preferred.

Students should practice creating several types of graphs using the same data in order to decide which is preferable for the various types of data sets. Emphasis should be given to the fact that variety in graphs for the same set can be expected. Students cannot be successful with graphing if they attempt to memorize some particular format for graphs. Graphs must be created uniquely for each data set because there is such variety in data sets and because different purposes for graphs also dictate different graph formats. Students should be reminded that the purpose of a graph is to convey information about a data set quickly, accurately, and interestingly. Thus, students should be cautioned not to make graphs that are "busy" or too small to be easily read. They should be shown graphs containing errors and should see and discuss the resulting misunderstanding or wrong impressions given by such graphs. (Some of these are presented in the section on interpreting and reading graphs.) It should be pointed out that appropriate labeling of parts of the graph is often the difference between a good and a poor graph even if the rest is well done.

Circle and Pictographs

Circle graphs and pie charts are common in texts and media and are sometimes easily read. Unless the fractional values are few and very common ($\frac{1}{4}$,

$^1/_2$, $^3/_4$, etc.), they are not easy to create. Where other values are to be used, graphing of this type should be reserved for sixth to eighth graders. The basic reason is that, to be reasonably accurate, creating a circle graph requires understanding of the angle measure of a circle (360°), ascertaining angle values representing percentages of 360°, and measuring those angles at the center of a circle. Only older children are capable of these skills and abilities. Unless there are only three or four categories and they are very close to half- or quarter-circle values, young children should not be encouraged to attempt circle graphs. Attempting to force data into circle graphs will create frustration and result in poor graphs.

Circle graphs become meaningless when there are too many categories. When there are more than five or six classes or when more than two or three of the classes are very small (less than 5%) and about the same size, another type of graph should be chosen. Under these conditions, the circle graph does not effectively represent the data set.

Activity for Grades 6 Through 8

Students in groups will attempt to circle-graph data collected from the class—each group doing the necessary computation and creating the graph on a transparency so that it can easily be presented to the whole class. The following subjects may be used for beginnings.

- Proportions of M & M's of a given color in a bag

- Preferred movies (class poll)

- Preferred CD (class poll)

- Political candidates (class poll)—these could be national, state, local, or in school.)

- Preferred professional teams

- Preferred TV shows

In each case, the categories should be described by the teacher so that some results will create good circle graphs and others will be poor circle graphs. In this way, counter-examples will be demonstrated and discussed by the class. The class then experiences the situations in which another type of graph should be chosen. In order to make the point, groups may have to be encouraged to go ahead with their graphs, even though they are messy and difficult.

Extension

The class chooses and creates better graphs for those data sets where circle graphs were inappropriate.

Pie charts are closely related to pictographs, a popular means used by the media and industry to present information to the public. These are pictures or caricatures with some of the features of graphs. The picture, sketch, or cartoon forming the graph is usually directly related to the topic or situation the data set describes. Examples can be seen in the section on graph interpretation. Considering some of the categories in the activity described above, students might use a picture of a CD separated into sectors of the circle of the CD to create a pictorial circle graph. Pictures of horses in a race with different horses identified as different candidates could be used. Care must be exercised to ensure that the information to be conveyed by the graph is not lost in the picture or that the picture is misleading. This is especially true when pictures of different sizes are used to represent larger or smaller values. A larger picture has two dimension differences—length and width (area)—and, if used to represent difference in one dimension such as distance, will be very misleading.

Activity for Grades 4 Through 8

Students will make pictographs for each of the categories in the activity above and explain and discuss each of them with the class, citing the advantages of their use.

Caution and Reminder

Students must be reminded often that creating graphs is not just a mathematical exercise. It is an attempt to present a clear pictorial description of an object or situation, using all the data obtained from that object or situation. Students must assume that someone will read and attempt to learn from their graphs.

Stem-and-leaf and box-and-whisker plots fall somewhere between charts and graphs. They are really organizational schemes to give the reader a sense of dispersion or distribution of the data items within a set. Typically a stem-and-leaf plot is used when numbers in a data set may be helpfully displayed according to decimal categories and the plots list all the data items in this organized fashion (Figures 13-4 and 13-5).

Examples

The 1's in the first line indicate that the data item 21 occurred twice in the set, and the 3 in the third line shows that 43 was an item, etc.

FIGURE 13-5   Stem-and-Leaf Plot for a Data Set

$$
\begin{array}{r|l}
20 & 1, 1, 3, 7, 8 \\
30 & 2, 5, 5, 6, 6, 6, 9 \\
40 & 3, 7, 8, 9 \\
50 & 2, 3
\end{array}
$$

FIGURE 13-6   Stem-and-Leaf Plot for a Decimal Number Set

```
.1 | 3, 4, 7, 8
.2 |
.3 | 2, 3, 6, 5, 6
.4 | 8, 8, 9
```

The data items are 0.13, 0.14, 0.17, 0.18, 0.32, 0.33 etc.

The stem-and-leaf plot can be used helpfully to obtain a sense of the dispersion of the data prior to graphing so that the grapher makes a good choice regarding the type of graph that will be most helpful. However, the stem-and-leaf plot may be sufficient in itself to organize the data in an at-a-glance form.

Box-and-whisker plots look at the data in a more general form showing at a glance the bunching of the data. They are used helpfully when there are outlying data items. These graphs require a little more computation and graphing, but also provide more specific information. They are used to analyze one set of data, not the interrelationship between two sets of data, so only one axis or scale is used. The axis is usually horizontal with an appropriate scale adequate for the whole range of the data. It must be possible to identify the median, mean, and 25th and 75th percentiles on the scale. (Other percentiles or standard deviations can also be used).

Examples

The box contains all the data points but 5. (Those are indicated by dots on the line outside the box.) The bulk of the data points lie between .3 (25th percentile) and .6 (75th percentile). The median is at about .45 and the mean is at about .5.

Two box-and-whisker plots may be combined to give a quick comparison of the relative positioning of data in two sets.

Grades on an exam given to two classes:

FIGURE 13-7   Box-and-Whisker Plot for Two Classes' Exams

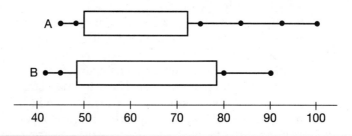

Students in the sixth grade and above can create box-and-whisker plots successfully. They can use them in science and in social studies reports may also put this math skill to practical use.

Activity for Grades 6 Through 8

Students in groups will, from given sets of data (perhaps collected by the class), create:

- a frequency distribution line graph

- a histogram

- a stem-and-leaf plot

- a box-and-whisker plot

- a circle graph

- a pictograph

Each should be on a construction-paper-sized sheet for display. The class will then discuss and decide which graph would best be used for each of several purposes, including: a presentation to the school board, on posters for a student campaign, an article in the school paper, in a letter sent to the mayor, etc.

Using Computers

Many computer software packages have graphing capabilities. They can be used to produce all sorts of colorful graphs of various types and will present them in pictograph forms if desired. Children should have a good understanding of graphing and be able to produce their own graphs before they use graphing software. Not only will the computer-produced graphs be more meaningful, but children will know whether the computer graph communicates what is intended about the data set.

Reading and Interpreting Graphs

As stated previously, reading and interpreting graphs, rather than creating graphs, should be emphasized. People seldom create graphs unless they work in a job in industry or the media that involves information sharing. However, in daily life people will very often be presented with graphs to read and interpret. Almost every newspaper contains at least one graph. News magazines and advertising media contain many graphs.

Students, then, must be given instructions and practice examining graphs to learn from them and to learn how to understand what graphs can and cannot do. Students must learn, too, how to avoid being misled by poorly constructed graphs. The difficulty is that some of the graphs presented to the public are misleading because they were poorly constructed, not adequately labeled, or intentionally designed to give a wrong impression. Apart from that, an uninstructed person may not be able to glean all the possible information from a well-constructed graph.

In order for graphs to be accurately and usefully interpreted, they must meet several requirements. Teachers should describe these requirements and help students note them as graphs are examined and interpreted. Graphs that do not meet one or more of the requirements should be disregarded because they will be misleading or difficult to understand.

- The graphs must account for all the data from the set under consideration.

- The data from which the graph was created must be good. (The sampling and collection procedures were sound.)

- The categories must be comparable. (The widths of the classes must all be the same.)

- The scales must be appropriate. (Consistent intervals and correct starting points.)

- The pictures and sketches must not obscure the information to be obtained from the graph.

- Two-dimensional figures must not represent one-dimensional data unless one of two dimensions is held constant.

- The graph must be clear and easily readable. (The reader should not have to do calculations and involved analysis to find the information.)

Activity for Grades 6 Through 8

Students will collect graphs and copies of graphs from newspapers (*USA Today* is a good source), news magazines, texts, and other sources and bring them to class. The graphs will be sorted as to type and each group of students given the graphs of a particular type. Each group will analyze their graphs and write a report answering the following questions:

- What were the errors in graphing?

- Were the purposes of the graphs clearly indicated?

- What were the strengths of the good graphs?

- What were the weaknesses of the poor graphs?

Alternatives

- Each group examines one graph (preferably a graph on a subject of real interest to students of that age—dating, pro teams, movies, TV, toys) and analyze it as to effectiveness.

- Groups examine several graphs on a particular subject such as year-to-year changes in demographics or popularity of TV personalities, toys, clothing, etc. and discuss the adequacy of the graphs.

The preceding activity could accompany, precede, or follow the examination by the teacher and class of several graphs such as those included in Figures 13-8 through 13-12. Some of these are good graphs which clearly convey correct impressions; the characteristics of those graphs should be noted. Other graphs have serious, but perhaps not obvious, flaws. These flaws should be pointed out and discussion about the errors and the misinformation portrayed and carefully noted.

The important parts of Figure 13-8 are clearly labeled and the graph is not too "busy" (it does not include lines for 5 other cities, for example); one can make comparisons at a glance. A slight distractor might be the use of the Celsius scale rather than the Fahrenheit. That could be remedied by placing both scales on the graph; one on the right and one on the left. Another slight problem is the bottom of the temperature scale. Since the Charleston line begins and ends at about 9°, the horizontal baseline (axis) should probably be at the 9° mark. Because it is a temperature scale (ordinal rather than interval), there is no need to start the scale at 0°. Another question concerns what tem-

FIGURE 13-8 Monthly Temperatures in Charleston and San Diego

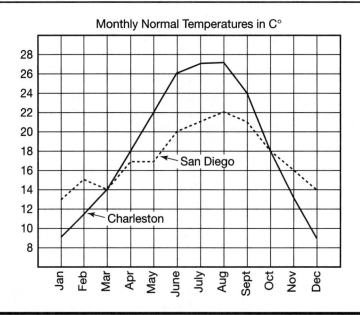

FIGURE 13-9   Circle Graph Example

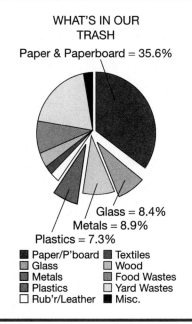

WHAT'S IN OUR
TRASH
Paper & Paperboard = 35.6%

Glass = 8.4%
Metals = 8.9%
Plastics = 7.3%

■ Paper/P'board	■ Textiles
▨ Glass	▨ Wood
■ Metals	■ Food Wastes
■ Plastics	▢ Yard Wastes
▢ Rub'r/Leather	■ Misc.

peratures are recorded. Are they daytime highs, mean daytime high temperatures for the month, medians, etc.?

The circle graph in Figure 13-9 is difficult to read because there are so many divisions, including several about the same size; the labeling is not clear and consistent. It is necessary to have an attached legend since the graph cannot be read at a glance. The reader must refer back and forth to understand the information conveyed.

The pictograph in Figure 13-10 is clearly labeled, and the picture attracts attention to the point of the graph. The bars are of equal width, making the categories comparable and easy to read.

Two-Dimensional Graph Comparisons

The pictograph in Figure 13-11 showing the different quantities of a substance contained in different types of cereals is misleading because of its two-dimensional presentation of one-dimensional data. The gram amounts, 20, 13, and 8, are respectively proportional to the heights of the grain piles. That is correct. However, the appearance of the graph conveys the impression that the amount in the 20g pile is much more than $1\frac{1}{2}$ times the amount in the 8g pile ($20 = 1\frac{1}{2} \times 8$). The area of the 20g pile is $2\frac{1}{4}$ times the area of the 8g pile ($1\frac{1}{2} \times 1\frac{1}{2} = 2\frac{1}{4}$).

The relative cost of a car information in the graph in Figure 13-12 is not

FIGURE 13-10 Pictograph

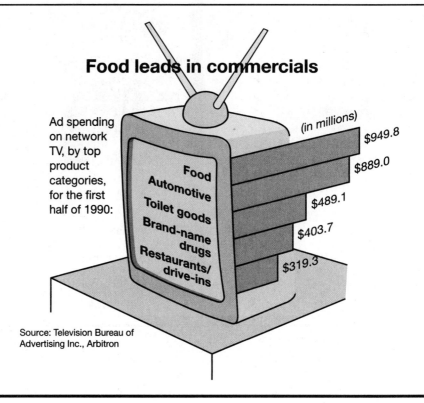

Food leads in commercials

Ad spending on network TV, by top product categories, for the first half of 1990:

(in millions)

Food — $949.8
Automotive — $889.0
Toilet goods — $489.1
Brand-name drugs — $403.7
Restaurants/ drive-ins — $319.3

Source: Television Bureau of Advertising Inc., Arbitron

clearly presented for two reasons: The suggestion in the title and apparent intention of the graph is that the percentage has increased over the three decades, but of the three, the middle value shows a significant decrease. This would make the thoughtful reader wonder if the next decade would again show a decrease. In other words, a regular upward trend may not be the case. Also, the length of the bars and "busyness" of the graph make it hard to grasp the information at a glance.

FIGURE 13-11 Two-Dimensional Pictograph of One-Dimensional Data

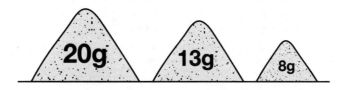

20g   13g   8g

FIGURE 13-12 Relative Cost of a Car

Cars take bigger bite of income

Since 1970, the price of a new car has risen from
40% to 51% of a family's income:

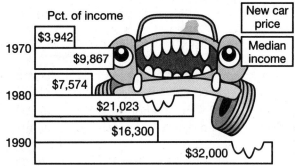

Pct. of income

New car price

Median income

1970 $3,942 / $9,867

1980 $7,574 / $21,023

1990 $16,300 / $32,000

Source: Commerce Dept.; American Auto Datam

Probability

Children often hear and occasionally use statements of probability in their daily lives. They note the weather forecasts when they wonder whether a game will be held or school canceled. They also use more ambiguous general phrases such as *not likely*, *no way*, and *probably* but, as with much of everyday speech, there are many misuses of probability terminology and concepts. Children may even have heard the term, *the law of averages* and wondered what that means.

Activity for Grades K Through 3

Students, working in groups of three or four, will *shake-and-spill* 3 two-color counters, then 4 counters, then 5. For each number they will *shake-and-spill* 10 times. Each *shake-and-spill* result will be recorded by a spot or symbol on a chart:

The groups will discuss and report to the class any patterns or trends that they notice. The teacher will ask why the larger and smaller numbers occur in certain places.

Activities for Grades 6 Through 8

Students will make a collection of everyday words and phrases relating to probability, list them on a poster and as lessons on probability and statistics progress, write on the poster the definitions and/or the errors connected to them. (In addition to those above, students might include *chance*, *odds are*, *give him odds*, *percent probability*, *very likely*, etc.)

FIGURE 13-13 *Shake-and-Spill* Charts and Results

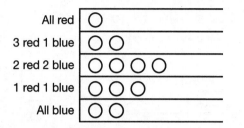
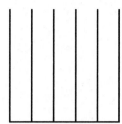

Students will write a report on the meaning of "the law of averages" and base their report on definitions given by people they interview.

The next task for students is to formalize probability ideas starting with the concept of probability itself. The probability of an event is calculated by dividing the number of specific occurrences by the number of possible occurrences.

$$\text{Probability of event 1, } P(E_1) = \frac{\# \text{ of } E_1 \text{ occurrences}}{\# \text{ of all possible occurrences}}$$

Teachers should lead students in discussions about probabilities and probability statements that are of interest to them. A cross-subject project that will incorporate probability concepts can be found in describing weather. In science or social studies, projects can include weather-predicting activities. Children can learn about and explore the means (including the use of probabilities) that weather forecasters use to predict the weather in the near and more distant future (SMSG, 1966, Primary).

Students may want to duplicate some of those techniques in the classroom by collecting data, drawing graphs, counting events, and calculating probabilities. They may then compare their results with those reported on local television. This project may take on special meaning if the class makes a prediction for some future specially scheduled day, such as a field trip or ball game. A sample probability unit is included in Appendix G.

It would be instructive, too, to arrange for a discussion about the way daily decisions are made and the fact that probability principles are often used unknowingly. For example, if a big dog scared Sally three of the four times she walked by a certain house, she will avoid that house because she believes that it is very likely (there is a high probability) that she will be scared by the dog there.

There are many opportunities in the study of probabilities for advanced students to work on projects and study probability concepts. These would not necessarily take the students into mathematical concepts and processes scheduled later for the whole class.

Certain Probabilities

Students need to understand that probability values between 0 and 1 can be expressed as fractions less than one or by percentages less than 100. When an event is believed to be certain, it is said to have 100% probability. Events like sunrise and winter are *taken for granted*; they have probabilities of 100%. The computation is:

$$\frac{\text{Number of times the sun rises}}{\text{Number of mornings}}$$

In a given period of time, say September, this would be $30/30 = 1 = 100\% = P$ (sunrise in September).

Since these numbers are the same, for any period of time, the value of the fraction is $1 = 100\%$.

When the event is as likely to happen as not to happen, people say its probability is 50-50. They are expressing the idea that the probability it will happen is 50% and the probability that it will not happen is also 50%. Alternatively, out of 100 possibilities, the event would occur 50 times.

$$\frac{50}{100} = 50\% = \frac{1}{2}.$$

"60–40" and "70–30" are similar common expressions (SMSG, 1966, Intermediate).

Zero Probability

Zero probability should also be considered. Children often say, "No way." Using that expression as a discussion starter, a teacher can help children understand 0 probability. They might be asked, "What is the probability the class will choose a math exam over a pizza party?"

$$P \text{ (exam is chosen)} = \frac{\text{Number of votes for exam}}{\text{Number of votes}} = \frac{0}{25} = 0.$$

Note

A teacher will note, in these probability considerations, the opportunity to review and practice fraction, decimal, and percentage concepts. In computing probabilities, there are many practical applications for using rational numbers.

Activity for All Grades

Students will cite and list different events and the occurrence of probabilities. For some events there may be disagreement over probability values; these provide opportunities for class discussion, decision, and justification. The class may want to make probability-based predictions to be checked out when the events occur.

Extension Activity

Students will consider probabilities that (E_1 or E_2) occurs and that (E_1 and E_2) occurs when the probabilities of E_1 and E_2 are known.

Summary

The purpose and value of statistics and probability were discussed both for K–8 students and in the context of preparing them for life outside the classroom. Emphasis was given to the need to keep a consistent focus on understanding and describing objects and situations clearly and accurately. It was pointed out that often the only way to do this is by collecting and/or analyzing the data that comes from the object or situation. Statistics was presented as a kind of measurement device. Because people in daily life seldom create graphs, but often need to read and analyze graphs, the necessity of studying the latter more than the former was highlighted. In examining graphs, the principles of good construction and the features to look for were outlined. Different types of graphs were described along with best uses and problems specific to certain types. The statistics, mode, median, and mean were discussed with activities that help students understand these and their interrelationships, including how they connect with the normal distribution. The definition of probability and its practical use in our lives was presented.

Exercises

1. Prepare a unit on reading and interpreting graphs using graphs found in newspapers and magazines. The graphs should include examples of both good and bad graphs.
2. Learn how to compute standard deviation, demonstrate to the class how to do it, and explain to the class how this measure on a set is used and useful.
3. Prepare sets of data in which the respective means, modes, medians, and ranges are the same, but the sets have different standard deviations and demonstrate the necessity of the standard deviation measure.
4. Prepare a unit (or lesson plan) to teach the application of probability and statistics to a practical problem (e.g., predicting the weather for a certain date or month. Consider the example in Appendix G.)

References

Hopkins, Marty. (1997, September) It's the berries. *Teaching Children Mathematics.* Reston, VA: NCTM.

National Council of Teachers of Mathematics (1989). *Curriculum and Evaluation Standards for School Mathematics.* Reston, VA: Author.

Nuffield Foundation (1967). *Pictorial Representation.* New York: Wiley.

Piaget, Jean, and Barbel Inhelder (1975). *The Origin of the Idea of Chance in Children.* New York: W. W. Norton.

School Mathematics Study Group (1966). *Probability for the Intermediate Grades.* Stanford, CA: SMSG, Stanford University.

———— (1966). *Probability for the Primary Grades.* Stanford, CA: SMSG, Stanford University.

Shulte, Albert P. (1987). Learning Probability Concepts in Elementary School Mathematics, *Arithmetic Teacher*, 34(5), 32–33.

Shulte, Albert P., Ed. (1981). *Teaching Statistics and Probability,* National Council of Teachers of Mathematics. Reston, VA: NCTM.

🔲 Suggested Readings

Botula, Mary Jean, and Margaret I. Ford. (1997, September) All about us: Connecting statistics with real life. *Mathematics Teaching in the Middle School.* Reston, VA: NCTM.

Dixon, Juli, K., and Christy J. Falba (1997, September). Graphing in the information age: Using data from the world wide web. *Mathematics Teaching in the Middle School.* Reston, VA: NCTM.

Edwards, Nancy Tanner, and Gary G. Bitter (1989). Teaching mathematics with technology: Changing variables using spreadsheet templates. *Arithmetic Teacher,* 37(2), 40–44.

Russell, Susan Jo, and Antonia Stone (1990). *Used Numbers: Counting: Ourselves and Our Families.* Palo Alto, CA: Dale Seymour.

Shielack, Jane F. (1990). Teaching mathematics with technology: A graphing tool for the primary grades. *Arithmetic Teacher,* 38(2).

Teaching Middle School Algebra

One of the children's problems: Jerry does not understand how letters can represent numbers or why they should.

Teacher's problem: The transition from arithmetic to algebra seems traumatic to most of the class and this causes them difficulty in getting started in algebra.

> **Problem:** *Learning algebra concepts presents special problems to many children.*

Understanding the Problem

Traditionally, algebra was reserved for high school students, but in recent years the course of study has worked its way down through the grades and now it is quite common for eighth graders to take the first course in algebra. It is possible, too, to find seventh graders studying algebra formally. This means that preservice teachers being certified for K–8 must prepare themselves for the possibility of teaching algebra. The difficulty for some who plan to be teachers is that algebra came as a shock to them when they were in high school and they have avoided algebra ever since. It comes to many students as an unpleasant surprise. This feeling of surprise and shock and the inability to cope with sudden change could cause preservice teachers real hesitation as they realize that there is a possibility they could be required to teach algebra (Herscovics & Linchevsky, 1994).

The difficulty seems to begin in the very early grades. Through examples in textual materials and in classes, there is a consistent reference to specific numbers as though there is no uncertainty in mathematics, even when there are mathematical sentences such as $3 + \square = 5$ to be dealt with. Educators often fail to make reference to variable concepts early. There is insufficient use of manipulatives and non-number symbols to represent numbers; even when there is extensive use of symbols, teachers may not point out to children what is being done and why. There is too little encouragement given to children to develop their own symbols to replace words or phrases.

It is recognized that young children are developmentally incapable of *operational* thinking and tasks. Piaget contends that children do not become *operational* until in their teens. They can, however, function at the level required by: "What number fits into the box to make $3 + \square = 8$?" and "Try some numbers in the box to see what makes the statement correct." (We expect young children to understand and use the fact that the 2 in 25 does not stand for 2 but for 20. That is a rather significant symbolic understanding. It is perhaps more subtle and difficult than to understand that $N + 3 = 5$ means that N stands for 2 and that when we later write $N + 3 = 6$, we mean that N now stands for 3.) White and Mitchelmore (1996) point out that a major source of difficulty for students is an underdeveloped concept of *variable*. They found that students frequently understand variables as symbols to be manipulated rather than as quantities to be related.

One of the difficulties experienced early by first-time algebra students is connected to the idea of variable. Up to this time students have dealt exclusively with constants. This background sometimes leads to situations such as the following:

✦ Example

Mr. Wilson: "If $K \div 5 = 8$, what is K?"

Student: "K has to be 40."

Mr. Wilson: "Right, $K = 40$ because if K is replaced by 40, we have $40 \div 5 = 8$, which is true."

Mr. Wilson: "Now examine this equation: $8 K = 4$. What is K?

Student: "K is 40."

The student is still dealing with constants. In the student's mind, once K is established as having the value 40, it continues to have that value.

Because of the lack of the use of symbols to represent numbers and number ideas in the early grades, the sudden use of non-number symbols in seventh or eighth grade surprises students. Many students feel betrayed by a dramatic change in the rules of the game. They are just mastering operations and concepts with whole numbers and fractional numbers, and they are confronted with a radical new idea—a variable. They are expected to cope with the idea of a variable and simultaneously with unusual procedures which in no way seem to resemble what they have been doing for the six years previous.

It may be worth considering those times in traditional mathematics education when there are dramatic changes in mathematics learning and which are a significant shock to children's mathematical thinking. Teachers should take note of these and take special care to help children cope with these sudden shocks. The quantum leap from arithmetic to algebra is perhaps the most obvious of these. Some others are:

from counting to operations

from whole numbers to integers

from integers to rational numbers

Different children will react in different ways to these transitions. Some make the transitions with apparent ease, but others experience considerable trauma—even math anxiety. These are points where an observant teacher can really make a difference in a child's ability to function effectively with learning in mathematics.

Some specific topics transitions and times are:

1. Operations with fractions—about the 5th grade

2. Formal problem solving—(in some curricula) about the 6th grade

3. Algebra—about the 7th or 8th grade

4. Geometry—about the 10th grade

5. Calculus—about the first year in college

At these transition times, students are presented with new sets of symbols that are supposed to be manipulated using all the terminology and processes previously used with numbers. However, in algebra there is an additional new terminology to be mastered: *variable, terms, binomial, polynomial, equation, inequality,* etc. Furthermore, it is assumed that all of this can be assimilated in a few days or, at the most, a few weeks when six or seven years has been spent on the arithmetic system. Often added to this is a teaching method which deals in abstractions only. Little explanation and elaboration with clearly understood examples are given. And all this is combined with algebra topics and processes for which there are no nice real life equivalents. Students then find themselves struggling with such contrived and unreal problems as: "Jerry is now 10 years older than Terry and in 2 years will be twice as old as Terry was 3 years ago. How old is each?"

Because students have practiced what they have previously learned in fraction and whole number problem situations and have actually used many of the operations in daily life activities such as buying items in stores, they can often see at least the possibility of applying that knowledge. Algebra, though, presents a real challenge to educators as they try to place particular algebraic processes in similar real life contexts. What child or adult can imagine a use for $x^2 - y^2$ at work or leisure? If children have been encouraged repeatedly during the first six grades by the statement, "You are learning this because it will really be helpful to you outside of school," they can experience real frustration because that rationale seems no longer to apply. The justification has to change to, "This will be very helpful in later mathematics," which generates very little motivation for the typical middle schooler.

Solving the Problem

Teachers should begin to lay the groundwork for children's understanding of algebraic concepts in the earliest grades. The usual practices of manipulating sets of objects, writing numerals, and counting contain opportunities for children to form the ideas that will develop into algebraic understandings. These teachable moments, however, must be capitalized upon by the teacher. It is important for the teacher to point out and help the children think about the ideas which underlie algebra.

Activity for K Through Third Grades

Students will sort and count attribute blocks.

1. The teacher will ask the students to record their results.

2. The students will write: Red, Green, Blue, etc.

3. The teacher will point out the insufficient room to write all the words.

4. The teacher will ask if it would be all right to use just one letter to represent each color category.

5. Upon agreement, the teacher will ask what letters should be used.

6. The students reply, *R* for red, *B* for blue, etc.

7. The teacher asks. "Could we use other symbols, say, *G* for red, *B* for green, etc.," or "How about placing a block at the top of the list for all like that block in some way?"

8. The teacher will ask if it would be acceptable to write: $R + B = 11$?

By this kind of questioning and encouraging students to think about and to question themselves, teacher help students begin to develop necessary basic concepts needed for algebra.

- A class of objects or numbers can be represented by a symbol.

- The same symbol can be used for different representations.

- One symbol may be better than another for a particular use.

- A symbol is a convenient tool.

- Users must remind themselves of the meaning for the symbol.

The teacher will not comment excessively on these points, but rather point them out as the opportunities occur. Attention to these ideas should be given repeatedly. Whenever children can develop and use symbolizing, create their own symbols, and make decisions about symbols cooperatively, they should be encouraged to do so (NCTM, 1989). The following example will illustrate a slightly more advanced concept.

Example and Activity for K Through Third Grade

Students are classifying clothing items including shirts, shoes, socks, pants, and coats.

Teacher: "Let's list the following categories":

s	s	s	p	c

Students: "How will we know which *s* means what?"

Teacher: "How should we change the letters for the categories?"

Students: "Perhaps

sh	sh	so	p	c

or

I	o	s	p	c

(discussion).

Students: Discussion and decision on the best scheme and development of a code list.

In the situation described above, the students are encouraged to identify the difficulty with using a kind of counter-example, and to think through the means for making symbols helpful and useful. At the next stage children are writing sentences and filling in blanks in forms such as $3 + \square = 5$. These exercises are used by children to work on basic facts and operations, and they also provide an introduction to algebraic forms such as $3 + x = 5$. Here also teachers should ensure variety in the children's experiences. It may be wise to give more emphasis to the letters than to the boxes and, as will be pointed out later, to emphasize the concept of balance (equality) from one side of the equation to the other.

 Example

Variety in formats and symbols should be used:

$3 + = 5$	$9 \div 3 = \bigcirc$	$* - 3 = 7$
$* + = 6$	$\square \times 4 = 12$	$4 = S + 12$
$8 = 16 \div 8$	$6 = 15 - N$	$a = 4 + 8$
$3 = X - 6$	$N - 5 = \square$	

Work with these expression should be coupled with allowing children to write their own expressions. Developing their own secret codes with symbols can motivate children to experiment with symbols and develop ease and facility with them (Sfard & Linchevksi, 1994).

 Activities

- Students will generate lists and models or drawings of various symbols common in everyday experience (FF, $\triangleright\triangleright$, $\otimes$, $\Rightarrow$, $\square$).

- Students will write a story with rebus devices using various symbols including those from mathematics.

Introducing Algebra

When students are familiar with working with symbols and manipulating objects as representatives of numbers, they are ready for the introduction to formal algebra. Students should be informed at the beginning that algebra is a mathematical tool, a system that, when learned, will be helpful to them in at least two important ways. It will assist them in problem solving and in learning other mathematics. They should understand that algebra provides short-cut rules and techniques by using symbols to represent numbers. In some ways it is like another language, a mathematical language, and in those ways needs to be learned the way another language is learned. It should also be explained and pointed out through examples that the operations and operation characteristics have not been changed. When students understand some of these ideas as they begin to study algebra, many of their fears are alleviated and the shock of transition is lessened. Two examples that may help are given here.

 Activity

Students will be asked to write out, entirely in words, the operation and steps for adding sixty-seven and thirty-eight. Absolutely no numerals or other symbols are permitted. As students experience the frustration of the time and difficulty of writing out all the words, they should discuss the wisdom of using symbols, numerals, and other forms.

Illustrations from their experience should be given to start with. Those who are aware of measurement in sports may readily understand adding 10k and 6k to find the distance covered by a runner running in a 10-kilometer race followed by a 6-kilometer race. The number of bottles of drink required for a group might be $5 \times 21 = 101$. Ten pounds of candy divided equally among 20 children would yield one-half pound per child.

Teachers should remind students of the transition they have already experienced when they moved from working with whole numbers to working with fractions.

- The symbols (fractions) were radically different.

- There was no place value system to organize the new symbols.

- A person could no longer tell at a glance which fraction is larger (Is $7/8 > 15/19$?).

- The algorithms for the operations were radically different.

Teachers should also point out to students that, in spite of these changes, they learned what the symbols meant and how they could be used in operations. Students should be asked how they made the transition to working with fractions. It should be made clear that the same techniques are used in learning to work within the system of algebra.

1. Relate the new ideas to known facts.

2. Translate new material to known forms.

3. Learn new terms.

4. Reason about information so that it makes sense.

There is also a need to develop the idea of *equation*. For a student at this early stage, maintaining the truth of these mathematical sentences is not a clear need. This is especially true of statements such as $x + 10 = 16$. Students often say, "How can I believe the statement is true when I don't know what x is or if x can change?" How should teachers go about helping students to develop the idea of equivalence, or equation?

 Activity

1. Students will use beam balances with known and unknown weights to illustrate equation statements and determine, by experimentation and algebraic processes, the weights of unknown value.

2. After solving the teacher-provided problems, the students will create their own unknown balance (equation) problems.

3. Students will write in their papers or journals full descriptions of reasoning to solution.

In all of these exercises, the teacher must emphasize the equality in balance (equivalence of both sides), the underlying principle of the algebraic equation. The terms and symbols may not appear similar on opposite sides of the equal sign, but they do have the same value.

Caution

1. Initially the items on the left and right should be hung at the same distances from the fulcrum. To hang some items at 4 units and others at 6 units from the fulcrum (even though balance is achieved) can greatly confuse the idea of the algebraic equation, which does not incorporate the concept of weighting. Recall that the issue here is the algebraic equation, and that should be the focus of the use of the manipulative. The other principles that this particular manipulative can be used to illustrate should be bypassed. They can be applied in science and statistics.

2. A simple pan balance or other weighing devices should *not* be used to attempt to demonstrate the idea of equation. The weighing process with many of these does not illustrate the equivalence idea in clearly visible ways. There are hidden springs or levers. A double pan balance tempts one to place different objects like markers or pennies on the pans. It then becomes difficult to find quantities that balance each other. Also, if the balance is a sensitive scientific machine, the difficulty in getting it to balance may seriously detract from the object of the activity (to show equivalence).

Teachers and students often struggle with a semantic problem which simply takes time to overcome using repetition with many examples. We call = the *equals sign* and we read $3x = y$ as, "Three x equals y." Equals, to a student, usually carries the idea of exact numerical equality. However, in algebra we usually are working with the idea of equal value or equivalence. When we write $3x = y$, we mean that with appropriate values for x and y, the expression will be a true statement. When using the balance beam to examine such expressions as $3x = 15$, the teacher should talk naturally about "doing the same process or *equivalent* processes" to both sides of the beam and maintaining balance.

 ## Examples

1. We can add or subtract 5 one's on the left and 1 five on the right and the beam remains horizontal (balanced).

2. We can divide in thirds both on the left and on the right and then remove two-thirds of what is on each side and the beam will remain balanced.

3. Consider the equation $3x + 10 = 22$ as two sides of a balance beam.
    Using the principle of item 1, above, subtract 10 from each side and the beam (equation) will stay balanced.

$3x + 10 = 22$ becomes $3x = 12$.

Divide into thirds: $x + x + x = 4 + 4 + 4$.

Using the principle of item 2, above, take two thirds ($x + x = 4 + 4$) away from each side, leaving $x = 4$ which still will leave the beam (equation) balanced. (The statement $x = 4$ is true.) The statement $x = 4$ is the solution to the equation and is the simplest form of the equation.

 ## Another Possibility

4. Consider the same equation: $3x + 10 = 22$.
Recognize that if 5 is added to each side, the numbers on each side of the equation would be divisible by 3 and the beam would remain balanced.

Add 5 to each side, giving $3x + 15 = 27$.

Divide each side into thirds:

$(x + 5) + (x + 5) + (x + 5) = 9 + 9 + 9$

Remove two of the thirds from each side:

$(x + 5) + (x + 5) = 9 + 9$, leaving $x + 5 = 9$.

Check the unknown x, and 5, for balance with 9.

Replace the 9 with $4 + 5$.

Remove 5 from each side, leaving x balanced with 4.

Conclude that x (the unknown) must be equivalent to 4.

(An interesting feature of the process above is that, at the beginning, 5 was added to both sides and, at the end, 5 was taken away from both sides. The 5, then, was a kind of catalyst to help make the process feasible and not really an integral part of the process.)

Note

When using the balance beam, it is instructive to have two students sit facing each other with the beam between them. Each writes the equation from that perspective. Thus, one writes: $3x + 10 = 22$, while the other writes $22 = 10 + 3x$. The class should discuss the relative merits of each expression and should note that they are equally correct and useful. Examples of this type will help students avoid the difficulty of believing that the "x" expression must always be on the left in order for work on the equation to proceed properly.

5. Have students recreate the activity using different weights and unknowns. It is preferable to have a balance beam and known and unknown weights for each group of four or five students.

The natural transition to thinking about equations as balanced beams should continue so that students (and teacher) talk about adding *equivalent* expressions to both sides or dividing both sides of the equation by *equivalent* numbers, for example. It is best not to use the term *equal* at first. It may also be helpful for students to regard work with equations (usually *solving* equations) as successive translations where they should employ their translation skills.

Example/Activity for Seventh or Eighth Graders

Solve: $3x + 10 = 22$

Note

(The terminology *solve the equation* is not very helpful at the beginning. It is better to say, "Find the value for x that makes the sentence true," or "Find the value of x that makes the equation balance," or "Find the value of x so that when x is replaced by that number, the result on the left is equivalent to what is on the right." The *solve the equation* terminology will come along naturally.)

- Point out to students that the purpose is to find out what the value of x is.

- Ask students to figure out what x is and to take note of their methods.

- Discuss the different legitimate methods used to obtain the value of x.

- Point out that any method that consistently yields the correct results is OK.

 Examples:

a) $3x + 10 = 22$
$3x + 9 = 21$
$x + 3 = 7$
$x = 4$

b) $3x + 10 = 22$
$3x = 12$
$x = 4$

c) $3x + 10 = 22$
$3x + 15 = 27$
$x + 5 = 9$
$x = 4$

d) $3(1) + 10 = 13$
$3(2) + 10 = 16$
$3(3) + 10 = 19$
$3(4) + 10 = 22$

Caution

It is critically important that work with equations *not* be taught as a one-and-only-one algorithm method, only one of which is correct. That simply is not true, and students who get this impression are seriously hampered in their progress and their ability to work successfully with more complex equations.

Method (d) above, a try-and-modify approach, is quite legitimate and very effective for some situations. Students should feel free to use the method, but encouraged to think carefully about the method and to realize that it would be extremely cumbersome in $x \div 13 = 28.52$, for example. Where would one begin to experiment and how long would it take to try enough values?

Teachers and students should note the opportunity here to un-operate, that is to rewrite numbers to different forms to make the expressions easy to work with. The whole effort should be presented in a very pragmatic light. We do what makes sense and what is likely to be effective. We organize and manipulate and make the numbers and mathematical tools work for us. In all ways possible teachers must avoid giving the impression that algebraic processes are magical, that they just happen without sound rationale. It is easy for students to develop the idea that algebra is done in ways that no one can really understand. When no sensible reasons are given, students believe that they have to memorize enough rules and procedures to get through the course, which contains material actually impossible to understand.

Examples

$$13x + \frac{1}{4} = 3\frac{1}{2}$$

$$13x + \frac{1}{4} = \frac{7}{2}$$

$$13x + \frac{1}{4} = \frac{14}{4} \quad \left(\frac{7}{2} \text{ is unreduced.}\right)$$

$$13x = \frac{13}{4} = 13\left(\frac{1}{4}\right)$$

$$x = \frac{1}{4}$$

$$3x + 10 = 22$$
$$3x + 10 + 5 = 22 + 5$$
$$x + x + x + 5 + 5 + 5 = 27 = 9 + 9 + 9$$
$$x + 5 = 9$$
$$x + 5 = 4 + 5$$
$$x = 4$$

In this example several sums were unadded (broken into easily usable *factors*) so that the balancing process could be easily done.

Students should also be given examples and exercises in which complete reduction is not desirable because it doesn't directly produce the desired results and because it involves unnecessary work. These examples also show the value of careful common sense thought about what is happening in working with algebraic expressions (Perrenet & Waters, 1994).

Factoring

Traditionally, much time and emphasis has been given to manipulating algebraic expressions. This has usually come prior to studying equations so that the skills can subsequently be used in solving equations. It may be, however, that for the introductory course in algebra, equations should come first. The danger is that students are likely to become bored and frustrated with all the exercises in factoring and operating with algebraic expressions, all of which are abstract and unconnected to any meaningful process. It is very difficult to provide any kind of real life and practical application of manipulations of these expressions. The reason for presenting equations first in this chapter, and recommending that equation solving should be taught first, is to help with this difficulty. Equation building, analysis, and solution provide a placed to use operations and other manipulation in meaningful contexts. If the equations are, in turn, related to real life problem solving, students can attach meaning to the various procedures. In this way, work with meaningful equations and practice with the operations using algebraic expressions can go hand-in-hand.

Children who really know operation concepts, and who have not relied solely on memorizing mysterious processes and facts, are ready to operate with variable expressions. One of the critical and basic concepts that needs to be well developed is the idea that only like objects can be added, multiplied, etc. Recall that 5 oranges and 4 applies cannot be added. The combination set must be renamed to *pieces-of-fruit*, *things*, *objects*, or *items* in order to use the number 9 meaningfully. Furthermore, students realize that one can add a set of 5 apples to a set of 4 applies and obtain a set of 9 apples, but cannot multiply a set of 5 apples by a set of 4 apples and get 20 apples (or square apples!). It is wise to begin the discussion and work on algebraic operations with these basic considerations. A wise teacher will bring the students along in stages, examining these ideas with many examples and counter-examples. A direct transition from the above would be to the following:

1. Write 5 apples + 4 oranges = ?

2. Write $5a + 4o = ?$

3. $5a + 4a = ?$

4. $5a - 4o = ?$ and $5a - 4a = ?$

5. Consider: $5a \times 4o = ?$ $5a \times 4a = ?$ $5a \div 4o = ?$

6. Ask the students to discuss these and make sense out of them. What modifications are necessary for these to make sense?

7. Consider: $5 \times 4a$ or $4a \times 5$. Could these have useful meanings?

8. Is there any time when $5a \times 4a$ could make sense? How about 5 in. $\times$ 4 in.?

Next, place these operations in the context of an equation which expresses a real problem situation:

 ### Example

For the banquet there are twice as many 6-place tables as there are 8-place tables and 300 people are to be seated. How many of each type of table are there?

Equation: Number of people at tables = total number of people.

If t is the number of 8-place tables then there are $8t$ 8-place tables.

There are $2t$ 6-place tables and $6 \times 2t = 12t$ people at 6-place tables.

The equation to solve is: $8t + 12t = 300$

Solving: $20t$ people = 300 people
$t = 15$ tables (8-place tables)
$2t = 30$, the number of 6-place tables.

Checking: $8 \times 15 = 120$ people
$6 \times 30 = \underline{180 \text{ people}}$
300 people

In the problem solving context, multiplying $6 \times 2t$ makes sense and adding numbers of people, $8t + 12t$ seems reasonable too. Obviously, experimentation with numbers—trying 10 and 20, 12 and 24, etc.—would eventually yield the result too. Students need to note that the operations using the algebraic expressions shorten the process. They make an organized and logically flowing argument that is easy to check and to communicate with someone else.

Note

The $20t$ people = 300 people equation expression above has the words *people* written in. Here that does not signify *units*. It helps ensure that what is being written is, in fact, an equation, that two entities that are comparable are being equated.

Operating with Algebraic Expressions

For adding and subtracting polynomials, an almost place-value-like form can be used; it should be pointed out to students that this is the case. The form can help students keep track of the different terms and ensure operating with like terms.

 Examples

$3x + 5$	$7a + 6$	$7a - 6$
$\underline{4x + 6}$	$\underline{-(4a + 8)}$	$\underline{-(4a - 8)}$
$7x + 11$	$3a - 2$	$3a + 2$

Note

Parentheses are used to indicate the extent of the subtracted terms.

Addition and subtraction are also done effectively by simply regrouping (putting all like terms together) and then performing the required operating. Still another method is to use the distributive properties.

 Examples

$$5x + 3 + 7x - 2 - 3x + 4 = 5x + 7x - 3x + 3 - 2 + 4$$
$$= 9x + 5$$

$$5x + 7x - 3x = (5 + 7 - 3)\, x = 9x$$

Again we emphasize the importance of helping students understand that there is great variety in legitimate methods that can be used. Students must be encouraged to take control of the processes themselves, and not let themselves become dependent on methods of memorization of some process they have seen in a book or in the examples the teacher has given.

Multiplication

Multiplication, other than of constants by variables, depends on providing categories for each type of term. This is similar to what must be done in the other operations. Students may be assisted by remembering that it was important in decimal multiplication to ensure that the place holders held the appropriate values. Here, too, different kinds of expressions must be kept in the appropriate categories, but there is not a preset order of categories, as there is with place value. The arrangement is at the discretion of the student. This should be pointed out so that students also note that, because of associativity and commutativity in addition and multiplication, the order and arrangement of terms may differ from correct result to correct result.

 Examples

- $3 \cdot 5x = 3 \cdot 5 \cdot x = 15x$

- $x \cdot 3 \cdot 5 = x \cdot 15 = 15x$

- $x(3 + 5) = x \cdot 3 + x \cdot 5 = 3x + 5x = 8x$

- $3(x + 5) = 3 \cdot x + 3 \cdot 5 = 3x + 15$

- $a(x + 5) = ax + 5a$

- $(a + b)x = ax + bx$

- $(a + b)(x + 5) = a(x + 5) + b(x + 5)$

  $$= ax + 5a + bx + 5b$$

There is an obvious question in considering the last two examples above concerning which form should be used. Is $(a + b) \cdot x$ or $ax + bx$ the desired result? Students should learn, at this point, that the form selected is chosen because of its ease of application or because it fits the situation more directly than the other. The form in the third example would usually be $(3 + 5)x = 8x$ directly rather than $3x + 5x$. One can, however, imagine a situation in which there were other $3x$ and $5x$ expressions, so that the $3x + 5x$ would be more convenient to use. The first term could be taken in combination with the other $3x$ terms, and so forth. In fact, the process might be to start from the other direction and translate (by unadding), changing $8x$ to $(3 + 5)x$ and then to $3x + 5x$. To reiterate: *It is extremely important for students at this level to understand that there are many possible arrangements and that memorization of the "correct" procedure and result is impractical and counter productive.*

Note

It becomes necessary to use parentheses and brackets to indicate which numbers are being used in the operations in order to avoid ambiguity.

Students need to understand that the use of parentheses and bracketing is essentially a controlling technique. This is a way of giving clear indications of what is to be done in the operations. They should realize that this gives them control over the process so that they know clearly what operation is to be done and how it is to be done. This use of parentheses should not be memorized, but rather done from a foundation of thoughtful decision making about the operation the problem calls for. Counter-examples and remainders should be given to the students to illustrate the difficulties encountered when brackets are not used.

 Examples

- $3 + 2 \cdot 5 = 5 \cdot 5?$ or $= 3 + 10?$
  $(3 + 2) \cdot 5 = 5 \cdot 5$ (No uncertainty)
  $3 + (2 \cdot 5) = 3 + 10$ (No uncertainty)

- $x + y \cdot a + b = (x + y) \cdot a + b?$
  $\qquad\qquad\quad = xa + ya + b$
  or is it $= (x + y)(a + b)$
  $\qquad\qquad\quad = xa + ya + yb + xb?$

The careful use of parentheses means that algorithmic rules about which operations are done first do not have to be memorized. Later confusion in remember just how the rules work is also avoided.

Note

The word *simplify* is often used to instruct algebra students. The difficulty is that there is often a difference of opinion as to which form is the simpler. Is $(a + b) \, x$ or $ax + bx$ simpler? This term should be avoided unless there is an accompanying clear statement of what the simplified forms are.

The reverse process, *factoring*, is important, particularly as an aid to division. The usual form factoring uses is the distributive property of multiplication over addition or subtraction. For more discussion of this process, return to the section on *unmultiplying*.

 Examples

- $3x + 3a = 3(x + a)$

- $ax + ay + az = a(x + y + z)$

- $bx - by + cz = b(x - y) + cz$

- $ax + ay + bx + by = ax + bx + ay + by$
- $$= (a + b)x + (a + b)y$$
$$= (a + b)(x + y)$$

Note

These processes using unmultiplying and distributive properties are difficult for many students for the following reasons:

- Students have been almost exclusively unidirectional in multiplying:
$9 \times 14 = 90 + 36 = 126$

- Students are accustomed to the fact that there is only one correct result of multiplication.

- Students find that in factoring there are multiple possibilities:

$$126 = 2 \cdot 63 = 3 \cdot 42 = 2 \cdot 3 \cdot 21 = 2 \cdot 3 \cdot 3 \cdot 7$$

for example. Which is correct?

- Factoring requires organization, planning, and consideration of many possibilities; thus it is time consuming.

- Factoring cannot be memorized.

Students should be informed and reminded of these characteristics of the process of factoring, to use their problem solving skills, and of the value of factoring to problem solving and other process in mathematics.

Two- (or More) Variable Algebra

Following studies of one variable equations and expressions, algebra continues into multivariable expressions, including systems of equations. Most of this occurs in the second year algebra course and is not usually studied by seventh or eighth graders. However, middle schoolers should be exposed to the basic expressions of interrelationship between two variables. These are often expressed by simple two-variable equations such as $y = 3x$ and equations arising from measurement and conversion formulas. These should be discussed to some degree by middle schoolers because they occur in what students learn in science and mathematics, and they are expected to be able to graph and work with common interrelated variables.

 Examples

$$C = \pi d$$
$$A = \pi r^2$$
$$F° = 9/5 \, C° + 32°$$

Activity

Students will:

1. Measure the diameter and circumference of 8 cylindrical containers of different sizes (accuracy to 0.1 cm).

2. Record d and C values on a chart:

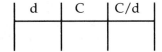

d	C	C/d

3. Graph (d, C) ordered pairs with d on the horizontal axis and C on the vertical axis.

4. Be asked to describe the relationship between d and C.

5. Calculate the C/d ratios for each set and compare the results with the result of item 4, above.

A number of hints may be needed. These are perhaps best offered in the form of questions: "If d increases by 1 cm, how does C change?" and "Is that increase (rate of increase) changing?", etc.

6. Develop an understanding of what kinds of interrelationships are linear and which are nonlinear.

Students need to learn what types of equations describe linear relationships between two variables. For example, $y = 3x$ and $y = 3x + 2$ are graphed by *lines* and the slope of those lines is 3. They should recognize that, for $A = \pi r^2$, the relationship between A and r will not be graphed by a line, but rather by a quickly ascending curve (a quadratic). The r values will be on the horizontal axis and A values will be on the vertical axis. It needs to be understood that graphs, equations, and lists of ordered pairs are all representations of the relationships between the two variables. Additionally, students should begin, at this point, to become familiar with the ways in which the values of one variable are affected by changes in the other variable.

 ## Examples

■ Problem: The equator of the earth is nearly circular and about 25,0000 miles long. If an imaginary rope were laid on the equator, making a complete circle, then raised 1 ft. above the equator all the way around the earth, How much longer would the rope have to be in order for its ends to meet?

■ $A = \pi r^2$. If the radius is increased by 1 inch, how will the area of the circle be changed?

- $F° = 9/5 C° + 32$. If the Centigrade temperature increases by 5 degrees, how does the Fahrenheit temperature value change? Is there a point at which the temperature values for $F°$ and $C°$ are equal? What is it?

- At a fixed temperature, pressure times volume is a consistent value, e.g., k: $PV = k$. As pressure increases, what happens to the volume value?

With good exposure to these ideas and practice with these concepts in the first formal encounter with algebra, students will be well prepared for high school algebra. This exposure and practice should occur in the middle school. Seventh and eighth grade students can learn one-variable algebra with good success if the way is carefully prepared for them, not only in content but in attitude creation. This can be accomplished by sharing with them openly what learning is expected and why and how it all fits neatly together in a system and structure and how it can be applied in practical problem solving (Brahier & Speed).

▣ Summary

This chapter outlined the difficulties children experience when algebra is "dropped on them" in the seventh or eighth grade. They have been told horror stories by peers and parents and are shocked by the apparent major transition from well-practiced material from six years experience to an entirely new and unfamiliar system. The reasons for their unfamiliarity were explored and then dealt with in suggestions and principles for introducing algebraic ideas and teaching algebra. The initial focus described is on becoming familiar with symbol manipulation. It was noted that this process should be begun in the very early grades and pre-algebra aspects of the traditional topics pointed out and discussed along the way through the grades. Teachers should also carefully develop the idea of *equation*, taking care that procedures are more problem solving than algorithmically oriented. Various operational processes such as *factoring* and *polynomial manipulation* were discussed. Finally, simple two-variable equations with emphasis on their interpretation as defining a relationship between two variables were discussed.

▣ Exercises

1. Find three real life situations in the daily lives of seventh or eighth graders in which simple algebraic procedures could be used or are naturally applied by the students. Explain this for each and describe each in a paragraph which could be used with an eight-grade class.

2. Place an example each of factoring and multiplying binomials in the con-

text of solving an equation in order to solve a practical problem, thus demonstrating the value and usefulness of factoring and multiplying binomials.

3. Develop the quadratic formula showing the unoperating techniques of reformulating parts of the expression in order to make the steps neat and concise.

4. Create a) a list of real-life algebra applications other than in academic subjects.

   b) lists of examples and counter-examples for basic algebraic concepts such as: equation, polynomial, solving equations, etc.

5. Explain thoroughly the reasons and rationale for the argument:

$$\text{Let } a = b$$

$$\text{then } a^2 = ab$$

$$\text{then } a^2 - b^2 = ab - b^2$$

$$\text{now } (a - b)(a + b) = (a - b)b$$

$$\text{then } a + b = b$$

$$\text{now } b + b = b \text{ (since } a = b)$$

$$\text{or } 2b = b$$

$$\text{and therefore, } 2 = 1$$

References

Brahier, Daniel, and Bill Speed. (1997, September). Worthwhile tasks: Exploring mathematical connections through geometric solids. *Mathematics Teaching in the Middle School*. Reston, VA: NCTM.

Herscovics, Nicolas, and Liora Linchevski (1994). A cognitive gap between arithmetic and algebra. *Educational Studies in Mathematics*, 27(1), 57–78.

National Council of Teachers of Mathematics (1989). *Curriculum and Evaluation Standards for School Mathematics*. Reston, VA: Author.

Perrenet, Jacob C., and Miriam A. Wolters (1994). The art of checking: A case study of students' erroneous checking behavior in introductory algebra. *The Journal of Mathematical Behavior*, 13(3), 335–358.

Piaget, J. (1970). *The Science of Education and the Psychology of the Child*. New York: Orion Press.

Sfard, Anna, and Liora Linchevski. (1994). The gains and pitfalls of reification—The case of algebra. *Educational Studies in Mathematics*, 26(2–3), 191–228.

White, Paul, and Michael Mitchelmore (1996, January). Conceptual knowledge in introductory calculus. *Journal for Research in Mathematics Education*. Reston, VA: NCTM.

🔲 Suggested Readings

Hilgart, Faye. (1996, March–April). Now and then: Livestock production by the numbers. *Mathematics Teaching in the Middle School*. Reston, VA: NCTM.

Kaur, Berinderjeet, and Sharon Boey Huey Peng (1994). Algebraic misconceptions of first year college students. *Focus on Learning Problems in Mathematics*, 16(4), 43–58.

McClain, Kay (1997, September). A weighty problem solved. *Mathematics Teaching in the Middle School*. Reston, VA: NCTM.

National Council of Teachers of Mathematics (1989). *Curriculum and Evaluation Standards for School Mathematics*. Reston, VA: Author.

Odafe, Victor U. (1994). Students' perceptions of myths about mathematics. *AMAYTC Review*, 15(2), 60–67.

Scavo, Thomas R., and Nora Conroy. (1996, March–April). Conceptual understanding and computational skill in school mathematics. *Mathematics Teaching in the Middle School*, Reston, VA: NCTM.

Using Computer Technology In Mathematics Education

One of the children's problems: Dave has used all the "drill and practice" programs on the school computer and needs to do some real math using the computer.

Teacher's problem: Software which is closely related to the concepts being taught is not available.

> **Problem:** *How may computers best be used in teaching and learning mathematics?*

▣ Understanding the Problem

Recently various educational and governmental groups have promoted the idea of having a computer in every classroom in the United States. This movement is generating much-needed discussion concerning the specifics about how this can happen. Of special interest to mathematics educators is how computers could and should be used in the mathematics classroom. Questions and concerns about using computers to aid in teaching mathematics center around several key issues. Can computers actually be used to teach mathematics, or only as expensive "flash card" machines? Are there concepts in mathematics which can be taught using computers? Are there concepts in mathematics which cannot be taught using computers? Does the use of computers hinder teaching in some ways? Are there certain facets of mathematics for which the use of computers in teaching mathematics is counter-productive?

Many people's first thought about teaching with computers is that they are perfect for teaching mathematics but perhaps not much else. However, experience tells us that the typical use of computers in schools today is predominantly as word processors. The most common usage is to run software programs on various subjects, only one of which is mathematics. As we explore the uses of the computer for teaching and learning mathematics, some of the reasons for the limited use of computers in the mathematics classroom will become evident. Until recently most of the only software available for mathematics has been designed to assist students with drill and practice, primarily in computation or in terminology learning. More recent developments in the writing of software have concentrated on problem solving (in some cases using spreadsheets) and on manipulation of objects on the screen.

The way computers can be used in the math classroom depends heavily on software availability and on the topic in math which is being studied. It also depends on whether the task is to teach concepts, processes, or facts. Most software is effectively used for only one of these objectives (teaching facts) and may function rather well in helping students with learning facts. Some software assists students with computation processes, but these only indirectly help with concept development. It is critically important that a teacher have a clear focus and objective in order to select appropriate software or to choose other uses of the computer. The teacher should be aware of the fact that software that claims to teach all three objectives is likely to do none of them well. Software programs should be examined carefully so that the teacher knows whether a program has a clear focus and will assist students with specific learning that fits into the teacher's curriculum.

Some concepts are difficult, if not impossible, for a computer to present to students, while for others, the computer is an excellent aid. If the software does not allow the student to interactively manipulate objects (or the representations of objects), it will not help children develop conservation concepts, for example. Additionally, many measurement concepts cannot be conveyed through the computer screen. Children need to experience the sensation of holding an object weighing 1 pound or 1 kilogram. They need to apply measurement tools to real objects. On the other hand, concepts of angles, various plane geometrical shapes, and three-dimensional figures can be much more effectively presented by the computer than by concrete manipulatives. For example, students can work with electronic tangram pieces by clicking and dragging them where they want to place them. The computer can produce infinite variety in examples and counter-examples. Not only can the computer produce various figures on demand, but some software is interactive. It permits the user to alter angle size and side lengths, for example, offering the possibility of experimentation and exploration to an extent simply not possible with paper-and-pencil activities or manipulation of concrete objects. Created figures can be rotated and "viewed" from all angles. Even in the case of the now relatively old LOGO program, which is very simple and plain by today's standards, students of all ages can use it to develop many important geometrical concepts (Demana and Waits, 1990).

Teaching Concepts

When using computers to help in the teaching of concepts, teachers must ensure that the program actually deals with the particular concept in question. For example, a program which helps students to be competent in adding will not necessarily ensure that the students have a full grasp of the addition operation concept. It is important to remember that the critical components in teaching and learning concepts are the examples and counter-examples of the concept and the contextualizing of the concept. That includes the concept's connections and interrelationships with other concepts. As mentioned, where the computer can give examples of a concept, it is a most powerful tool. Some programs, while giving many examples of a concept, do not give adequate counter-examples. This means that to use the programs to teach concepts, the teacher would have to supplement the software material. Obviously this would be time consuming and perhaps impossible for the teacher to do adequately. What a computer can do to assist in teaching and learning concepts is almost completely dependent on the software, which must be written intentionally to present a particular concept. This means that the program must be interactive, allowing the student to select concept attributes, question them, and be questioned about them. When counter-examples are presented the student must identify the differences and note the attributes which are critical yet missing. Repetition and variety should be evident in the program before it is selected for classroom use.

Teaching Processes

A different approach is required for teaching mathematical processes such as operation algorithms. To be useful, the program must guide students carefully through the process being taught and must point out pitfalls and important steps. Since the order of the steps is often critical, appropriate emphasis must be given to order. The program then must provide opportunity for repetitive practice using every kind of number or entity to which the process applies. The computer should also monitor the practice so that errors are detected and the student guided to correct them before they are practiced too often and become difficult-to-change bad habits. The computer, if the software is well written, is especially effective in this role because it is infinitely patient; it never tires of repeating examples, making corrections, and showing correct procedures. There is a need for caution here too, though, because the computer cannot be depended on to teach every mathematical process students need to learn. If, for some reason, a student cannot learn the particular algorithm being taught by a piece of software, it is unlikely that the program will be able to identify the student's difficulty and to find alternative algorithms. The processes of geometrical constructions, for example, have to be done with compass, pencil and paper. The computer can illustrate them and describe the steps, but students have to do some of these—hands on—to understand the process fully. In other words, the computer may be quite adequate for explaining and demonstrating processes pictorially but cannot assist with the next steps in which the students must do the hands-on practice. In addition, some students need to hear verbal descriptions along with visual and written instruction. While some newer computers have sound cards and speakers, it is impractical to have computers speaking out loud to children in the classroom or computer lab. One solution to the noise and distraction problem is to provide each computer with earphones.

Teaching Facts

A third type of software program is necessary for presenting mathematical facts and knowledge to students. This type of information needs to be presented to learners in all possible contexts and interconnections with other facts. Computers are uniquely capable of presenting facts and knowledge with color, sound, and fascinating graphics. Unfortunately, too much of the available software covers the absence of substantive content with flashy sound and color. There is also the danger that programs may be written to make the computer function only as a very expensive flash card machine. When this is coupled with the tendency among many students to memorize facts (without the necessary development of interrelationships), the usual flash card kinds of software and the trivia game formats may not actually help the students. Teachers must carefully examine the software that purports to help children develop their factual knowledge in mathematics. Does it present the facts that are needed for the particular curriculum at hand? Are the facts accurate and properly perceived by the children? If the information is presented in the context of a game, are the children able to play the game (and enjoy it) and not really take note of the facts they are to be learning or reviewing (Cognition and Technology Group, 1993)?

Examining Software

Whatever use is to be made of particular software, teachers must find a way to look past the beautiful graphics for mathematical substance. This is usually not easily done, because it is time consuming actually to use the program sufficiently to see most of what the students will see and do. Fortunately, most software allows for a 30-day examination and approval period. Provided in Appendix C is a checklist to be used when examining software.

Software comes in essentially two formats. Some programs are on individual floppy disks or CDs. These are purchased separately and loaded onto desktop computers as needed for individuals or small groups. Unfortunately the cost (usually the responsibility of the individual teacher) of providing more than one of these for a class is prohibitive. Teachers should remember that there is additional software demand for other subject areas as well.

The second type of software format occurs in the classroom or computer lab where computers are networked. These programs usually are permanently installed, not removed after use or when topics change. Usually they are professionally installed and serviced under some kind of ongoing agreement with hardware and software providers. Clearly programs of this type need to be quite general and will likely be drill-and-practice types as far as mathematics is concerned. They are not likely to be tutorial in nature because of the large amounts of computer memory necessary for tutorial programs (Hirschbull, 1996). The typical small system in a school will have insufficient memory to contain a broad range of tutorial programs in mathematics, especially if programs for other subjects are also installed. One of the advantages of a network system is that such program arrangements can include record-keeping capabilities. This enables the teacher to monitor children's uses of the various parts of the program. The teacher can quickly note the extent of the child's capability to do certain tasks and answer certain questions. The tool can provide for testing, record keeping on test results, and analysis of those results. The teacher might use the networked program to create a test that all students take on the computer. For certain aspects of mathematics this can obviate the difficulties students have when they cannot write or draw well enough to communicate what they actually do know.

Solving the Problem

Over the last decade Computer Aided Instruction (CAI) software has become more and more sophisticated, but the primary focus in mathematics is still on drill and practice. Programs such as *Number Munchers* and *Fraction Munchers* attempt to motivate students to memorize mathematical facts by placing the information in arcade video game formats. These programs rely on students having certain levels of knowledge and certain concepts in place. For grades 1–6, exploration of number patterns, estimation, fractions, decimals, and percentages is provided by programs such as *Math Blaster: In Search of Spot* on CD-ROM.

Another level of computer application includes tutorial programs. These present concepts, question students to determine understanding, provide explanations, and give feedback. Tutorials can fill gaps, reinforce learning, and patiently give responses to students' questions. These programs must be used in contexts familiar to the students who use them. They need to provide obvious connections to the concepts and knowledge the students already possess. An example of the few mathematics tutorials available is *Mastering Mathematics: Decimals*. The development time, the computer time, and the memory space required for a tutorial on just one concept are so great that not many true tutorials are currently available. Furthermore, it is prohibitively expensive to provide tutorials for a class in all the topic areas where they could be used. Ideally, a sixth-grade class would have tutorial programs in decimals, fractions, percentages, angles, geometric shapes, measurement, probability, graphing, and a number of others. All of this is simply not feasible (Merrill, 1996).

Simulation Programs

Math simulation programs are also powerful teaching tools, particularly as they provide real life settings for the applications of mathematics. The majority of these are science related, providing mathematically accurate interactive science explorations. *The Physics Explorer* is a good example of a simulation program which includes graphing and spreadsheet analysis of pictorial, graphic, and numeric data to observe, analyze, predict, and evaluate outcomes. *Math Sleuths* is a real life problem solving simulation program. It is designed to provide video clips of problem scenarios and resources such as graphs, maps, and periodical literature reports. In these, students are required to use skills of estimation, computation to determine costs and profit, and measurement involving geometric properties. Many of these are on video disks or use video disks in conjunction with computer programs. Among the values of using video disks are the motivational attraction for children and the capability of presenting more complex and interconnected problems than is possible in written form. Another important benefit provided by video disks is the incredible capacity for storage of data and information students can readily access for use in problem solving.

Research on the results of using one of these, *The Adventures of Jasper Woodbury*, shows that students taught using this format "are better at solving one-, two-, and multiple-step problems, are more successful at generating problems, have more positive attitudes toward mathematics" (Allen, 1995).

Simulations of manipulatives and their manipulation can extend the capability of students to explore shapes and objects far beyond the possibilities that in-the-classroom, hands-on experiences can provide. An important aspect of these programs is their versatility and interactivity capability. Students can change colors, and enlarge and examine different characteristics by manipulating the objects in all sorts of manners and configurations.

Problem Solving

Much software experimentation continues in the area of writing problem solving tutorials. Some of these, unfortunately, take a didactic approach by trying to classify problems as to type and teach children the steps required to solve that kind of problem. As discussed in the chapter on problem solving, to give students the idea that one can learn to solve problems algorithmically is to do them a serious disservice. The programs that help students with various problem solving skills such as translation are much more effective in teaching students to be good problem solvers. One such program is *Read and Solve Problems*, which focuses on translation of worded problem statements to numerical and mathematical symbol formulations. Other good software programs focus on developing problem solving strategies that will aid students in working toward solutions. In *Math Blaster: Mystery*, students break problems into intermediate steps or into smaller problems and inductive and deductive reasoning are highlighted. Students are guided through examples of helpful logic using highly motivating stories and graphics. The intention is that, having seen successful problem solving and noting the step-by-step process of reaching solution, students will be able to apply the same techniques on other problems.

In the series, *The Wonderful Problems of Fizz and Martina*, students are required to work in groups and solve problems as teams. All of these applications require extensive computer time and memory space, just as problem solving in other contexts requires time and involvement on the part of the problem solver. This means that the hardware necessary for using computers to teach and to practice problem solving must be quite sophisticated and have large memory capacity. It may not be possible to use computers extensively in this manner before the fifth or sixth grade when reading and keyboard and other control skills are fairly well developed. Students learn to solve problems by solving problems, using whatever skills and aids are available.

Caution

Caution: Students must not come to regard a computer as a device only for teaching them how to solve problems, but must, instead, come to understand that the computer is a powerful problem solving tool to assist the problem solver.

Spreadsheets

The one directly useful tool for problem solving that students now have available on most computers and must be taught to use is the spreadsheet. This tool is widely used in real life by all sorts of businesses and industries, so that learning to analyze, discover, and problem solve using a spreadsheet will serve the additional purpose of preparing students directly for the workplace. Within the classroom, the tool has a wide range of uses in many subject areas including mathematics. It can be used in meeting several mathematics lesson objectives on topics such as estimation, variable relationships, applications of operations, understanding of formulas, measurement conversions, and many statistical concepts. Since one of the difficulties significantly troubling many mathematics students is the inability to organize information in order to work with it meaningfully, and since a spreadsheet's strength is in its organizational capabilities, learning to use a spreadsheet might well come before learning to use the computer in other ways (McClain, 1997). If the particular spreadsheet on the computer in a school does not do sufficient graphing, it may be necessary to acquire graphing software as well. Teachers should be reminded that reading, interpreting, and constructing tables, charts, and graphs is one of the 10 basic skills to be taught and learned in mathematics as outlined by the NCTM's *Curriculum and Evaluation Standards* (1989). For the specific use of the teacher, a spreadsheet can also be very valuable for record keeping. If the teacher's computer does not have some kind of gradebook software (essentially a dedicated spreadsheet), a spreadsheet may be used to keep and analyze grades and other student records such as lists and a variety of other information important to teaching the class (Edwards & Bitter, 1989).

Networking in Mathematics Education

The benefits of a within-the-school network of computers either in the lab or throughout the school have been mentioned. There are also significant benefits attached to interschool networks that are districtwide or larger. There are statewide educational networks in many states and more and more schools are going online with these and the Internet as well. There is not much in these networks yet which is dedicated directly to student mathematics learning. That is, there would be little value in a student logging on to the network to find a program to help with learning the concept of equivalent fractions, for example. There would, however, be much to be gained when a student or a class could E-mail back and forth with a student or a class in another city or state (or nation) to share problems and problem solving ideas. Also of practical help would be access to data bases that could be analyzed statistically for mathematics-based real life problem solving and project work. There are, on the Internet, sources of geometric art and architecture which could significantly enhance geometric concept studies. Furthermore, the information on the history of mathematics and the stories of the great mathematicians, both men and women, are accessible through network sources. This kind of material is increasing in quantity and availability all the time (Dixon & Falba, 1997).

Beyond the direct classroom uses of networks are the phenomenal resources for the mathematics educator. For example, the Eisenhower National Clearing House stores and has readily accessible all the journal articles, professional writings, and books written for mathematics and science education. In addition to this marvelous resource, there is, on file, current information on all projects for improving mathematics and science education and for professional development of teachers, programs for schools and classrooms, and even lesson plans that have been successfully used to teach many different aspects of both science and mathematics. Classroom projects and experiments at all the different grade levels are described for a wide variety of topics. All of these are being constantly updated and are open to mathematics teachers. In addition to stored resource centers like this, many states have teacher- or school-dedicated networks such as the *Discovery Net* in states where the Project Discovery program has been operated. This network, like others, provides a forum where teachers can exchange views and ideas on teaching methods and strategies. It has been the source for a wide variety of cooperative efforts for small groups of teachers from various parts of a state or for schools to band together to work on projects in mathematics education. As schools are able to get on these networks, teachers will be empowered to strengthen their own teaching and knowledge and thus are enabled to improve mathematics education in their classrooms. For those teachers in non-networked schools, the home computer can be used to the same effect (Lynnes, 1997).

Future of the Computer in Teaching Mathematics

Some of the capabilities mentioned above are still in the future for many teachers and schools, but they are probably not very far in the future. There are, however, some very exciting prospects for using the computer in the mathematics classroom that are farther out on the horizon. First is the improvement in quantity and coverage of the software for teaching material interfaced more directly with the school's curriculum. The software needs to be much more compact (covering more topics adequately with fewer pieces of software) and much less expensive. Fortunately, that is in the not-too-distant future. The hardware will have to be more versatile, constantly upgradable, and also less expensive so that more students can be one-on-one with computers more of the time in mathematics. The installation of this kind of hardware is currently underway in many schools. More futuristic are networks which include industry and business as well as other agencies where there are persons engaged in applying their mathematics in their workplaces. When these networks do provide students with real-time views and even interaction with the direct application of mathematics at work, that might spell the end of the student comment, " 'When will we ever use this stuff? (Kinnaman, January 1995).

Distance learning is already a reality in many areas of our nation. This is essentially a two-way interactive network connection among learners and teachers. It could be in the form described above, between two schools or classrooms, among several learners or groups of learners, or between home and school. The variety of possibilities seems endless. The child ill in a hospital or disabled in some way and using this system would be, in effect, in the classroom. The teacher at home in the evening could monitor each child's homework being done on the child's home computer and even mark it online. (And perhaps the teacher can ascertain the extent to which the parent was helping or hindering). The dog could not eat the homework because as it was being done it was being recorded at school. With each child working on mathematics on an individual computer (at least an individual keyboard), the teacher could at a glance monitor each child's work and key the computer to analyze the specific difficulty the child was having and possibly give the remedy in immediate and personalized feedback. The child could move at his or her own pace through certain kinds of material being closely monitored and guided all along the way. All of this could be arranged to free the teacher and students to work on the in-class activities with hands-on manipulative, discussion, and interaction needed for projects and cooperative learning. A classroom system that included only a keyboard at each desk, a central processing unit, and TV-like monitors or large-screen projections could enable every student to use a computer as a tool in the way they now use calculators (Bitter & Mikesell, 1990). Or perhaps the laptop sized computers will become inexpensive enough to allow each child to have one, and they could be networked for whole-class work and monitoring. Whatever the system, one can envision the powerful tool of the computer becoming even more powerful and providing much more direct benefit to the mathematics classroom for both teachers and students at all levels than it does currently.

▣ Summary

This chapter examined the various ways in which the computer is effectively and ineffectively used in teaching and learning mathematics. The differences in software requirements for teaching concepts, processes, or factual knowledge were noted. Cautions were given that the computer cannot teach all that is to be taught with the same level of effectiveness; in fact, the computer cannot be relied on at all for certain topics. It was noted that to obtain software for each concept, process, or set of facts would be prohibitively expensive, and to place a significant portion of it on typical school hardware (which has very limited space) would be impossible. The important and successful applications of the computer in teaching mathematics were noted, and the future of computers in teaching mathematics were discussed.

▣ Exercises

1. Find a piece of mathematics software for the use of students between grades 1 and 6 and analyze it critically as to its content, appropriateness for topic, grade level, and method of presentation. Rank it against other comparable software using your analysis as justification for your ranking.

2. Create a spreadsheet to record pre- and post-grades on a concept lesson evaluation with actual or imaginary grades from a class and cause the spreadsheet to do appropriate analyses (compute pre- and post-means, plot pre-vs. post-scores graphs, calculate percentile rankings, etc.).

3. Find and use thoroughly a mathematics tutorial program for a particular concept. In a paragraph describe the salient characteristics of the program and answer the question, "Could a typical child at the appropriate level work through this program and end without having acquired the concept correctly?"

4. Carefully observe a child using (extensively) a grade-level-appropriate piece of software and note in a report the following: What is the child's level of interest and motivation? How long is the interest maintained? Are concepts, processes, or facts learned? Is skill improved? What levels of activity are maintained?

📖 References

Allen, Denise (1995). *Creative Problem Solving: Teaching K–8*. New York: Early Years Inc.

Bitter, Gary, and Jerald L. Mikesell (1990). *Using the Math Explorer™ Calculator*. Menlo Park, CA: Addison-Wesley.

Cognition & Technology Group at Vanderbilt University (1993, April). *Arithmetic Teacher*, 474–478, Reston, VA.

Demana, F., and B. Waits (1990, January). The role of technology in teaching mathematics. *Mathematics Teacher*, 27–31, Reston, VA: NCTM.

Dixon, Juli K., and Christy J. Falba (1997, March-April). Graphing in the information age: Using data from the World Wide Web. *Mathematics Teaching in the Middle School*, Reston, VA: NCTM.

Edwards, Nancy Tanner, and Gary G. Bitter (October 1989). Changing variables using spreadsheet templates. *Arithmetic Teacher*, 37(2), 40–44.

Hirschbull, John J., and Dwight Bishop, Eds. (1996). *Computers in Education* (7th ed.). Guilford, CT: Dushkin Publishing Group.

Dyrli, Ovard, and D. Kinnaman (1995, January). *Technology in Education: Getting the Upper Hand*. San Rafael, CA: Peter Li Inc., pp. 38–43.

Lynes, Kristine (1997). Mining mathematics through the Internet. *Teaching Children Mathematics*. Reston, VA: NCTM.

McClain, Kay (1997). The farmer's dilemma resolved. *Mathematics Teaching in the Middle School*. Reston, VA: NCTM.

Merrill, Paul F., et al. (1996). *Computers in Education* (3rd ed.). Needham Heights, MA: Allyn & Bacon.

National Council of Teachers of Mathematics (1989). *Curriculum and Evaluation Standards for School Mathematics*. Reston, VA: Author.

▣ Suggested Readings

Bobis, Janette F. (1991). Using a calculator to develop number sense. *Arithmetic Teacher*, 38(5), 42–45.

Hiatt, Arthur A. (1987). Activities for calculators. *Arithmetic Teacher*, 34(6), 38–43.

Pagni, David L. (1991). Teaching mathematics using calculators. *Arithmetic Teacher*, 38(5), 58–60.

Activities and Problems

Task 1: Measurements

First Level. Build the pictured block. Count to determine length, width, height, perimeter, area, and volume, then write the values in the chart. Build a new block twice as long, twice as wide, and twice as high; again find P, A, and V. Repeat using three times the dimensions. Write your conclusions about the relationships: P to A and P to V.

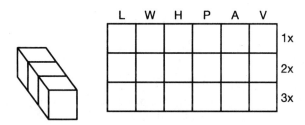

L	W	H	P	A	V	
						1x
						2x
						3x

Second Level. Same as above, except draw the blocks and use calculations to obtain the values.

Task 2: Create a Triangle

Create a triangle whose sides are the same lengths as these segments.
(a) _____   (b) _____   (c) ___

Can a triangle be created (as above) using any three line segments? Justify your response.
(d) Use these three segments to create a triangle.

Task 3: Volume of Solids

Measure the volume of the following solids built from C-rods.

(a) 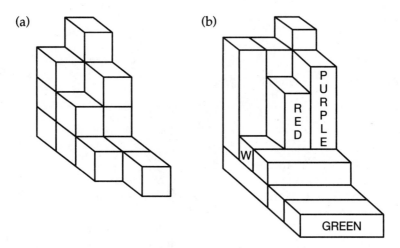 (b)

Activity: Counting/Visualizing/Understanding Cubes/ Detecting Patterns/Generalizing

Painted Cube Problem

1. Imagine (or create) cubes of various dimensions by stacking small (unit) cubes together.

2. Imagine next that the constructed cube is fully painted on all six faces.

3. For each size cube in numerical sequence, count the number of unit cubes that have no faces painted, one face painted, two faces painted, etc., and fill in the chart below.

4. Describe any patterns evident in the chart below.

5. Generalize to an $n \times n \times n$ cube and write the general statements in words or symbols.

Cube Size	No. of Unit Cubes with This Number of Sides Painted								Total Number Unit Cubes
	0	1	2	3	4	5	6		
$1 \times 1 \times 1$									
$2 \times 2 \times 2$									
$3 \times 3 \times 3$									
$4 \times 4 \times 4$									
$5 \times 5 \times 5$									
$n \times n \times n$									

Creating Figures

Create each of the figures described and convince the group that you have done what was required.

1. Create a three-sided polygon with one right angle and no two sides equal.

2. Create a three-sided polygon with one right angle and two sides equal.

3. Create a three-sided polygon with one right angle and a side not forming the right angle equal to a side forming the right angle.

4. Create a three-sided polygon with three equal sides.

5. Create nine different polygons, each with an area of four square units.

6. Create a polygon with three pegs on the perimeter and none inside. What is its area?

7. Create a polygon with three pegs on the perimeter and one inside. What is its area? Create another. What is its area?

8. Create a polygon with four pegs on the perimeter and none inside. What is its area? Create another. What is its area?

9. Create a polygon with four pegs on the perimeter and one inside. What is its area? Create another. What is its area?

10. Create a chart of results. Look for patterns. What pattern do you see?

Sample Assignment and Exercise Questions

1. Describe the use of *partial reflectors* (Miras) in:
   - teaching symmetry, angle duplication, angle bisecting
   - constructing: perpendiculars, parallels, circle centers
   - checking: symmetry, congruence

2. Give rationales for teaching: symmetry, geometrical shapes, angles, geometrical formulas, geometrical facts.

3. Explain the appropriate balance between teaching plane geometry and solid geometry, with a justification of your position.

4. Describe your position on this topic: Measurement should be taught before/concurrently with/after geometry.

5. Argue the question: Only nonmetric geometry should be taught in the first six grades.

6. Describe three pieces of software that are valuable for teaching geometrical concepts and list the strengths of each.

Activity: Folded Pentagon

It's not easy to create a regular or near-regular pentagon.

1. Give students pieces of adding machine tape (or other paper strips, preferably wider than one inch).

2. Ask students to "tie" the simplest knot in the strip. It will take some care to make the knot tight. Students should adjust the folds so the knot is as tight as possible.

3. Ask students to make measurements to determine if all the sides of the pentagon have the same measurement.

4. If the students feel that, within the accuracy permitted by the instruments, the sides all have the same length, ask the students if this is truly a regular pentagon.

5. Discuss the fact that two requirements for regularity exist.

6. Discuss methods for checking for equal angles. Note that it is very difficult to measure angles accurately in terms of degrees. Consider symmetry checks as equal angle checks. Could partial reflecting devices (Miras) be used?

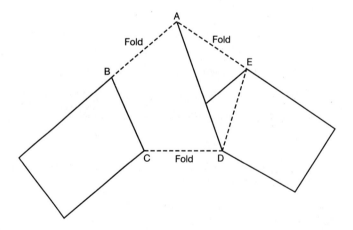

Activity: Help the Archaeologist Find the Center

Ask the students to consider the sketch below as the outline of a pottery fragment found in a dig. To deal properly with this fragment the archaeologist must assume that it is a piece of a circular plate and will need to know the diameter (accurately) in order to describe the artifact in her report.

Ask the students to suggest ways to solve this problem.

Lead them to use properties of chords, diameters, and tangents. Ask them to use Miras or compasses as tools.

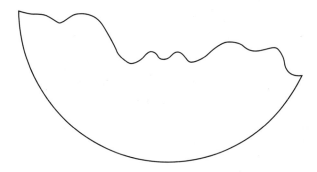

Activity: Inside/Outside

Ask students to consider the figure below and determine whether the indicated points are inside or outside the closed loop.

Direct students to start with simple closed loops and build gradually more complex ones, making the attempt to generate a pattern that will yield an algorithm for determining whether points are inside or outside of any closed loop.

Hint: Draw a line segment from the point to the outside of the figure and consider the number of crossing points.

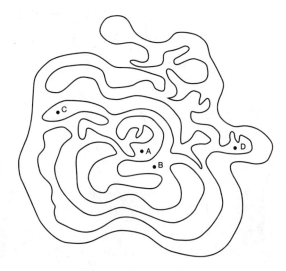

Activity: Construct Vernier Calipers

Many students don't know a practical way of measuring the diameter of a circle or circular object. Some have the idea that the diameter can be measured with accuracy using a straight edge and moving it until the maximum value is found. It should be pointed out that this method cannot be used effectively, especially with larger circles. A Vernier caliper is the tool of choice.

Construction

Using 5 × 8 cards, cut each of two into L-shaped pieces with the legs the same width (about 2 cm), as shown in the sketch below. Using tape and two strips cut from another card, make the slide guides. If desired, the L pieces may be marked with a measuring scale. (Larger calipers may be made with tag board or foam core.)

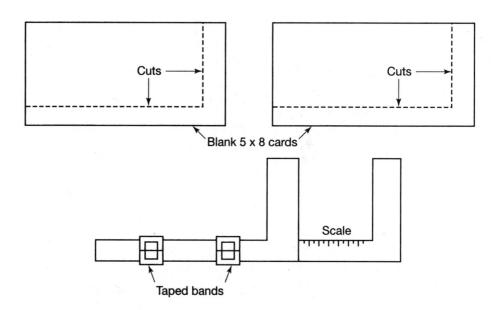

Activity: Examining Fraction Concepts in Real Life

Which of these figures represent ½?

(a)

(b)

(c)

(d)

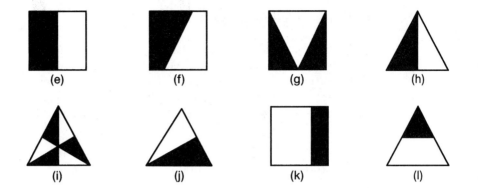

Do the blocks each represent ½?

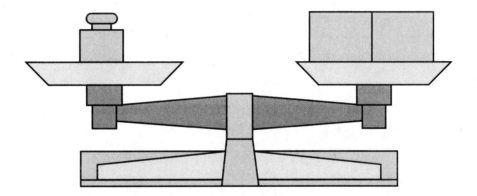

Is the geoboard divided into eighths?

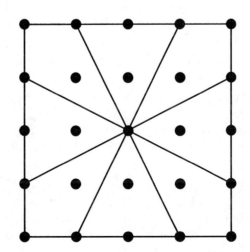

Activity: Broken Calculator

Some teachers believe that calculators should not be used by children who are learning to compute. There are, however, ways to use calculators effectively while learning to compute and, in so doing, to learn proper use of calculators.

Each student has a calculator—basic four operation ones are adequate. Give students a task such as: Add 25 and 39 assuming that:

- the addition key is broken.

- the addition and multiplication keys are broken.

- the above and using the memory.

- the above without using the memory.

With each solution (and there should be several successful methods), ask for an explanation of the principles and an explanation of the operations used.

Give the students other tasks such as subtracting, multiplying, dividing, squaring, and finding square roots, and vary the types of numbers. Different sized numbers, decimals, fractions, and so forth, should be used.

Ask students if the ease or difficulty is dependent on what numbers are used and why.

Sample Problems

1. If 6 horses eat 6 bales of hay in 6 hours, how many hours are needed for 3 horses to eat 3 bales of hay?

2. Kay has a basket full of eggs. If she takes out 5 eggs at a time, at the end there are 4 eggs left. If she takes out 4 eggs at a time, at the end there are 3 eggs left. If she takes out 3 eggs at a time, at the end there are 2 eggs left. If she takes out 2 eggs at a time, at the end there is 1 egg left. How many eggs are there in the basket?

3. Show and describe how to measure accurately (to 0.01 mm) the thickness of a single sheet of paper like this page, using only a standard ruler and sheets of paper.

4. For a class trip, the bus will cost $67.50, meals $6.50 each, and the museum admission $6.00 each for groups of 20 or less. There is 50¢ off each admission for between 20 and 50 in a group and $1.00 off each admission if there are more than 50 in the group. If there are 45 students in the group, how much should each bring for the expenses listed above?

5. Find the number of intersections possible for a given number of lines. Record also the number of possible arrangements of intersections. It is possible to have the same number of intersections with different arrangements, for example: 4 lines, 3 intersections.

6. How many nails are needed to balance the block on the last scale?

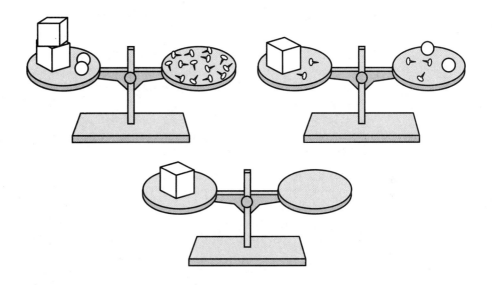

Example Problems with Specific Skills and Strategy Notations

Problem.   Kevin is responsible for planning for a racquetball single-elimination tournament at the YMCA. For how many games must he plan if there are 100 players in the tournament? Find a general rule so that he can plan for different numbers of players.

1. What problem-solving skills and strategies do you use in solving this problem?

2. What problem-solving skills and strategies can be taught effectively using this problem?

3. What mathematics can be taught effectively using this problem?

Solution 1.   Translate the idea of a tournament into a diagram—a bracket diagram showing the position for each of the players; chart the games and count the number of games. (99 games)
    (Skill: Translating words to diagram)
    (Strategy: Creating a diagram, making an organized chart, and checking the chart for a procedure for solving)

Solution 2. Realize that each time players play one wins and the number of players is reduced by half. List the successive halves: 50, 25, 12 (1 left), 6, 3, 1 (1 left), 1, 1. Add these numbers to obtain 99 games.

   (Skills: Deducing reduction by half, and the use of addition of the halves)

   (Strategies: Breaking down the problem into parts, working with parts, reassembling parts)

Solution 3. Consider the number of games in a small tournament of 2 people (1 game), 3 people (2 games), 4 people (3 games). See a pattern of: 1 less than the number of players. Check the solution of 5, 6, 7 players. Conclude that for 100 players, 99 games would be played.

   (Skills: Translation, deduction, generating a pattern, verifying)

   (Strategies: Breaking the problem into smaller, simpler problems and solving those to obtain an idea for a solution strategy)

Solution 4. Reasoning that one person will be the ultimate champion, having lost no game. Every other player (99 of them) will have lost one game; thus there were 99 games played.

   (Skill: Deduction)

   (Strategy: Reason about the conditions of the problem)

Find all the numbers which, when added, give the same result as when multiplied.

1. What important-problem solving skills and strategies do you use when solving this problem?

2. What problem-solving skills and strategies can be taught using this problem?

3. What mathematics may be taught effectively using this problem?

Using the cryptarithm: $\dfrac{I}{AM} = .HOTHOTHOT$

1. Solve the problem explaining steps, reasons, strategies, and skills used.

2. Describe the use of this problem and the solving process to teach problem-solving in a middle school setting.

3. Describe the mathematics that can be taught, learned, reviewed, connected, and so forth in the process of solving the problem.

Instructions

1. Draw 7 chords that pass through the point P in the circle.

2. For each chord, measure the length of the segment in the shaded region and enter the measurement value in the X column; measure the length of

the chord segment in the unshaded region, and enter the measurement value in the Y column.

3. Graph the ordered pairs on the graph.

4. Determine the relationship between X and Y.

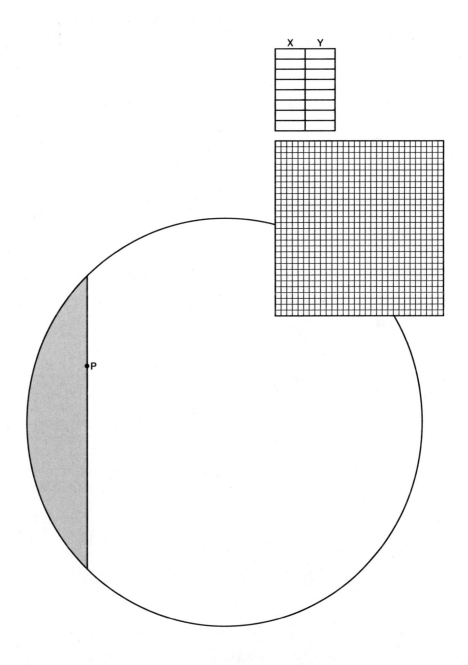

Sample Hundreds Chart

1	2	3	4	5	6	7	8	9	10
11	12	13	14	15	16	17	18	19	20
21	22	23	24	25	26	27	28	29	30
31	32	33	34	35	36	37	38	39	40
41	42	43	44	45	46	47	48	49	50
51	52	53	54	55	56	57	58	59	60
61	62	63	64	65	66	67	68	69	70
71	72	73	74	75	76	77	78	79	80
81	82	83	84	85	86	87	88	89	90
91	92	93	94	95	96	97	98	99	100

Algorithms

▣ Types of Algorithm Difficulties

Addition

1. a. $\begin{array}{r} 48 \\ +56 \\ \hline 914 \end{array}$ b. $\begin{array}{r} 97 \\ +25 \\ \hline 1112 \end{array}$ c. $\begin{array}{r} 39 \\ +13 \\ \hline 412 \end{array}$ d. $\begin{array}{r} 63 \\ +37 \\ \hline 910 \end{array}$

Nature of the difficulty:
Reason for the difficulty:
Corrective teaching:

2. a. $\begin{array}{r} 954 \\ +32 \\ \hline 1274 \end{array}$ b. $\begin{array}{r} 7600 \\ +36 \\ \hline 7960 \end{array}$ c. $\begin{array}{r} 624 \\ +27 \\ \hline 831 \end{array}$ d. $\begin{array}{r} 4327 \\ +17 \\ \hline 4434 \end{array}$

Nature of the difficulty:
Reason for the difficulty:
Corrective teaching:

3. a. $\begin{array}{r} 48 \\ +56 \\ \hline 94 \end{array}$ b. $\begin{array}{r} 37 \\ +25 \\ \hline 52 \end{array}$ c. $\begin{array}{r} 32 \\ +45 \\ \hline 77 \end{array}$ d. $\begin{array}{r} 55 \\ +28 \\ \hline 73 \end{array}$

Nature of the difficulty:
Reason for the difficulty:
Corrective teaching:

4. a. $\begin{array}{r} 15.7 \\ +2.8 \\ \hline 4.37 \end{array}$ b. $\begin{array}{r} 19.27 \\ +6.23 \\ \hline 8.157 \end{array}$ c. $\begin{array}{r} 2.137 \\ +4.1 \\ \hline 2178 \end{array}$ d. $\begin{array}{r} 1.301 \\ 41.2 \\ \hline 1.713 \end{array}$

Nature of the difficulty:
Reason for the difficulty:
Corrective teaching:

Subtraction

1. a.
$$\begin{array}{r} 1176 \\ -\ 37 \\ \hline 860 \end{array}$$
b.
$$\begin{array}{r} 1342 \\ -4\ 1 \\ \hline 941 \end{array}$$
c.
$$\begin{array}{r} 1231 \\ -75 \\ \hline 526 \end{array}$$
d.
$$\begin{array}{r} 4321 \\ -29 \\ \hline 4112 \end{array}$$

Nature of the difficulty:
Reason for the difficulty:
Corrective teaching:

2. a.
$$\begin{array}{r} 35 \\ -45 \\ \hline 10 \end{array}$$
b.
$$\begin{array}{r} 17 \\ -18 \\ \hline 1 \end{array}$$
c.
$$\begin{array}{r} 29 \\ -37 \\ \hline 8 \end{array}$$
d.
$$\begin{array}{r} 756 \\ -841 \\ \hline 76 \end{array}$$

Nature of the difficulty:
Reason for the difficulty:
Corrective teaching:

3. a.
$$\begin{array}{r} 87 \\ -38 \\ \hline 59 \end{array}$$
b.
$$\begin{array}{r} 63 \\ -45 \\ \hline 28 \end{array}$$
c.
$$\begin{array}{r} 54 \\ -28 \\ \hline 35 \end{array}$$
d.
$$\begin{array}{r} 42 \\ -17 \\ \hline 35 \end{array}$$

Nature of the difficulty:
Reason for the difficulty:
Corrective teaching:

4. a.
$$\begin{array}{r} 97 \\ -38 \\ \hline 61 \end{array}$$
b.
$$\begin{array}{r} 86 \\ -39 \\ \hline 53 \end{array}$$
c.
$$\begin{array}{r} 34 \\ -26 \\ \hline 12 \end{array}$$
d.
$$\begin{array}{r} 71 \\ -38 \\ \hline 47 \end{array}$$

Nature of the difficulty:
Reason for the difficulty:
Corrective teaching:

Multiplication

1. a.
$$\begin{array}{r} 23 \\ \times 45 \\ \hline 95 \end{array}$$
b.
$$\begin{array}{r} 17 \\ \times 23 \\ \hline 41 \end{array}$$
c.
$$\begin{array}{r} 18 \\ \times 47 \\ \hline 96 \end{array}$$
d.
$$\begin{array}{r} 98 \\ \times 13 \\ \hline 114 \end{array}$$

Nature of the difficulty:
Reason for the difficulty:
Corrective teaching:

2. a.
$$\begin{array}{r} 17 \\ \times 24 \\ \hline 68 \\ 34 \\ \hline 102 \end{array}$$

b.
$$\begin{array}{r} 51 \\ \times 13 \\ \hline 153 \\ 51 \\ \hline 204 \end{array}$$

c.
$$\begin{array}{r} 72 \\ \times 21 \\ \hline 72 \\ 144 \\ \hline 216 \end{array}$$

d.
$$\begin{array}{r} 37 \\ \times 34 \\ \hline 148 \\ 81 \\ \hline 229 \end{array}$$

Nature of the difficulty:
Reason for the difficulty:
Corrective teaching:

3. a.
$$\begin{array}{r} 33 \\ \times 19 \\ \hline 297 \\ 23 \\ \hline 427 \end{array}$$

b.
$$\begin{array}{r} 47 \\ \times 18 \\ \hline 376 \\ 47 \\ \hline 746 \end{array}$$

c.
$$\begin{array}{r} 53 \\ \times 27 \\ \hline 371 \\ 106 \\ \hline 1331 \end{array}$$

d.
$$\begin{array}{r} 28 \\ \times 47 \\ \hline 196 \\ 112 \\ \hline 1216 \end{array}$$

Nature of the difficulty:
Reason for the difficulty:
Corrective teaching:

4. a.
$$\begin{array}{r} 77 \\ \times 14 \\ \hline 288 \\ 77 \\ \hline 1058 \end{array}$$

b.
$$\begin{array}{r} 89 \\ \times 13 \\ \hline 247 \\ 89 \\ \hline 1137 \end{array}$$

c.
$$\begin{array}{r} 96 \\ \times 15 \\ \hline 450 \\ 96 \\ \hline 1410 \end{array}$$

d.
$$\begin{array}{r} 65 \\ \times 47 \\ \hline 425 \\ 260 \\ \hline 3025 \end{array}$$

Nature of the difficulty:
Reason for the difficulty:
Corrective teaching:

Division

1. a. $3\overline{)310}$ with quotient 133

b. $7\overline{)721}$ with quotient 130

c. $4\overline{)428}$ with quotient 170

d. $8\overline{)831}$ with quotient 138

Nature of the difficulty:
Reason for the difficulty:
Corrective teaching:

2. a. $4 \div 5 = 1.25$ **b.** $3 \div 1 = .33$

c. $7 \div 2 = .285$ **d.** $6 \div 7 = 1.1\overline{66}$

Nature of the difficulty:
Reason for the difficulty:
Corrective teaching:

3. a. $\dfrac{1}{4} = 4$ b. $\dfrac{2}{5} = 2\dfrac{1}{2}$ c. $\dfrac{4}{8} = 2$ d. $\dfrac{2}{3} = 1\dfrac{1}{2}$

Nature of the difficulty:
Reason for the difficulty:
Corrective teaching:

4. a. $2.3\overline{\smash{)}54.9}$ with quotient 2.38 b. $46.2\overline{\smash{)}75.32}$ with quotient $.163$

c. $3.5\overline{\smash{)}72.1}$ with quotient 2.06 d. $841.1\overline{\smash{)}753.23}$ with quotient $.089$

Nature of the difficulty:
Reason for the difficulty:
Corrective teaching:

Checklists

▣ Manipulatives Checklist

Manipulatives should:

_____ be appropriate to the topic being taught.

_____ not be distractive because of multiple attributes.

_____ not be dangerous because of sharp edges, toxicity, or the danger of being swallowed.

_____ be able to support the specific learning intended.

_____ have multiple uses where possible.

_____ be attractive.

_____ be easy to use.

_____ not be trivial either because of the way they are used or because of their appearance.

_____ not be restricted to a very narrow topic such as being usable for only one lesson during the year.

_____ not be too easily modified or turned into playthings.

_____ encourage inventiveness.

_____ be sturdy.

_____ be easily maintained and stored.

_____ be cleanable and not easily stained.

_____ not leave marks on kids, clothing, or furniture.

▣ Problem-Solving Checklist

A. Skills

1. Classify (Note facts)

2. Deduce (If this, then)

3. Estimate

4. Hypothesize

5. Generate patterns

6. Translate

7. Try and Modify

8. Verify

Strategies

1. Make an organized list

2. Make a chart, table, graph

3. Work backward

4. Work a simpler problem

5. Detect patterns

6. Break problem into parts

7. Translate the problem: reword, sketch, diagram, use models/ manipulatives

8. Collect relevant information

9. Act out

10. Consult

11. Create a logic construct

12. Modify problem requirements

Work on problem

1. Analyze problem

2. Accept the challenge

3. Spend time on problem

4. Break and return with new approach

5. Describe problem nature

D. Nature of solution

1. Type of solution understood

2. Account for parts of solution

3. Ensure completeness of solution

4. Verify and justify solution

5. Consider solutions to related problems

6. Transfer of information to other problems

7. Find a "better" solution (better strategy)

Software Worksheet

Title _____

Subject _____ Level _____

Source _____ Cost _____

Applications _____

Use: General or specific _____

    Progression (fast or slow) _____

    Purpose (Practice skills or facts) _____

        (Introduce topics, concepts) _____

        (Source of information) _____

        (Problem solving) _____

        _____

        _____

Evaluation: (Motivation) _____

        (Entry/re-entry) _____

        (Extent) _____

        (Interesting because:) _____

        _____

        (Value to subject/purpose) _____

        (User-friendly) _____

        (Clarity, instructions/material) _____

        _____

Rating: _____ Have to have

      _____ Good, will buy asap

      _____ Good, will buy when extra money is available

      _____ Fair, will buy after the above are filled

      _____ Will accept as a gift

      _____ A real dog, will not accept

Constructions in Mathematics

▣ General Observations

1. Construction usually proceeds from the simple to the complex; starting from a carefully laid foundation and occurring in a conducive environment.

2. Differentiation should be made among constructing concepts, constructing processes, and constructing facts or mathematical knowledge. Each requires a unique construction approach.

▣ Constructing Concepts

1. Give examples of the concept which vary over as many noncritical attributes as possible. Include especially those attributes which are often misunderstood.

Illustration: Concept—Operation of addition

$$75 + 38 \qquad 75 \qquad \text{What is 75 and 38?} \quad \$75 \text{ plus } \$38 =$$
$$\underline{+38}$$
$$0.75 + 0.38 = \qquad 75 + 3.8 =$$

$$38 + 75 \qquad 38$$
$$\underline{+75} \qquad X = 75, Y = 38 \text{ What is the value of } X + Y?$$
$$38 + (75 + 38) \qquad (38 + 75) + 38 \qquad 75 + (38 + 38)$$

2. Give counter-examples of the concept which vary over the critical attributes of the concept.

Illustration: Concept—Operation of addition

$$X = 75, \quad Y = 38, \quad \text{What are the values of } X \text{ and } Y?$$
$$75 \, (38) \quad 7538 \qquad 38$$
$$\underline{75}$$

Concept—Triangle

 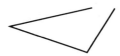

3. Give examples of interrelationships with other concepts.

Illustration:

Multiplication is repeated addition

Polygons can be subdivided into triangles

Constructing Mathematical Knowledge

1. Begin with a modification of a known fact or demonstrate the need for a new piece of information.

Illustration:

Basic facts for 6 + 7, 8 + 9, etc. are doubles + one.

A square is a special rectangle—all sides equal.

2. Do not begin with a definition or abstraction like a name, especially if the name has multiple meanings.

Illustration:

Circle: ring, go around, loop

Addition: The number, $a + b$, of the union of two sets, A and B where the number of set A is a and the number of Set B is b.

3. Build the definition of the fact by adding attributes from examples and nonexamples.

Illustration:

A rhombus is a square with unequal angles.

A baseball diamond is a rhombus.

A rhombus is a squashed square.

4. Reference the fact in a variety of contexts and forms; especially using it in problem solving.

Illustration:

Use the fact of the sum of angles in a triangle to determine the sum of angles in a polygon.

> Use the fact of the angle total for a circle to show that there are only five regular polyhedra.
>
> Fractions: 0.21, 3/4, 34%, one-half, 2/x, 17/12, . .

5. Revisit the fact in connection with new facts, concept development, and learning processes.

Illustration:

> Recall that a fraction can be thought of as division when converting fractions to decimals.
>
> Use the fact that a straight angle is 180 degrees when constructing a right angle.

◨ Constructing Processes

1. Begin with real life child-understood activities.

Illustration:

> Operation order—Child puts on socks before shoes.
>
> Division—repeated take-away

2. Show that an algorithm is simply a shortcut, that there are multiple algorithms, and that there are reasons for the steps involved.

Illustration:

$$78 + 39 = 70 + 30 + 8 + 9 = 100 + 17 = 117$$
$$78 + 39 = 70 + 40 + 8 - 1 = 110 + 8 - 1 = 110 + 7$$

3. Demonstrate a variety in processes for a particular result and that certain processes are better for certain situations.

Illustration:

> Problem: Find the number of games in a tournament when the number of players is 20.
>
> Process: Draw a bracket and count.
>
> > If the number of players is 32, do successive divisions by 2.
> >
> > If the number of players is 200, reason about the number of losses.

4. Give an abstract algorithm only after the underlying process and concept is well developed.

Illustration:

> Don't give the standard long division algorithm until the idea of repeated subtraction and a scaffold type algorithm has been used.

Don't give the "invert and multiply" algorithm until division of fractions is understood.

5. Avoid the use of abstract terminology particular to the process. Use meaningful terms.

Illustration:

Use "take away" rather than "subtract"

Use "top number" rather than "numerator"

Glossary

Algorithm: A set of steps or procedures for obtaining the result of an operation. An algorithm is not synonymous with an operation; it should be thought of as a tool for obtaining the operation results easily and accurately. The steps may closely reflect real life operation applications or the algorithm may be very abstract. Good algorithms are always accurate, have easy, clear steps, and are concise. Operators should know many algorithms and how to select the one best suited to the operation situation.

Bar graph: A graph composed of rectangular elements such that the lengths of the bars indicate the frequencies of the classes. The bars may be either horizontally or vertically oriented.

Cardinal number: The number indicating the number of items in a set. The cardinal number is contrasted with ordinal number which indicates order in a set.

Concrete object: An entity which is physical, can be touched, handled, and manipulated.

Conservation: The ability to understand that objects do not change in number or weight when rearranged or reshaped.

Constructivism: The philosophy that holds that ideas must be constructed by the person in order to become fully understood and functional. Memorization and exposure are insufficient to accomplish the integration of new ideas.

Counting: Basically, placing objects or constructs in one-to-one correspondence with the positive integers greater than zero starting with 1, taking the integers in increasing order, and noting the value of the last integer paired. Simply reciting a set of words in correct order is not counting. There are many ways to count including using operations, comparing measurements, and estimating. Measuring is essentially counting.

Cryptarithm: A problem that involves finding the numerals to replace letters in an algorithm format so that the resulting algorithm is correct.

Equation: A mathematical statement, usually in numbers and symbols, that shows two expressions to be of equal value.

Exercise: A mathematical activity used to give students opportunity to practice a mathematical process.

Fraction: A number representable in a wide variety of ways and usable to express (among other concepts) *division, parts of wholes, rate,* and *ratio.* Fractions comprise a class of numbers which includes integers as special cases; thus the operation attributes apply to these numbers too. The algorithms that are place-value-dependent can be applied only to the decimal forms of fractions. The most common representations for fractions are: *a/b,* decimals, and percentages.

Hierarchy: A system of numbers, procedures, or concepts ranked one above another. A hierarchy of algorithmic steps suggests that the steps must be done in a specific order in order for the algorithm to be done correctly. Within problem solving there is usually no hierarchy of complexity or difficulty. Two problems might deal with the same numbers and be very similar, but have very different difficulty levels; solving one may not help in knowing how to solve the other.

Integer: A number expressible with a symbol involving no fractional part. Integers include counting numbers and 0 and may be positive or negative.

Mean: The result of dividing the sum of the numbers in a set by the number of the numbers in the set. The mean may be thought of as the balance point of the set and/or graph of the set. It is a measure of the center of the set.

Median: The middle number of the set or the mean of the two numbers at the middle of a set that has an even number of items. The median is also a measure of the center of a set.

Mode: The most often occurring item in a set or the largest class in a frequency distribution for a set of numbers.

Preoperational: A person who has not progressed to the developmental level where it is possible for the person to reason (operate) with abstract concepts in the mind.

Problem: A task involving mathematics in its presentation and/or in the process of solving, for which there is no algorithm available to the solver. A problem presents a challenge and a need to solve to the solver. It may require importing information or the application of many different skills and strategies. Typically more than one step or set of steps will be necessary to reach solution. Answering questions may or may not be a part of working toward solution.

Problem solving: The application of various skills and strategies to resolve the blockage, dissonance, or apparent contradictions in the statement of the problem. The application of the skills and strategies often involves try-and-modify activities. Since solving is a challenge and there is often no obvious indication of how to proceed, trials have to be made and experimentation done.

Puzzle: A problem which likely does not have any practical or real life application. Some problem solvers enjoy puzzles simply because they are abstract and have no connection to other issues. Others see puzzles as a waste of time for the same reason.

Real numbers: Numbers which can be used to measure real objects. The *reals* include whole numbers, integers, and rational numbers. They do not include imaginary numbers.

Rational numbers: Numbers, including fractions, decimals, and percentages which can be used to express parts of wholes.

Rebus: A story line in which pictures or diagrams replace some of the words.

Solution: A statement, usually general, which resolves the blockage, dissonance, or contradiction in a problem. Solutions are typically not one-word or one-number answers to some question (The word "answer" should not be used in the sense: The answer to the problem.) Solutions will likely have multiple parts or conditional statements of the type: "When this is the situation, then this . . . will be the solution." and "All of the numbers of this kind . . ." "A solution" connotes one-symbol solutions and thus suggests a misunderstanding of solution as does "complete solution." If the solution is not complete it hasn't solved the problem.

Tesselation: A repeated pattern or design in which the parts of the design fit together so that they cover a surface.

Topology: The study of characteristics of geometrical shapes which do not depend on measure. Important characteristics are closed or not closed regions, the number of closed regions, and intersections of curves.

Un-operating: Reversing the operations of addition, multiplication, subtraction, or division. Un-adding, for example, 35, would be to write 20 + 15, or 30 + 5, 25 + 10, etc. in place of 35, in order to find a form more feasible to use. This technique can be used to assist with computation; it is especially helpful for mental computation.

Math Assessment and Diagnosis Scheme (MADS)

This is an outline of a plan for assessing the status of mathematical knowledge and process ability of a child using a one-on-one interview/observation method. Included here are checklists, effective questions, and an outline in five areas of mathematics teaching. An individual teacher may need to modify the items and questions to suit a particular situation considering the needs and experience of the child and the current mathematics activity in the classroom.

The teacher, in preparation for this assessment, will prepare a worksheet covering the topics under consideration or an activity to engage the student. As the student works on the activity, the teacher will observe and gently question. It will be necessary for the teacher to set the stage for this activity so that the child is accustomed to work in this environment and will feel comfortable being watched and talking about what is being thought and written.

Teachers may attach a value and scoring scheme to the checklists so that students assessment results may be compared and/or a whole class status may be described.

Algorithms and Computation

Algorithms

The child uses:

- the algorithms currently being taught in the class
- algorithms learned before child-invented algorithms
- a mix

The child uses:

- algorithms correctly
- algorithms incorrectly

    difficulty with basic facts

    uses correct steps but in wrong order

    omits steps

algorithms don't apply to this operation

difficulty with place value

lining up columns

placing decimal point

"carrying/borrowing"

Ask:

- Do you enjoy computing? Why? Why not?
- Which algorithm do you like? Why? Why not?
- Which algorithm do you not like? Why? Why not?
- How did you come up with that way of doing it?
- Can you tell me another way to do this?
- Would you like to know a 'neat' trick to do this?
- Can you see how this is related to what is done with objects?
- How could you use this to solve a problem?
- Is this like another way of doing this operation?

Basic Facts

Addition and Multiplication

The child:

- has no hesitancy with noting/using 1–9 facts
- hesitates with certain facts
- doesn't know certain facts
- works out some facts using others using:

  addition

  multiplication

  subtraction

  division

- will not use facts uncertain about
- knows additional facts beyond 1–9

0 facts

10 facts

- applies facts inappropriately
- applies facts inconsistently
- is not sure that facts always remain the same

Subtraction and Division

The child:

- doesn't know/use subtraction facts
- has learned subtraction facts
- uses subtraction facts without reference to other facts
- works subtraction out using other facts
- has only a few basic facts
- uses facts inappropriately
- feels compelled to use subtraction facts rather than addition facts

🔳 Estimating

In numeracy the child approximates:

- small numbers near 1
- numbers to the nearest decade
- numbers to the nearest hundred
- fractions near 1
- fractions near 0
- fractions by decimals or percentages
- decimals by fractions

In computation, the child:

- uses front-end estimation
- uses back-end estimation
- by estimation verifies results
- recognizes when an estimate is sufficient

- recognizes when the result must be an estimate
- uses estimation to shorten the process

In measurement, the child:

- recognizes that all measurement is an estimation
- knows what level of accuracy makes sense
- compensates for inaccuracy when operating with measurements
- chooses units based on estimation needs
- uses fractional numbers appropriately in estimating
- changes units for better estimates
- expresses estimates properly

Operation Concepts

The child

- recognizes that: algorithms are not the same thing as operations
  many different algorithms can be used to get correct results
  some algorithms work better than others for a given operation
- recognizes that operations are binary and uses that fact in operating
- knows and uses the commutativity of addition and multiplication
- recognizes that subtraction and division are not commutative
- does not commute in operating with subtraction and/or division
- knows and uses associativity of addition and multiplication
- recognizes that subtraction and division are not associative
- does not use associativity in operating with subtraction and/or division
- recognizes and uses multiplication as repeated addition
- recognizes and uses division as repeated subtraction
- recognizes and uses the inverse relationship between addition and subtraction
- recognizes and uses the inverse relationship between multiplication and division
- recognizes and uses the distributive property of multiplication over addition and subtraction (both right and left)

- recognizes and uses the right distributive property of division over addition and subtraction
- recognizes the properties of operating with 0

▣ Problem Solving

The child:

- recognizes a problem as distinct from an exercise or operation
- understands the nature of solution to a problem
- considers the possibility of "multiple" solutions
- generalizes the solution statement
- recognizes that one number "solutions" are not typical
- is willing to accept the challenge of working on a problem
- has and uses the skills: *Has (sufficiently)*   *Uses*

  Classifying

  Deducing

  Estimating

  Generating patterns

  Hypothesizing

  Translating

  Trying and modifying

  Verifying

The child uses the strategies:

- Making an organized list
- Making a chart, table, graph, etc.
- Working backward
- Working a simpler problem
- Detecting patterns
- Breaking problem into parts
- Translating the problem statement

Rewording

Sketching

Diagraming

Using models/manipulatives

Collecting relevant information

Acting out

Consulting

Creating a logic construct

Modifying problem requirements

Model Lesson and Unit

▨ Lesson on Place Value

Objective/Purpose: To demonstrate and reinforce a place value based algorithm for adding by using a nonbase 10 system

Set: The class is familiar with a base 10 place value addition algorithm for 2 digit addition.

Set Induction: Ask the class when $5 + 3 \neq 8$? Tell them they can confound their friends with a secret math they can use with a system that has no 8's or 9's in it.

Materials: Paper—columns
Counting line for base 7 (drawn on the board)
Counters

Procedures:

1. T. will form groups of four.

2. T. will guide the class in solving the problem of finding out how many weeks and days until Columbus day.

3. T. will ask each to write as the T. has written: 1 week, 0 days plus 1 week, 6 days plus 1 week, 2 days.

4. T. will re-form into classic add form and add weeks and days.

5. T. will ask groups to make up two of the above and add, each time using no more than two 'times' with 2 weeks and more than 3 days in each.

6. T. will ask the groups to repeat the above using the 2w. 3d. format.

7. T. will ask the groups to repeat the above using the columns on the paper.

8. T. will ask the groups to repeat the above using the 2–3 format and point out the use of the counting line.

9. T. will ask the groups to discuss and report the similarities and differences with the base 10 process and the easiest way to get the addition result.

10. T. will ask each student to make up and add two weeks/days numbers showing the work on the students' columns' sheet.

11. T. will ask each student to write sentences at the bottom of the column sheet stating how adding these numbers is the same/different from adding base 10 numbers.

Evaluation: Teacher will circulate and look for difficulty and/or hesitancy in trading, recording, or following known procedure. Written papers will be handed in and examined for correct use of algorithm and any misconceptions expressed in the writing.

Note

An obvious extension is to ask, try, and discuss whether the known subtraction algorithm also works in the same way.

🔲 Unit on Probability

Duration: 1 Week
Objectives:

1. To study basic probability concepts

2. To solve a problem with probability

3. To apply probability in a practical, real-life setting

Preparation:

1. Review writing fractions to express real situations.

2. Review and practice writing equivalent fractions.

3. Review and practice adding, subtracting, and multiplying fractions.

4. Announce a 'Probability Week' and probability project, 'Predicting the weather for the first week of February.'

5. Provide materials for counting and probability experiments (colored counters, bicolor counters, calculators, newspapers, magazines, which include articles of interest to 7th graders.

6. Arrange for a TV weather forecaster to visit the class and arrange for the equipment needed (TV and VCR, overhead, etc.).

Day 1: Pose the problem: Create a prediction of the weather for the first week of February.
  Organize the groups who will work on different tasks.
  Give overview of the week and instructions for day 1.

Post straightforward probability questions—obvious (for 7th graders) — which clearly illustrate the basic ideas of probability.

Experiment with counters (shake and spill) to answer the questions.

Chart probabilities, and experiments' results, guiding students to $P(A) + P(B) = 1$ if $A \cup B = U$ and $A \cap B = \varnothing$, $P(C) = 0$.

Decide with class what specifically will be forecast. (temp., precip., wind, sun/cloud, etc.)

Assign homework: Write down or bring newspaper, magazine references to probabilities.

Day 2: Quick review of Day 1's learning

Answer questions and solicit comments

Using transparencies of print material brought in, lead a class discussion centered on the questions:

1. Why was this (weather fact, projection, etc.) presented with probabilities?

2. Who is interested—needs to know?

3. How will interested persons use the info?

4. How did producers arrive at these numbers?

   a) What data was used?

   b) What calculations were done?

(If students did not bring what is required, do the above briefly with teacher provided materials.)

Group 1. Discuss and decide what distant past info to collect, how many years back to go and how and where to get the info.

Group 2. Discuss and decide what recent past info to collect, how many months back to go and how and where to get the info.

Group 3. Discuss and decide what current measurements to take, and how to do them.

Group 4. Discuss and decide what charts, formats, and calculations should be made.

(Each group will record its recommendations.)

Prepare classroom arrangement and equipment for the speaker.

Assign homework to begin the collection of information.

Day 3

Prepare questions, perhaps one major question from each group, that will be asked of the speaker.

Listen to the speaker.

Record the answers to the questions and other important information.

Assign homework: Continue information collection.

Day 4

Prepare a large wall/chalkboard chart to organize and record each group's recommendations, and modifications due to the speaker's presentation, and any of the speaker's information.

Have the groups do their information collection and record data, process plans, etc., on the chart.

Discuss $P(A \text{ or } B)$ and $P(A \text{ and } B)$ as needed.

Day 5

Perform the calculations and record on the final chart, posters, etc.

Decide on how to judge for accuracy of results and how to compare forecast with actual.

Plan for sharing the results: Posting in hall, school office, sending to TV broadcast, storing for next year, etc.)

Professional Organizations and Publications

National Council of Teachers of Mathematics

Journals

Journal for Research in Mathematics Education (JRME)

Teaching Children Mathematics

Teaching Middle School Mathematics

Instructor

Learning

Books

Assessment Standards for School Mathematics

Curriculum and Evaluation Standards for School Mathematics

Professional Standards for Teachers of Mathematics

Standards Emphases

K–4 Mathematics

Emphasized

Number

Number sense
Place-value concepts
Meaning of fractions and
  decimals
Estimation of quantities

Operations and Computation

Meaning of operations
Operation sense
Mental computation
Estimation and the reasonableness
  of answers
Selection of an appropriate
  computational method
Use of calculators for complex
  computation
Thinking strategies for basic facts

Patterns and Functions

Identifying and using functional
  relationships
Developing and using tables,
  graphs, and rules to describe
  situations
Interpreting among different
  mathematical representations

De-emphasized

Number

Early attention to reading, writing,
  and ordering numbers symbolically

Operations and Computation

Complex paper-and-pencil
  computations
Isolated treatment of paper-and-
  pencil computations
Addition and subtraction without
  renaming
Isolated treatment of division facts
Long division
Long division without remainders
Paper-and-pencil fraction
  computation
Use of rounding to estimate

Patterns and Functions

Topics seldom in the current
  curriculum

Algebra

Developing an understanding of
variables, expressions, and
equations
Using a variety of methods to solve
linear equations and informally
investigate inequalities and
nonlinear equations

Algebra

Manipulating symbols
Memorizing procedures and drilling
on equation solving

Statistics

Using statistical methods to describe,
analyze, evaluate, and make
a decision

Statistics

Memorizing formulas

Probability

Memorizing formulas

Probability

Creating experimental and
theoretical modes of situations
involving probabilities

Geometry

Developing an understanding of
geometric objects and relationships
Using geometry in solving problems

Geometry

Memorizing geometric vocabulary
Memorizing facts and relationships

Measurement

Estimating and using measurement
to solve problems

Measurement

Memorizing and manipulating
formulas
Converging within and between
measurement systems

Instructional Practices

Actively involving students individually and in groups in exploring,
conjecturing, analyzing, and applying mathematics in both a mathematical and a real-world context
Using appropriate technology for
computation and exploration
Using concrete materials
Being a facilitator of learning
Assessing learning as an integral
part of instruction

Instructional Practices

Teaching computations out of
context
Drilling on paper-and-pencil
algorithms
Teaching topics in isolation
Stressing memorization
Being the dispenser of knowledge
Testing for sole purpose of assigning
grades

5–8 Mathematics

Emphasized	*De-emphasized*

Problem Solving

Pursuing open-ended problems and extended solving projects

Investigating and formulating questions from problem situations

Representing situations verbally, numerically, graphically, geometrically, or symbolically

Problem Solving

Practicing routine, one-step problems

Practicing problems categorized by types (e.g. coin problems, age problems)

Communication

Discussing, writing, reading, and listening to mathematical ideas

Communication

Doing fill-in-the-blank worksheets

Answering questions that require only yes, no, or a number as responses

Reasoning

Reasoning in spatial contexts

Reasoning with proportions

Reasoning from graphs

Reasoning inductively and deductively

Reasoning

Relying on outside authority (teacher or an answer key)

Connections

Connecting mathematics to other subjects and to the world outside the classroom

Connecting topics within mathematics

Applying mathematics

Connections

Learning isolated topics

Developing skills out of context

Number/Operations/Computation

Developing number sense

Developing operation sense

Creating algorithms and procedures

Using estimation both in solving problems and in checking the reasonableness of answers

Exploring relationships among representations of, and operations on, whole number, fractions, decimals, integers, and rational numbers

Number/Operations/Computation

Memorizing rules and algorithms

Practicing tedious paper-and-pencil computations

Finding exact forms of answers

Memorizing procedures, such as cross multiplication, without understanding

Practicing rounding numbers out of context

Developing an understanding of ratio,
proportion, and percent

Geometry and Measurement	**Geometry and Measurement**
Properties of geometric figures	Primary focus on naming geometric
Geometric relationships	figures
Spatial sense	Memorization of equivalencies
Process of measuring	between units of measurement
Concepts related to units of	
measurement	
Actual measuring	
Estimation of measurements	
Use of measurement and geometry	
ideas throughout the curriculum	

Probability and Statistics

Collection and organization of data
Exploration of chance

Patterns and Relationships

Pattern recognition and description
Use of variables to express relationships

Problem Solving	**Problem Solving**
Word problems with a variety of	Use of clue words to determine
structures	which operation to use
Use of everyday problems	
Applications	
Study of patterns and relationships	
Problem solving strategies	

Instructional Practices	**Instructional Practices**
Use of manipulative materials	Rote practice
Cooperative work	Rote memorization of rules
Discussion of mathematics	One answer and one method
Questioning	Use of worksheets
Justification of thinking	Written practice
Writing about mathematics	Teaching by telling
Problem solving approach to	
instruction	
Content integration	
Use of calculators and computers	

Instructions for Addition Slide Rules

▣ Ruler Addition

1. Obtain two strips of heavy paper or tag board 15 to 20 inches long.

2. Orient them horizontally.

3. Mark equally spaced vertical marks and on the bottom edge of the strip that will be used above the other. The marks should be between $\frac{1}{4}$ and $\frac{1}{2}$ inch apart.

4. Number the marks starting with 0 and continuing until the end of the strip is reached.

5. Do the same to the top edge of the other strip.

Illustration

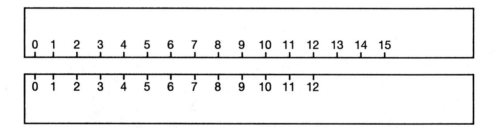

▣ Circular Slide Rule

1. Obtain two circular pieces of heavy paper, preferably tag board. One should be 6 to 7 inches in diameter and the other, one inch less in diameter. The important dimension is one inch less.

2. On each circular piece mark the center.

3. Place the smaller piece on the larger with the centers matching and place a pin or small nail through the centers into a small board. If a board is not used as a base, a paper brad can be used.

4. Using a ruler, place equally spaced marks on the outer rims of both

pieces. The ruler should line up with the centers and the marks, which may be made using a protractor or a ruler, spacing the marks ¼ to ½ inch apart.

5. Number each set of marks starting with 0 and moving clockwise until all the marks are numbered on each circular piece.

Illustration

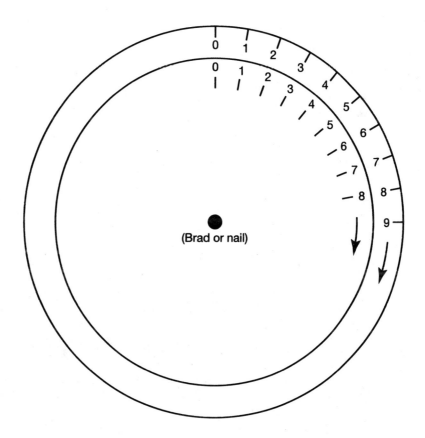

(Brad or nail)

Index